THE IMMORTAL CLASS

 VILLARD NEW YORK

THE IMMORTAL CLASS

BIKE MESSENGERS AND THE CULT OF HUMAN POWER

TRAVIS HUGH CULLEY

All rights reserved under International and Pan-American Copyright Conventions.
Published in the United States by Villard Books, a division of Random House, Inc.,
New York, and simultaneously in Canada by Random House of Canada Limited,
Toronto.

VILLARD BOOKS is a registered trademark of Random House, Inc. Colophon is a trademark
of Random House, Inc.

Library of Congress Cataloging-in-Publication Data
Culley, Travis Hugh.
   The immortal class : bike messengers and the cult of human power / Travis Hugh Culley.
      p. cm.
   ISBN 0-375-50428-1
   1. Bicycle messengers—Illinois—Chicago.   I. Title.
HE9751.C85 2001
384—dc21   00-061452
Villard Books website address: www.villard.com

Printed in the United States of America on acid-free paper

9 8 7 6 5 4 3 2

First Edition

Book design by Barbara M. Bachman

To my grandfather, Bernard Fox,
founder of the Fox Firestone Bike Shop,
New Smyrna Beach, Florida, 1956.

Always keep your tools nearby.

ACKNOWLEDGMENTS

ACKNOWLEDGMENT IS A RARE THING IN THE WORLD I come from. The messenger is too often seen as a cranky drunk with little education, little understanding of the world, little concern for others, and a small paycheck to show for it. The messenger works because he must, because the dispatchers he works with are just as hard-boiled and socially maladjusted as he. The messenger can be himself because he is no one. Being no one, he decides of his own volition to do little for others. So the stereotype goes, and so it continues, giving the messenger, at least the stereotype, few reasons to be acknowledged.

ACKNOWLEDGMENTS

Naturally, the model does not fit the real thing. First, the messenger is by no means only male. There are female messengers who work to capacity every day of the week in every major city in America. They often outperform the men on the team by dint of their courage, their strength, and their commitment to succeed. Second, there are many significant contributions that messengers (male or female) make day to day that go completely unnoticed by the rest of the world. The problems of cycling in the American City are as real as the problems of driving in the American City. They are in fact the same problem, and the courier should be credited for overcoming the problems of transportation with such admirably simple tools. The strength and determination of these cyclists should be celebrated as much and as often as their shared obstacles are feared.

I think few people believed that I could accomplish the task of writing this book. For that lack of support I am neither surprised nor resentful. As the stereotype goes, I should be filled with small-minded complaints about cabdrivers and pedestrians. As the stereotype goes, I should dream big because I am scraping the bottom of society. As the stereotype goes, I should have a litany of excuses that would include all the reasons I was unable to succeed, and I should celebrate that list nightly over beer special at a dive bar. Failure and defeat are part of the typified world of the messenger that I am proud not to have embraced.

For those who did believe in me and those who do, I am for-ever grateful. The first and most important on my list, also a part of my story here, is Haewon. Though she may not play a big part in the narrative, she was an essential player in the development of *The Immortal Class.* I thank her not only for her strength and her

x

constant support but also for giving me the inspiration to write a book like this.

I thank my agent, John Ware, whose commitment to the book was so strong that at times he had to put the fear of god in me to assure that I was moving in the right direction. His standard of clarity and professionalism I can only hope to use as a model for my own life. I am blessed to have received his guidance, his confidence, and his friendship.

I owe a heavy debt of gratitude to my posse at the Villard house for their hard work and for their faith in the book. Bruce Tracy, Oona Schmid, Katie Zug, Brian McLendon, Daniel Rembert, Barbara Bachman, Bonnie Thompson, and Benjamin Dreyer—I thank them all for giving me the chance to work so closely with them. They were exhaustively considerate and sensitive to my image of the final product.

I have to thank my mother and my brother for the time they had to hear me cry and wail about the book. They were a tremendous support to me emotionally and, at time, financially. The encouragement of my brother, Joseph, was in large measure the reason that I could get up every morning and continue writing. His support and excitement were so deeply felt that I sometimes wondered if his heart was not, in fact, sitting right at the desk with me the whole time.

I have to add to this list a great deal of gratitude for the encouragement and support of friends so dear that I may as well call them family. It is impossible to measure what a help, what a friend, and what a teacher Richard Paul Janaro has been to me. The excitement and encouragement I have received from Richard and other friends like him, namely Jorge Mejia, Alex and Dean Swinfold, Nikki Rollason, and, more recently, Melissa Lawson, are deeply cherished.

I am especially thankful for having met and had the chance to work with Sandy Wisenberg, at the Chicago Poetry Workshop, and Roy Khoury, at the Actors and Artists Conservatory of Philadelphia. They, and their classes, were instrumental in the maturation of important pieces of this project, and I thank them for their insights and contributions. Eric Anderson, Kim Morris, and Jeff Benjamin all got their hands dirty in the development of many of the chapters. The work here benefited from the time and professionalism that they offered generously. The photographic work of Lenyr Munoz and Butch Connelly was instrumental in the development of the book. Their shots went out in every stage of the book's progress, giving an important and appealing visual aspect to the text that achieved exactly what I was looking for. Thanks go out as well for help in the photo process to Steve Greiner Photography, Daniel Kopald and Jimbo Daniels have been very good for allowing me, and at times helping me, to use as illustrations the shots they had on hand.

For their openness and genuine support of some of the ideas dealt with in this book, a special show of gratitude is offered to Jon Boub, who was cool enough to detail for me his experience with cycling and politics, and to Robert McBride, Sr., and the McBride family, who have shown immense trust in my capacity to write about a very challenging period in their lives.

As I suggested earlier, acknowledgement in the messenger community is often hard to come by. So I would like to take a moment simply to thank the people who have shown their dedication to the industry by working to improve the lives and the culture of the courier. Their leadership and hard work are helping to create a positive image for an industry that we should be proud of. Special thanks therefore go out to John Green field, Jimbo, Marcus Moor, Super-dave, Donny Quixote, Bobcat, Rod Richardson, and Eric Spratt-ling—may he be remembered always as the champion that he is. These dedicated bikers have all been inspirations to me and, in many cases, have also been a great help in the creation of this book.

On the national scene, I would like to acknowledge Joel Metz, John Kenda, Wendy Fallono, America, Sean Bega, Sheba Ferrin, Re-becca Riley, Rolland and Elle of Reload Bags in Philadelphia, Jack Blackfelt and Hermes-n-Pit of the NYMBA, Jacoob Allerdice of Hideous White Noise, Natasha of Citysplinter, and all the messengers of every city who are providing a sense of leadership in their com-munities. These committed people, and others like them, are the ad-vocates that the courier world needs in order to get better working conditions, better pay, and a higher sense of respect in our grueling occupation. I hope that they remember on many levels they are paving a path for others.

On the activist front, I am fretfully unable to even begin to ac-knowledge all the people whose hard work and dedication have influ-enced me personally and politically, but at the same time, I cannot deny the impact that the Redd house has had on this work. Jim Redd has been an enormous influence on the finer points of my political beliefs and the ways that they can be carried out. He is the best kind of friend and role model I could possibly have had in the last few years, and I would be proud to call my activism a mere articulation of his.

I am especially grateful to Service First Courier for keeping an al-most eternal open-door policy with me. Chris Coster, Dave Goldberg, Dave Knol, Dave Carter, Tom Willet, and Vern are gems in the field of the American Workforce and they deserve to be praised and sung about like the great warriors of history. Even in hard times they find a way to keep their spirits high, and I respect that.

To my heads in Philly and the bikers of brotherly love, I am exceedingly grateful. Loud Steve, Inbred Jed, Ol' Man Phil, Chris, Brother Bill, Corey The Courier, Big G, Lena, Marcus, Marcus, Rebecca, Frankie, Denny, and the entire crew at American Expediting have graced me with their hospitality, friendship, and support.

Special thanks go out to the J-mack brothers, all of them and the extensions of them, Clay, Sam, Serko, Devynn, and Rashid. I hold very dear all the time that we had together and the bonds we built on Cambridge Street.

With that, I must show my gratitude to you, the reader, for taking the time to go through these acknowledgments. I did not list these names to bore you. These people, all of them, have had a direct impact on this book you're reading and should be credited for the parts they played in its production.

CONTENTS

AT 5:22 P.M. MY EYES FEEL HEAVY AS SEWER GRATES. I lean against a *USA Today* paper box on Washington and Clark and think: *Who the hell are you to make such a claim?*

I stand in the heart of the lurching flow of self-consuming crowds, surrounded by a whirlpool of technological and economic development. It is a time called *rush hour* and I am nursing liquids from a polystyrene cup. The water was free, though the cup cost twenty-five cents.

An old man with no legs, a veteran who has served in numerous wars, sits in his wheelchair on an adjacent corner. Handmade signs surround him, making his case while he bows his head and sleeps. I would love to be in his body. I would love to feel the presence of so many thousands of people walking past, occasionally tossing pennies into his small box. I would love to feel such boundless brotherhood in the dreamlike landscape of his slow breath. In a dark way, I think, with coins clanging together in his lap, it must tickle to be so in the hands of the world.

The cup rests on the metal box next to me, still half full of the thick water that my system will have to pull the wetness out of. The water in the cup shakes lightly. I can see its smooth metallic surface rippling, but I cannot feel its vibration. Maybe the trains cause the vibration. Or the low-flying planes out of O'Hare. It could be the leather express, the platoon of loafers and heels, pounding the sidewalk around me. It could be the 17 million automobiles produced in this country every year, or the combined impact they have colliding on our highways. But something, something I cannot see, is disturbing this otherwise still life, and shaping it quietly. People rattle along with this vibration like magnetic hockey players on a tin field. They jiggle in place and circle on the sidelines. They too are subjects of this deep machinery that I cannot see from the surface.

Like the water in the cup, I can measure the movement but I cannot weigh the vectors that influence these waves of pedestrians that flutter across Washington Street and Clark and farther out across LaSalle, Wells, Franklin, Wacker. I am too close, burdened by the skyline, unable even to imagine a world built without the crude handiwork of mankind. I am stuck here, amazed, both loving and hating the city, loving and hating the humanity and the grand scale of my smallness in it. Yet I cannot keep my distance. No, I am all too close. Sometimes I am only a breath away from losing myself in it entirely, from being consumed.

And who am I? I am a bike messenger: a lackey, a laborer, a punk-ass kid who calls this place his home. I am part of this machine, and I am also its observer. I am in the mix most of the time, hardly a self at all, but then I get these flashes, these pictures that assemble not about me but about the city. It, too, is self-conscious; it asks the same question. I can hear its uncertainty rising up in my heart, making the nerves in my hands shake, making the water ripple without cause. I get taken by this question, overwhelmed. What is this spinning around me, passing through me in radio waves, passing beneath me in subways, crawling up beside me in elevators, flying overhead? Grasping the whole picture seems impossible. The cliffs that stand around me go up so high that I am dizzy just thinking about them. And yet someone, somewhere, thinks they can speak for a "USA today"? What do *they* know? How can *they* claim to understand all this when I, down in the heart of America, cannot?

Who am I? The question is difficult because my system has been hit with a virus. I am pixelized infinitely, a series of zip codes and floor numbers, drop schedules and street names. *Who I am* is a parallel pursuit, a city and a man.

My name is Travis. I am twenty-five now, in no position to generalize. I can only hope that maybe, just standing here, a drifter, a dreamer, a messenger both outside and inside this pinnacle of advancement, my position may be a valuable one. I don't have the degrees from old universities to call me an authority on urban development, but I do have this: I have the question and I have the city to relate it to, I have the imprint that industry has inscribed into the blackness behind my eyes, and burnt into my skin like a branding. If nothing more, for the spectacle and the injustice that give this place its edge, I've got one of the best seats in the house.

In my messenger bag, I have four dollars crumpled into a side pocket, a bike pump, a spare tube, and a paisley handkerchief. In my hand is a cheap ballpoint pen that advertises a marketing company I'll never use. My right shin itches from the sock that I pulled up over a deep gash there. My toes are still slippery from the blood that traveled down my foot. A wound like this will take months to heal, but then, in a world like this, everything gets infected.

I sometimes wonder if my perspective is valid, but then, don't we all? So many of us spend our days looking at LCD displays and NASDAQ tickers. We enjoy the journey of watching the little lights in the elevator travel from LL to 83. Our stresses come from the computer-generated futures of meteorologists and morning papers, and yet we wonder what happened to the real world. We wonder if the public is not a team of extras standing behind newscasters at ball games. We wonder if we can speak for ourselves or if we need polling statistics to do it for us. It is an important subject—the value of a human perspective—because it runs into so many bizarre illusions.

That's where I come in, where the daily news hits deaf ears. I can't offer you the daily headlines, the crime reports, and the details of who got shot on Harrison Street. I don't know where the bullet entered and I don't know what the motive was. But I can share with you something about standing here, about listening to the heart of the world, beneath the surface of this advanced condition, where I am at home with the shadowed fields of society and the highest peaks of capitalism. It is this inner life of mankind from the heart of the marketplace that is at issue here—a parallel: human life and city life, close up.

Outside of the accredited perspectives of academic social scientists, away from the politicians and their soft money, I am a free thinker, unbound to any precast vote, outwardly disrespectful to the "authoritative voice." I am not a layman to the academy, but so too I am not paid by it. So I stand, I circle, I cycle through the urban world at the speed of light, or sometimes just at the speed of earth still crawling out from beneath me.

You may say my perspective is unaccredited, but in the face of clouds reflecting across a sea of steel surfaces, concerning the meaning of street signs and the way the heart sinks at the sight of a tide of fuming freight trucks, who can claim to be anything other than an amateur? Can anyone really be *authorized* to cast a net over all this? I don't think so.

I can only stand here and let my thoughts go, trust these words to reflect what I see. This is all that I can hope for. Fighting for respect, hunting for the living I take home, working among the city's every articulation, a tribesman, a native, and yet also its critic, I just may have the constitution, tested in both crude and lofty verse, to attempt an understanding of the urban world, the nowness of city life.

I can see my reflection in a window, through a steady stream of predators seven heads thick. A hint of my red shirt flashes back through the shadowed glass. The streets move like rapids, turning frothy over noisy intersections.

My cup of water makes my mouth taste like old piping. Black steam from passing trucks swirls into the wake of passing men. My bicycle leans against the paper box. Here, on the street, among the couriers, it is a respected, elite machine. To the rest of the world, to the masses trotting through these trenches with me, it seems a toy, a feeble substitute for a Ford Expedition or another fucking Camry, those big and small tanks of the Interstate Highway System—the world's largest public works project, ever.

What these people don't know is that the bicycle is more than a sport and more than a job. The bicycle is a revolution, an assault on civilian territory, intent upon taking, from the ground up, responsibility for the shape of our cities. It is a mutiny, challenging the ever-one-way street. The bicycle is a philosophy, a way of life, and I am using it like a hammer to change the world and to redeem our war-torn cities.

With this simple story, and with the perspective of the lives involved, I challenge you to consider that in the overproduction of big media, we may have missed a few aspects of this "USA today." We may have overlooked the cult of human power that is reclaiming public space and giving it back to average people.

Where am I? I am at Washington and Clark, right outside of Chicago's Daley Plaza, and I am not alone.

THE IMMORTAL CLASS

CHAPTER ONE

DAYBREAK

THERE IS NO DISTINCTION BETWEEN MAN AND MACHINE when I mount a bike like this one. Trusting all of my weight to the right pedal of a simple pulley system, I overcome the resistance of two thin tires bound by an aluminum frame and a steel chain. A small disk at the axle of the back wheel, slowly giving way to the force of my weight, holds the pressure taut against the chain. As I lean forward, the weight of my body pulls the cog around the rear axle, turning it one inch. The wheels, held tight by a matrix of metal spokes fixed to a hub, are pulled around a set of ball bearings by the torqued cog. Eighteen inches of rubber wheel crawls forward.

My weight shifts from pedal to pedal, reversing the side-to-side tilt of the frame. Like a plucked guitar string, the sideways sway of the cycle is narrowed. Lateral motion is exchanged for speed. Ten yards. One block. One mile. This specific process repeats itself endlessly. The press and pull of my legs draw the chain around a disk attached to a set of crank arms and pedals. All the parts work as a single organism, absorbing the asphalt and the cold wind while adding power to the spin of the wheels to build momentum. My torso, held up by arms gripped to handlebars and toes clipped into pedals, yanks the seat side to side. The bicycle and I shoot forward, going south into the Loop as the Great Lake rolls to the east and another day begins in Chicago.

As I bolt headlong down from the Michigan Avenue Bridge to Madison Street, each dark Bauhaus shape blurs into the cold stone facade of its Gothic neighbor. I keep on, coasting in the pedals, taking a wide right turn westbound on a vacant three-lane street through the center of downtown. This first delivery of the day shakes off my morning lag, pumping warmth through my veins, bringing the first bit of sweat to my brow. The air is clean; my head is clear. I look for a left turn onto Wells.

This morning, before the computers are booted up, the banks unlocked, and the stock market scrolls clicked on, I am running delivery routes under the city's yellow streetlights. The elevator banks are empty and the traffic lights, at what will soon be congested intersections, hold and change for no one. Most deliveries I make at this hour are to locked offices, where packages are slid beneath dim glass doors. I move as quickly and efficiently as I can, preserving my energy. A day of messengering is like a hard drug: you never know how rough it will be until you've slept it off.

Out here, while I'm coasting unobstructed through the shadows of morning, the world seems at perfect peace. The whole city is still and relaxed. Even buildings get their beauty sleep. Coming out of the spinning doors of the Morton Salt Building, I keep a swift rhythm skipping down the cold steps, heading to the Grinch, my yellow Cannondale road bike, locked to the bridge railing overlooking the riverbank. While the sky changes with dawn, a steady stream of people crowd the revolving doors over my left shoulder. Their eyes are half open, their manner calm; they smile softly like babies still tucked into bed.

I enjoy this quiet time when the city's rhythm is slow. I can empathize with the early-morning modesty, and I share the reflective awe that I see in the pious postures of people walking. This respect will fall away when the colors in the sky turn blue and the city awakes. These same quiet faces will struggle for a spare minute, a phone number, a positive response from a supervisor or a client. Sincere people doing honest work will be driven into shouting matches, compelled to insult each other, tempted to quit right on the spot.

I'm with them every step of the way. I have seen the red faces and the feelings of distrust as shoulders brush in crowded yet silent elevators. I have seen the masklike smiles they wear through stressful meetings about bottom lines. And yet I know none of these wandering souls. I talk to very few of them; they are somehow another species. Their machinery, and their mythology, move in one direction only. They stand packed into tight spaces, they look up to the brass trim of elevators, and they rise like they are spirits ascending to a gilded afterlife. Is it a floor number they are after? A title that will follow their name? A certain number of digits in their salary? Perhaps they just want a little safety? I don't know. But they are on a path and they will kill to stay on that path.

Every day I see them, good people yelling at each other, running past each other, and stepping over each other. I see them at their worst: in the public space, on the street, where no one is looking and no one cares.

I don't have time to be caught up in the sorrow of this. As my eyes have grown tired of fanning over as many as a million people in a single day, my heart has grown weary of caring for them. My relationship to these people of the city is reduced to suffering the silence of elevators with them, or walking through the ritual pickup and drop-off of packages with them, or muscling through traffic where "please" and "thank you" are lost to the aggravating assault of car horns and uncalled-for profanities. I have found that these good people, so engrossed by their own private struggles, are often incapable of conversation or a courteous word. They are concentrating, holding up the weight of their self-made worlds, trying to find higher ground.

While these masses groan over the decisions they have made and the responsibilities they have undertaken, I float above. I am free of their ideas of good and bad, rich and poor, right and wrong. As an uncommon laborer I may not amount to much in their eyes, but I am free of their judgment. I am sometimes seen as a social misfit, a freeloader, a junkie, but I am also envied for the color, the vigor, the picture of America I can find while they push their way through the weekday treadmill routine.

I love my work and the people I work with. I admire the arrogant history of these old buildings, the monuments to the free market, and the avenues they are built upon. They tell epic stories of the city's forefathers, hinting at codes of conduct that apply to some and not all. Street names give credit to the elite like deep-rooted propaganda. Chicago remains a contentious city where big politics are played out on local levels, where lawmakers learn their craft from kingpins, where virtue and suffering are the poor man's plight. From its long history I still hear shouts of civil outrage that echo down these quiet streets, reflecting moments in history like the riots of '68, the burden of Black Friday, and the shock that came after the great fire of 1871.

There is always some heated debate going on in the public squares. Protesters walk the streets and chant in the courtyards of government buildings. Wanderers wear signs bearing political slogans. They are not asking for money or running for office; they simply believe in something, and they let you know it. I like being inside the arena, somewhere near the fight. I achieve this every morning with a radio, a set of wheels, and a team of dependable couriers out to make a living.

We wake the city along with freight trucks and the quiet tide of pedestrians pouring out of suburban trains. We read about the latest atrocity on the cover of the *Tribune* as the papers are cut from their bundles and loaded into curbside metal boxes. We ride familiar paths around the city's feet and palms, seeing the abuses of the night before on her scarred back. We call out her landmarks, as we need to, keying in over the airwaves the pet names we've christened.

"Thirty-nine to base."

"Number Thirty-nine go."

"I'm out of the Lockbox, with a bag full o' rags."

"Start rolling the Peat and call me on the Foote, Thirty-nine."

"Yeah, boss."

"And where is my Punk?"

"Thirty-three to base?"

"Hey, Punk, drop the coffee and call me out of the Litter Box. The Katz got an Oil Can with your name on it."

"But I am not drinking coffee—it's a *mochaccino.*"

"You're on route to the Kat, you rat, and Punk, make it snappy."

The banter is one of the joys of the job. Each courier company develops its own special brand of street language. That talk is shared between us during the day, after work, at home, making even the unseasoned courier feel accepted—part of a larger group. Though we may treat each other harshly, there is usually a great deal of respect among us.

Transcending age, sex, color, and all of that divisive sociopolitical bullshit, the courier industry is supported by a very like-minded people. Many of us are artists and musicians, usually in our twenties. Most of us have been broke long enough to be masters of survival and have dreamt big enough to avoid the constraints of a salaried existence. I came to this city to succeed in the theater. I survive as a courier. Cadence for cash and Money for miles—these are the mantras of many a struggling genius. We work for materials and we herald our poverty for the liberties it grants us. Every week or so on the street I meet another ambitious biker who has a bag full of handbills for their next big show or their next exhibition or their next club gig.

Beyond these surface similarities, there is a deep and unspoken bond between couriers. When one is down, others carry the weight. When one is hurt, others are there to help. Some days the work can be so intense that bikers dehydrate, panic, end up confused or lost, or get messages scrambled on the radio. We have to look out for one another. Bikers get hurt, and when we do, we are often our only family.

Today, we talk about the gender of pigeons on the two-way radios, we watch the world roll slowly before us, and we wait for pickups to be dispatched over the airwaves.

8:43 A.M.

IN MY ROOKIE days, when I was still amazed and daunted by this rectangular horizon, the job felt like some kind of sadistic punishment. I was clumsy, accident-prone, inefficient. The city was huge and complicated. I had to wonder if I could last out here more than a week or two. But I continued. I continued because I had to, pushing through every day with ghoulish resignation. In no time a few lessons about the city surfaced as tricks or shortcuts. With them, I could more easily navigate and plan my maneuvers. But these lessons grew deeper as time went on, more profound. Eventually they took the shape of philosophical insights that helped me position myself mentally for the work. It is true: how you see things determines how you live among them.

The first major lesson came after only one week on the job. I was exhausted from the miles I was putting on the bike. Mentally, I was fatigued by the effort of being awake at every instant, organizing the excessive stimuli, learning the streets, the daily shuttles, and, of course, the talk. Then one morning, I was called in to base to pick up some packages that were left undelivered from the night before.

I pulled into the Service First alleyway, which was clogged with illegally parked cars belonging to drivers who handled oversized orders and suburban runs. The office was a converted garden apartment with a propped-open back door leading into a kitchen without cabinets or a sink. Only some tables and chairs, littered with loose receipts, were scattered across the floor. An old refrigerator stood in the corner, loose water bottles and half-empty beer cans rimming its top. The messengers' smudge marks and bike parts had long ago scraped out the domestic feel of the apartment. Bedrooms were made into private offices, closets were used for file management, and the white walls were tinted light brown from the support staff's afternoon sessions of stressed-out chain-smoking.

When I arrived, the dispatchers talked to me through a Plexiglas window cut into the drywall of the cramped radio room. Chris

Coster, a.k.a. Zero, handed me a few large envelopes. I'd sat down to organize them in my bag when Pat, Number Thirty-four, lurched through the back door, bike in hand.

Pat had dreadlocks like short twigs pointing in every direction. He was muscular and tight, with tattoos tarred beneath his glistening black skin. His personality was part voodoo priest, part Wicker Park punk. "Man, fuck this," he spat. Sweating and panicked, he rummaged through his plastic bin for a T-shirt that didn't smell too bad and a new helmet. In broken sentences he proceeded to vent through the sliding window that he had just gotten into some shit with a cabbie.

Apparently, Pat was in the left lane trying to make a right turn when a taxicab accelerated, blocking his way. Pat sped up and signaled that he'd be cutting in front to make the turn onto Grand Avenue. Just when he felt safe to proceed, the driver sped up again, nearly swiping Pat off his bike. Pat swerved away and regained his balance. By this time the cab had driven ahead. Pat sprinted forward. (I know how he rides. The man has the dexterity of a mountain lion.) He pulled his U-lock out of his bag, came up from behind the taxi on the driver's side, and smashed in the window only inches from the cabbie's head. The driver hit the brakes and Pat was gone. Now, with a different colored helmet and shirt, he was ready to vanish into the early-morning streets again, free from any possible retaliation.

I was stunned into silence. I saw no point in relating to another human being with violence. How did it help Pat to smash in the window of even the most obnoxious driver? How would it alter that driver's behavior, even if he was wrong or rude or pushy? Beyond this, I was astounded that he would share this news with Chris and

11

Dave Goldberg. These were the people who had *hired* him. *Maybe it's okay,* I thought. *Jesus, maybe it's normal!*

"Are you okay?" Zero asked Pat, sharply looking for information, caring nothing for his feelings.

"I'm good—just a little shaken," Pat came back easily.

"No shit!"

Goldberg came to the window, asking if he thought the cabbie had seen the company name.

"Nah, he was a little distracted, I think."

"Yeah, boyyyy!" Chris erupted in laughter.

"Take a few, Pat. Cool down."

"Nah, man. I'm ready now. I'll call ya out of the Can in ten."

"10-4. You *go* girl," Chris called out as the back door closed.

Once Pat had gone, the dialogue between the two dispatchers continued.

"You shouldn't egg him on like that," Goldberg contended.

"Listen," Chris defended, "when it comes down to the biker on the street, I don't care about right and wrong. I need bikers alive and confident."

"Oh, I've heard this speech before."

"10-4, Dave. I'm just not going to be blamed when someone gets hurt. I've had enough of that shit."

The talk stopped here, leaving the issue unresolved in my mind. I thought about it the whole day. Pat would talk on the radio with anger in his voice, as if to say, "You can't pay me enough to do this." He felt put out. Number Thirty-four felt abused when, in my eyes, he should have been fired.

But then, I had never been in his position. I had not yet been put to the test, and I had not seen just how much of myself I would have to invest to survive out here on these congested streets. I had not been exposed to the breadth and scale of a world this extreme. In time I would learn that Chris's defense was justified. As a biker, I was alone against the traffic, the people, the elements, the awkward packages, and the authorities who arrest bikers for minor infractions. The company has nothing to do with my survival or success.

The bike messenger is a lone ranger; he comes in to the industry from god knows where and offers himself up to sometimes incomprehensibly extreme situations. Every day he overcomes an avalanche of obstructions, he makes miracles happen to win what is essentially a little game he plays with time. Companies will support a biker who can fight down any obstacle, who, like Pat, can almost cast spells and levitate. A biker like this is hard to replace.

If the company ever tries to discipline a messenger, two things can happen. An inexperienced biker will try to improve. This means going faster or trying to cover up mistakes—often losing his own inner calm, his *style* on the street. Eventually he will screw up and get hurt. If the biker is above being disciplined, if he is confident in his technique, he will just go to another company to work his magic.

Simply put, the relationship between the biker and the company is one of mutual gain. There is no ass to kiss and no contract to sign. It all comes down to the brutally simple premise that no matter the distance, the climate, the time of day, or the circumstance, if the package is on time the agreement between the courier and the company remains solid. But accomplishing this can be deadly. When it all comes down, the biker stands alone where there are no shadows, no one to help him, and nothing to hide behind. The messenger must take personal responsibility right down to the asphalt with him. This is lesson one.

I SIT WATCHING streams of cars and buses scuffling along. The sky ripples upward in a stream of rising fumes. I can feel the seconds pass as my thoughts keep time. Whenever there is a moment of rest I meditate on the world, the street, the day, the psychological wear and tear of modernism, of urbanity. I make sure that my pen is lodged in the right place and that I have a spare. I stretch my legs to keep my knees from tightening up. I think about the other bikers I can hear on the radio and what I should expect of the next ten seconds or so. I think about how I can do my job faster, with less effort. I forecast.

In another twenty minutes the streets will clear out. Cabbies will circle, looking for work, or sit in long lines at hotels, cracking open doors to lean out and spit. In offices, the phones will light up with personal calls and lunch plans will be discussed in private. I will get a group of daily shuttles that will occupy me for an hour or so.

The city that once seemed so chaotic and wild to me now seems like a perfectly choreographed ballroom dance. I have learned to see in the city a distinct sense of order, a special geometry, a realm of necessity behind each unplanned lunge and skid. The Loop has its own laws of nature that the biker must come to terms with. There are many such axioms, like *Cops north of the river are too corrupt to enforce laws* and *Bikes are invisible in traffic—always pass on the left.* These lessons come with experience and some common sense, but not all of these laws are so easy to learn or to integrate into a routine.

14 One of the most difficult lessons I've had to learn is that the city responds to the emotional, the philosophical—the *subjective pre-*

disposition of the messenger. Like in a dream or hallucination, the city comes to reflect the messenger, determining how long he will be able to sustain the job by how well he can live with himself.

Pat, Number Thirty-four, is an example. If you come into the job angry, the most unexpected obstacles will drive your temper into the ground. The aggressive drivers and slow-walking pedestrians will become your nemeses. Pat quit eventually, after getting into a fight with another cabdriver. As we all know, cabs are a great excuse for getting upset, but Pat rubbed the cliché to soreness.

If, however, you understand this law of reflectivity, you can avoid certain traumas before they happen. The best illustration of this I found in Matt, Number 6145, the lanky Buddhist messenger from Cannonball Courier. He quit biking a few years back because, as he put it, he could read the writing on the wall. He had been out there too long, and I think he'd begun to feel as if he were being hunted by the city, as if some kind of ghost were watching him. He got off the bike to keep from getting hurt. "I have seen it happen." He smiled sadly. "I didn't want to end up like my brother."

Matt's brother Max was also a bike messenger, one of the best. After nine years of working as biker Number 221 for Advanced Messenger Service, he was looking for a change of pace. He was trying to put in his last few months before moving on to a more predictable career. One afternoon he swerved into an oncoming lane to pass a van that was stopped at an intersection. This is a standard maneuver through dense traffic. But while Max was coming out from behind the van, a valet was gunning a red sports car through the same intersection, arriving suddenly in his path. Max was swept off his bicycle and thrown. He woke to find himself on a stretcher, losing blood quickly. The coming surgery put five pins and a metal plate into his right knee. Max was told that he would never ride again because the reconstructed joint and bone would not hold up to the stress. Instead of quitting, he spent three years recovering—without proper compensation.

The important difference between Matt and Max is that one valued his intuition more than his livelihood. Matt could tell that he was asking for trouble. Before getting into that trouble, he quit and cleared his mind.

It is sometimes hard to maintain a positive outlook out here in these trenches. The sheer volume of work can be crushing. Unforeseeable problems can surface, threatening serious injury, extreme fatigue, and frustration. But if a biker can keep a good outlook in the face of wrong addresses, rude recipients, flat tires, dying radio batteries, unruly cops, hotheaded security guards, and injured friends, he can become indispensable to a company.

During the height of the summer of '98, Service First was low on bikers. There were five of us, doing the work of at least nine people. But, as always, when word got out that we were hiring, experienced bikers, unhappy with their companies, came out of the woodwork.

One morning we were told that a new guy would be starting sometime that day. This news was a great relief, as we had been overworked and exhausted for weeks on end. We kept our frantic pace that day, waiting for some capable help to even out the workload. By that afternoon the dispatcher was still busting out orders like a machine gun. I had lost count of how many packages I had shoved in my bag and had no idea where they were supposed to be delivered to. The office too had lost track. This forced us, for convenience' sake, to switch envelopes with fellow bikers without bothering to confuse the dispatch room with the details. We were all frustrated and panicked, just trying to sort out the demoralizing mess. Then the radio did something I had never heard before.

"Thuribidabidop?"

"10-9?"

"Thirdybopda*clean,* da*Cock* 10-4? 10-4?"

"Number Thirty-five? Are you clean out of the Hancock?"

"Yubeyu gotcha!"

"10-4, spare me the R2-D2 lingo and pull a Looking Glass out of DDB."

"Tebelepde-gotcha, gotcha-boo."

"I'll take that as a 10-4, Thirty-five. Call me when it's on."

"T-four! Bg*out*! Whahoooo!"

Number Thirty-eight, Otis, keyed on to the radio: "What the hell was *that*?" Base introduced us all to the new guy, Todd, Number Thirty-five, who during the next few weeks confirmed my thesis about what can happen with a positive outlook.

Like a real-life member of the Jetson family, he was a tall man with cartoonish good looks, dressed in pseudocorporate clown garb. I remember him for dress slacks rolled up to his knees and a slender tie. When he was not wearing his helmet, he would ride with a Frank Sinatra–style hat and chain-saw protection glasses. He lived on Snickers bars and cans of Coke, and he swore on the combination as if sugar equaled life (and he may have had a point). There was a blinding speed about old Number Thirty-five and a constant irony. He could turn anything into a reason to cackle, like the Joker in the old *Batman* series. He would speak in tongues on the radio, which meant, because no one else did the same, that he would never have to identify himself. He would play in fountains, he would howl at the moon at daybreak, and he would jump to do any kind of work. Todd was eager and outgoing, but he was not a rookie. As a messenger at other companies, he had faced the worst of it, the slush and freezing rain, the cracking skin and perpetual darkness; but he had developed a spin on life that kept the job fun. His insanity made hellish days something to laugh about.

"I want a world like *this* one!" Todd would shout over the radio. He eventually got a job in a big advertising company, making utopian visions out of silly products like Drano and Tic-Tacs. Thesis confirmed: the city's law of reflectivity will bring a messenger into close contact with whatever nightmare or whatever bliss he comes to the job with. In Todd's case, this meant a high-speed, two-dimensional mania not unlike that of Saturday morning cartoons.

11:21 A.M.

WITH THAT REFLECTION, I am rolling right onto Randolph out of the Leo Burnett Building and I see, on what has become a gorgeous day, hundreds of tiny white particles flying through the air. The light wind is blowing soapsuds off a scaffold, suspended from the ledge of the Daley Plaza. It looks like snow falling through a perfect blue, late-summer sky. The flakes vanish into the Clark Street bustle below.

In these little things I achieve what I am looking for, instances of incredible beauty, stories of human struggle, great ideas, and religious highs. Many jobs can offer beautiful, challenging experiences, but none are quite like this.

Beyond all of the stress, the fatigue, and the often bizarre expressions of humanity that I find on a daily basis, I can appreciate this work for what it has shown me, how it has challenged me, and who it has allowed me to become. But this very deep satisfaction did not come quickly. It came only when I first realized that, as a bike messenger, I could *succeed.*

Success for a biker depends essentially upon two things: how well you can keep a rhythm and how well you can keep a temper. The first challenge is finding the rhythm of the city. This takes time, sensitivity, and a little bit of soul. The next challenge—keeping the temper—requires inner strength. But once you are *there* and you can hear the city's rhythm and look her in the eye, finding order in the chaos, then, at that instant, all of the obstacles that can confound an amateur will dissipate. The timing of when to hydrate, when to stretch, when to go headlong down Michigan Avenue—all becomes clear. Congested streets seem empty. Intersections and red lights are pierced effortlessly. The routine of locking up the bike is choreographed to perfection and can be accomplished in three seconds or less.

I discovered this secret after months of exhausting work. I was called off my route to "pull a Hinshaw out of the hospital." Hospitals are notoriously difficult to weed through, as there are often hundreds of rooms per floor. The package had just been called in, and it had to be off by 10:00 A.M. I looked at my watch; it read 9:43—this meant trouble. "Pretend you're clean, Thirty-nine, pick it, drop it, and call me with the POD." Dispatch knew I was still recovering from a knee injury and was burnt out from the weeks past. Part of me wanted to say, "Nah, man, you do that shit." But I knew he wouldn't pull me off a route unless this package was already starting fires on his desk. It was an important step for me as a cyclist to declare that I could do the impossible. I could make miracles happen. No matter what crossed my path, I could make this work—without interrupting the route.

"10-4, boss. I'm on it."

I hammered down Columbus, fought my way through the hospital, and got the package on board. I shot out of 680 North Lake Shore Drive and took Erie west. Erie took me to St. Clair, and St. Clair took me to Grand, so I could hit Lower Michigan. Lower Michigan led to Lower Wacker, the warp zone, where a blue Taurus was going just my speed. I got hold of the hub over the back passenger-side wheel (the blind spot). Usually I am not seen when I do this, but this time I noticed the posture of the driver, a young black woman now nervously bent over her steering wheel. She saw me skitch her hub. At first she hit the gas trying to shake me, but her car didn't have enough pickup. Watching her through her rearview mirror, I could see that she was frightened and determined to lose me. I was expecting her to hit the brakes or start swerving, but at the right moment, we happened to make eye contact in the reflective glass. I calmly nodded my head and mouthed the words "It's okay. It's okay." I could see that my speedometer was hitting forty-three miles per hour and, over my left shoulder, the exit ramp was coming up.

Watching my timing carefully, I let go of the car and coasted into the wind. The driver now had a surprised smile on her face. I touched the back brakes just enough to make the turn without sliding or being hit by the oncoming traffic and flew up the underground exit ramp, rounded the corner, and locked the bike. The moment I left 221 North Wells, having dropped the package, I checked my watch. It was 9:53 when I called in the proof of delivery. Dispatch didn't need to applaud my work. It is not like that out here. The work applauds itself; the work was on time and I was still rolling. It is called doing a job, but the sensation is much more like flying—except flying, in this world, is sort of normal.

I arrived back at the NBC building on City Front Plaza (we know this building as the "Peacock") by 9:59 for a 10:00 A.M. pickup and hurried in to avoid the black mass of rain that had been collecting above the city. The elevator mirrors confirmed my calm. Being calm meant that I didn't have to worry about how to get somewhere. I didn't have to think. I could trust my body; it knew how to accomplish what my mind would be too hesitant to even try.

By the end of the day I had run off sixty-one packages, weak knee and all. Some of the other bikers had just topped forty. I stood in the rain, remembering some of the things I'd seen.

Two cabs had tried to run me off LaSalle. I'd skitched a tow truck up the Fairbanks incline. I'd dropped thirty-two packages by noon. A woman had been hit by a black Mazda that spun its back end through a wet intersection. As I'd rolled past, the young woman had not gotten up. I'd been sliding everywhere; my tires couldn't seem to stick to the road. I'd delivered a very important package to a judge; he'd closed the door behind me before he signed the manifest. I'd taken a shortcut through the down ramp of the Apparel Center parking lot, where a BMW had lurched into my path. I'd hit the brakes and been thrown like a stone from its sling, landing only a few feet from the car (thank god for helmets). I'd come within a few breaths of a fistfight with a security guard at 200 Madison; I remained calm. I'd run over some guy's toes as he tried to scurry across the State Street traffic. I kept my tempo. For every close call I said to myself: *Take inventory and move on. Just keep the rhythm.*

Soon I began to feel that I was floating, softly looking down upon the city, pointing out my passage through all the blind corners and tricky buildings. Even through torrential rain and slippery brakes, from this godlike view, all of my motion seemed effortless. I savored the shifting, spinning weight of my body, the bicycle, and the street as a single organism. I was in the zone. By the time I could envision a destination I would arrive there as if by magic. I would appear rested, and yet behind me would be the distant reflection of what I had just encountered and just overcome.

Standing in front of the mirror after work that day, I saw that my tanned face was splattered with dirt. My hair was matted and wild. My body was wet, hot *and* cold. My legs were blackened, and my cracking fingers were saturated with soot. My bright red shirt was now a kind of burgundy. Taking off my black fingerless gloves, I saw clean white palms. My pale body, without the armor of biking gear, was nameless. The alter ego of the messenger had consumed it. I was no longer quite human. I was a messenger in the body of a human being. I felt like a metronome: once I had the rhythm, it became very hard to justify stopping it.

Taking a shower, I watched the drain swirl black powder down and back out into the city through the drainpipes. But it was not dirt I washed off. It was sweat and burnt fuel. I smelled like a muffler. My thighs felt so tight that sitting was painful. Cleaning my ears, I pulled out swabs of black wax. While my muscles spasmed in random fits, I leaned back in a comfortable chair to relax. My eyes seemed burnt, torched out of their sockets. But behind them, my mind still hurled itself forward, compensating for the lack of speed I found in the chair. Even rest seemed to require energy. Then unexpectedly, like a possessed man, channeling from the world of the dead, I spoke:

"Life sucks, but work is really cool."

I tried to laugh but my face hurt, tired out from the hard wind. My thoughts kept spinning and rolling and ranting through my head, until I woke the next morning to don the armor again.

1 1 : 5 5 A . M .

I FIND IT difficult to paint a picture of messengering as a blissful day job, a worklike recreation for sunny days in a big city. Yes, there are many moments that feel like celebrations of human power and personal freedom. When the sun is high and the breeze is cool, amid streams of joggers and tourists crowding parks for music festivals, with blue skies all around, I am the first to stop and be grateful for this side of my work. I savor the scenes I can stumble across on my way through the Gold Coast with a hot package going to a high-rise condo in the park. There are days that end with the light radio banter of friends on a gorgeous afternoon, saying things with intended coolness like:

"Thirty-nine to base. I am clean here in *heaven,* holding a cold Sam Adams and hoping to stay that way."

"10-4. You've had a hard day, Number Thirty-nine. Why don't you kick your heels up and watch the girls. Will I be seeing you in the A.M.?"

"That's a big 10-4, boss. Heels are up. Thirty-nine is out."

I have a right to enjoy these rare times because, more often than not, I am trying to keep my knuckles from going numb, my safety glasses from fogging up in the cold, and my packages dry. As a messenger, I spend much of my time in steel freight elevators that whistle at high speeds through tall shafts of stale air. Scratched into their industrial gray sidings are the senseless and profane scribbles of mailroom clerks. I deliver thick checks to old men in spacious condos who get twenty-four-hour care from live-in nurses. I spend some part of my day with young women who answer phones behind big desks. They scramble for pens because they know I am in a rush, and sign for each package as if it's urgent. I suppose it *is* urgent, but they can take all the time in the world and I won't rush them because they are, for me, probably the one part of my day I can always enjoy. The rest of my day is spent sprinting through traffic or waiting in a courier center with six other smelly bikers who are in line for packages from the Sears Tower.

Some of my day is spent back at base matching the day's delivery receipts with the dispatcher's floaters (the office's crudely cut paper forms that each order is written on). Throughout a workday, these floaters are collected in a stack and pinned together by magnets against the board, a metal sheet that is leaned up above the dispatcher's desk. After an order has been dispatched to a biker, Zero scribbles down the biker's number on the floater and sticks it on this board, under that biker's magnet, for him or her to go through later. We turn this matching time into bitch sessions that have us laughing to tears, making party plans or racing plans for the weekend. When our paperwork is done, we usually leave behind us a table littered with torn receipts and half-empty beer bottles, some of which end up atop the old refrigerator.

Messengering is not an easy job. It can be filled with anguish and humiliation, it can offer hardship so much deeper than the minor frustrations of traffic and rude doormen. In my time on the street, I have been hunted by cars, and hit by them. I have been chased and have returned chase to many unruly antagonists. I've been doored, thrown, clobbered, threatened, and pinned between cars. I have been in fistfights with motorists. I have cracked mirrors and scratched paint jobs. I have stood in the middle of traffic with my arms spread wide, demanding to be run down by a vehicle. This kind of conflict is just part of the job; such trials are so common now that I only talk about them if there are injuries or court dates. Somehow, through the unique difficulties that the journey of every single day brings, the job gets done and the board gets cleared, bringing with it a feeling of victory that never tires because each day seems only to get worse.

The longer you work out here, the sooner you begin to see yourself as somehow different, somehow exempt from the so-called universal laws of life and death. You become part of a class that, in order to continue, must believe itself unstoppable. This heightened feeling gives the messenger a confidence, a speed, and an agility of almost metaphysical proportions.

We cling to the dream of being untouchable, part of an immortal class of winged angels, hailed for speed and strength. It moves us forward when danger comes too close, when "Man down" is heard on the radio and we can't be distracted, and when we feel too exhausted to go another mile but yet we will continue. We will find our destinations, catch the elevator to the right floors, deliver the packages, and be ready for more. We messengers fight through extreme fatigue, overstimulation, frostbite, and dehydration. With resilience and determination we are able to survive stunts and endure stresses that seem impossible to the casual observer. The pride taken in this feat makes us part of a unique world of young, colorful soldiers who look death in the face and make a living evading her.

CHAPTER TWO

FREEDOM IN THE AMERICAN CITY

Borne on a cloud, I followed the lightning's
Blazing trail from the eternal heights.
But the cloud sank, and still is falling.
Tell me, great Father Indra, to what region
Am I come? The air's so dense, so hard to breathe.

August Strindberg,
A Dream Play

I T WAS AN AWFUL DAY. THE MORNING'S WEATHER REPORT advised anyone with a heart condition to stay indoors. I could hear the DJs on passing radios teaching drivers how to recognize heat stroke. I flatted out on South State under the Fifteenth Street Bridge. To change the tire I had to tear out the old tube. It had melted down to hot rubber, which stuck to my fingers. Our staff was low because Rod, Twelve, had not been let out of the holding cell from the night before. He'd been harassed and arrested for coasting through a red light on the empty Ashland Avenue Bridge around two that morning. I picked up the AmEx shuttle, a daily stack of plane tickets with numerous destinations, from the dock of the *Tribune* building.

After I made a few deliveries, scratching the drop times onto the manifest, I noticed a problem. One of the items on the AmEx manifest did not have a corresponding ticket. I sat down outside the IBM building and rifled through the five-inch stack of computer-generated forms that were rubber-banded together like a small bundle of hay.

The sun was bestial, sitting over my helmet like an Aztec god. I turned west to keep the light out of my face, but it reflected off a glass building. I faced north and the tickets lit up so white that I couldn't read the ink. I turned south and the sidewalk flashed like a strobe light. I turned east again and curled my head into the bag as if I was looking for a half-eaten meal or a cup of coffee in a garbage bin. When I arose empty-handed, I called the base on the radio and told them that the AmEx manifest must have been wrong. The base then called the client to report that there was a piece missing. The travel agent freaked out at the idea of a missing ticket, blaming the mistake on a new temp who was clearly not "fitting the bill." The temp then turned the entire office upside down to prove that she was not responsible.

I continued knocking out the route, moving on to deliver the R. R. Donnelley, the Nuveen, and the 180 Wacks to save time while all the parties, IBM included, panicked—all of us unaware that the missing ticket was tucked in with the rest of them, hanging out of the side pocket of my big shorts, cruising around with me through the bitch-hot summer day, slipped into the wrong envelope.

When I dropped the Jones on One South Wack, the lady at the desk shuffling through her stack of ticket stock looked up, smiled, and showed me an address for IBM. I gave her thanks as calmly as I could, took the misplaced ticket, and walked to the door, but *god* I felt like kicking out the plate glass of her twenty-first-story view and strangling the Tribune Building to death with my hands around its forty-second floor.

It shocks me how our market system can be so easily threatened by the culture of temps and administrative assistants. Little mistakes like these can make the rhythm of our business sputter and rattle like the tailpipe of a VW bus. The problem begins with a corporation's unwillingness to commit to its employees. They pad their lower ranks with part-timers and temps who are paid dog shit, given no benefits, and changed out like can liners. This turnover creates a quiet chaos beneath the surface of our entire corporate structure, which is choking on the issue of training.

Many times a week I find managers with little finesse, counting every minute they are wasting, standing over the shoulders of interns or temps and telling them every detail of the job at once. Meanwhile, under the pressure of their red-faced boss, the temps are going pale wishing they could have just stayed unemployed for one more day.

I saw a manager so fed up and frustrated by training that she reached up to me, leaning over her new assistant at the reception desk, signed for the package I had to deliver, and apologized: "It's so hard to find good help."

The new employee looked up at me and twisted her face as if to ask me, "Did I just hear that?"

Why should this temporary society, typically filled with eager and intelligent young people, bear the stress of an industry that seems so intent on screwing it? These people are more than mistreated. They are often dehumanized by mandatory, idiotproof, fully scripted reception talk filled with all the robotic courtesy of answering machines. *I should have strangled the forty-third floor,* I thought to myself, mounting up in the hot sun again.

Oh, injustice! I try not to overthink it while I'm on the clock because there is simply too much to go around. I just pick up the pieces from the old guy in the window of the underground Tribune dock and play the matching game.

Today this old man, who was carefully shaving peanuts down into tiny morsels on a paper towel, wrote down my name on a green log and handed me the brick of tickets. I saddled up and coasted carefully down the dock's ramp through the underground alleys. Behind me I saw peanut morsels fly out of the service window and get devoured by a little tornado of pigeons.

I pumped off the packages one by one like they were loaded into a small cannon. Each drop took me four to five minutes to aim and execute. Boom! One down. Kablam! Another. From building to building I saw the landscape change. New targets came into view and old targets burst into flames behind me.

To the client, I am an information mercenary, hired to pedal a little bit of peace of mind to the corporate world—and, with my blood and fire, that is just what I do. I may miss out on the steady pay, the stock options, and the health care, but I do get to avoid issues of bottom lines and personnel politics, the squabbles that tear apart the nerves of America. I am loyal to no one, responsible only to my landlord—and that's how I want it to stay. It is an idea I have of being unrestricted, of living as I want to. This detachment from middle-class shoulds and oughts just feels right for me.

I can do anything. I can impress a client with a smart-ass comment or a nasty weather report delivered in good humor. I can hang out and curse about politics with the stockholders. So long as I am forthright and honest, I can pull a CEO out of a crowded elevator, take his place, and let the doors close between us. It is as if there is a certain space around me, like a force field, that human bullshit just can't penetrate. It protects the urgency of my deliveries by telling people to get the hell out of my way. When the force field's up, I am untouchable, and everyone knows it. It is a matter of respect. Moving at the speed of commerce, shoveling through all the scales of mankind at once, saving a little bit of the world all day long, I require at least that much respect.

The force field comes on the moment I set a pair of clear protective glasses across my eyes. I can't work without them. They are all the protection I get from the social clatter, the dire poverty, and the proudly overbearing ignorance that these streets can offer. They are not just for dust and wind. They protect me from a well-deserved cynicism about the human race in an arena where all divisions between us as people are revealed in horrific nudity. I see the stress and hardship hidden beneath our paper-thin presentations of kindness. I see the diseases of our everyday lives bury themselves beneath a thin veneer of language, and I have got to just live with it, openly, brotherly, constantly; everything—constantly.

I don't have any fancy theories to hide behind. I just have these plastic glasses, this helmet, and this U-lock. I've got no tools outside of a two-way radio, a bottle of water, a pair of gloves, and a set of hex wrenches. I have room for little else. Going in, like a skydiver, I have to leave all of my fear and prejudice somewhere far in the distance.

AS THE SUN GREW higher and the heat felt like it could pile up in my open palm, I had another wave of bad luck. It hit me during a short break I was taking outside of the Equitable building. Sitting down next to my plastic pail of letters for Smith Bucklin, taking a few swigs out of my tupper of dry granola mix, I could feel a pressure slowly build. First, through my two-way radio I could hear the phones in the office begin to ring in a flurry. Then the dispatchers could not be reached. Bikers called in, looking for contact information. They gave their numbers and got nothing in return. Then Zero came back to the radio, his voice pitched up a few octaves, and listed off orders from the desk like a general on a losing battlefield. Number Thirty got sent to Hell (One North Franklin). Number Thirty-one, Lu, was hit with a rag that would take her all the way out to WGN, twelve miles northwest along Elston. I got a special from the ADA law library on nineteen.

"10-4, boss. I'm going to drop the bucket of Bucklin, grab a bouquet of Rosies, roll off the Fairbanks, and hit you on the outside of the Dentist."

"What else you got on board, Thirty-nine?"

"I am sitting on a pair of southbound rags, an MTA/Cock, and I got a Monkey on my back that needs a rear-end. Is that a 10-4?"

"10-4. Call me with the teeth on."

The American Dental Association is in a small ugly building on Chicago Avenue. Its gray facade alternates vertical pillars of gravel with clear, untinted glass. The overall effect is much like an old Volvo station wagon standing twenty-one stories high—except that Volvos are usually much easier to get in and out of.

I was still in the middle of five or six different deliveries, so I dumped the Bucklin, hit the Peacock for the Rosies and, after dropping a DDB on 541 Fairbanks, I hit the ADA with a sneak attack. I free-locked the Grinch in the arching colonnade and saw the security guard stepping out onto the wide front sidewalk to stretch his legs. I had a few seconds to make it to the glass doors without his seeing me. The door he'd opened was slowly swinging shut. I dodged behind the column and caught the door without making a sound, sped past the empty desk, and found an elevator waiting for me. I took the elevator to the nineteenth floor.

We call this kind of maneuver a "bum rush." It is meant to save a messenger the few seconds that it takes to sign in at a security desk and, in this case, to get your work bag past the security guard. It may sound ridiculous, but in some buildings it is a serious offense for messengers to carry their own bags up to a client's floor. The way I look at it, I am responsible for the contents of the bag, not him, and so I do what I can to bend the rules.

Sitting behind an old wooden school desk, the gray-haired librarian had a few *very* important things for me. She spoke slowly as if I were deaf or stupid; "originals," she stressed. The two books were cheaply bound, turning brown at the edges, like the preserved manifestos of Communist Russia, and wrapped with a small piece of cotton string. She held on to them carefully, like they were Scripture.

"They'll get there."

"Are you sure?"

"Listen, lady, this is what I do. Call the recipient in thirty minutes. If you need the number, call my office, but give me the package, 'cause I have got to get the hell out of here."

I stepped quickly out to the hallway and hopped into the same elevator as its doors closed, pressing the button for the lobby and mauling the CLOSE DOOR button, which had been worn down to a yellow smudge. The doors slowly came together and I was rolling like thunder! Like a child on a big set of drums! I put up my dukes in the muted reflection of the brushed steel doors—this is the gesture I afford myself when my timing is just right—and I thought about how I'd coolly walk past the security desk so that I wouldn't stir problems with the guard.

I was in a steel box now, realizing that the world, like a projected film, runs across my neutral surface evenly. I was not in control here. I knew that. My heart gulped as it endeavored to know itself once again on this mythic descension into the modern world. Under the hum I sank, sling in hand, aware of all the machinery.

I have square eyes. Close up, I could see their shape in the hazy reflection of the elevator walls. The lids are thin and cropped low from the hard times and hopeless situations I've seen. I considered myself a young man, but it had been a long twenty-five years. I ran away from home as a teenager, lived on rooftops and in the back of cars; some of my most influential years were improvised lessons in survival. I was an angry young man, an adolescent time bomb—a common sight, really, given the circumstances. In my blurred reflection, I could still see a hint of softness. As I focused my eyes into the reflection of the elevator's steel paneling, that softness vanished.

JUST A SCRAWNY white kid, I was raised on the 14400 block of the quietly run-down North Miami Avenue, about a half mile from I-95 and a mile from school. I would bike that mile every day in an eternal summer, much like this one, that numbed the mind with constant and often unbearable heat. September was the same as January, which was much the same as April and November and June. There is nothing glamorous about that kind of climate. It leaves only a dire complacency as it saps the energy out of you. Without water and cooling, the nimble faculties of the mind just wander off. Strangely, many memories of my youth are accompanied by this drained, slow-motion kind of suffocation, like I was always just a few breaths from giving up, falling into the silence and the anonymity of Miami's endless city grid.

Even then I could see how the streets seemed to slice through fields and marshes, cutting up and organizing the pasture into crude divisions. Traffic would pass in front of our old house, one lane north and one south, at full speed, like lines of fire and return fire. The street was so violent, busy, and dangerous that my father, in jest, would tell my brother and me to go play in traffic. *Ironic,* I thought to myself, tightening the nylon strap on my messenger bag.

When the doors opened on the twelfth floor, a man in a blue suit with a peach-colored bald head took notice of my smile. I flattened it out as best I could to be polite. The doors closed and I found myself laughing again. I never really did anything that my father told me to, and I am proud of that, even today. I was trouble in more ways than one, in more ways than I will probably ever know. As I continued to submerge, my cheeks filled with this embarrassing heat. I must have been red as a turnip, smiling like a boy.

The elevator stopped at the tenth floor and opened upon two men who were engrossed in a perverse snicker about a female coworker. One of them stepped aboard and took a position behind me. I could see in the lines of his pale face the same doughy texture of an old friend's and suddenly my chest heaved like I'd missed a beat.

"He is a dangerous man," I heard my mother say. This is how she used to describe Gill, the ghostly man who would walk slowly through the neighboring yard. His body was thin and his flesh was weak, like that of an old man, but his hair was long, curly, and black. Though many wrinkles were chiseled into his tight face, I could tell that he was still a young man.

I had been warned, and by the strained postures of friends around the yard, I could tell they'd all been warned the same. I remember seeing Scott Voice staring out at Gill's yard during a birthday party at our house. Scott had this deep look of dread in his eyes, the kind I had rarely seen among kids my age. We stood on the inside of our old stone fence, which had crumbled to being no more than a pile of stones in a line. This was the only barrier between my house and the untended yard of that man, *that sick man,* as my mother would say.

On the other side of his yard was a massive pink church with a large open parking lot that emptied out onto the same quiet neighborhood streets that I would take to school. Across the high weeds of his backyard I saw it—a perfect shortcut. I was having a conflict: Should I avoid Gill because he scares me and pay the price of a longer trip to school? Or should I open myself up to the things I don't understand and take the shortcut?

In the coming years, Gill's health slowly began to look up. The first symptom was that he began to mow his lawn—on a nightly basis. He would mount the huge orange tractor around eight P.M., turn on the bright headlights, and spend much of the evening running patterns through his yard. My family would eat dinner trying to ignore the noise. My mother and father would shake their heads in silent judgment. My father's expression was strangely conniving. It looked to me that he was thinking about how he could stop the noise by calling the police or having a man-to-man. But my father was too afraid to do either. He chose instead to ignore the problem, and my brother followed close behind, laughing at "the crazy man."

My mother looked concerned. She understood why Gill shunned the light of day, but I don't think she could show her pity.

Because of Gill's unusual gardening schedule, I would see him more often. After he'd plowed the yard at night I would find him the next day digging into the ground with a shovel and a few pipes, trying to repair the sprinkler heads he'd run over in the dark. As he leaned over the wet hole he'd dug into the earth one morning, I walked up to him to ask if I could ride through his backyard as a shortcut to school. His naked back, as I approached it, was bone white, and it twisted, showing me every rib, as he turned to look at me, hearing me coming into his yard. He still had one arm in the sprinkler hole, leaning on a long iron tool. He was sweating. His arms were nothing but bones, and seeing them covered with black soil gave me an image of a man coming out of the grave. A living skeleton. But then he smiled. "Through here? With your bike?"

"Yeah. For a shortcut."

"No, no. Ride your bike if you want to, man. That's cool. It would probably be all right for me to see kids in the yard sometimes. No, that's a really good idea. Yeah, anytime, man, anytime."

One day, about a year later, on what was now my normal route to school, I saw Gill standing outside his painted and patched gray wooden door with his forehead only a few inches from the peephole. He just stood there, motionless. I rode closer and slowed to a stop about ten feet behind him.

He wore faded jeans and a threadbare plaid shirt. His black hair hung down around his stretched features, making him look something like Mick Jagger or Steven Tyler on a bad day. He did not look good. As I put down the kickstand on my bike, his left arm rose into the air about four inches. I stood behind my bike waiting for him to notice me. He didn't. His arm fell as if he forgot he'd heard a sound. When I called his name he almost lost his balance and fell to the ground.

His breath was soft and his lips hardly moved: "Travis?"

Then, in a sustained strain of words, he complained that he had lost his keys and he needed help breaking into his converted garage through the ventilation window of his bathroom. Physically, I knew he could never accomplish this. He was barely standing. And his keys? I could see them lying in the grass about two feet from his left foot. I walked over and handed him the silver ring.

He leaned back so relieved he nearly fell, stumbling to the seat of his big riding lawn mower. He sat there, sweating. "Oh, man, I really thought I lost them for good! Jesus, thank you!" I found his weakness astonishing; he had the same frailty as Christ being brought down from the crucifix. A groggy conversation emerged.

"Where are you heading to?"

"School."

He laughed. "You don't have to wear a uniform, a tie or anything?"

"No."

"Things have improved!"

We talked for a few minutes about school. Before I left I told him that if he ever needed help doing stuff, I could help him. He was not a dangerous man. At the age of nine I was stronger and faster than he was. I could see more clearly, think more quickly, and I never stumbled. It wasn't like he had brain damage or anything. He was just weak, unclear, but so what?

Our friendship was solidified by incidents like this. I would help him clean his yard of sticks that fell in the heavy rain. I learned how to fit sprinkler heads. I would climb his trees with his small chain saw and cut back low-hanging branches. I remember holding these big branches straight up over my head like I was the trunk, a human trunk. I was strong and proud and I would carry these big branches to the back corner of his acre lot and throw them onto a mulch pile. Meanwhile, Gil (I had learned that he wasn't named after the gill of a fish) would have barely enough strength to pour orange soda into a coffee cup from a two-liter bottle.

One afternoon the vice principal of my high school took me out of my ninth-grade class just to tell me about his memory of a child he knew as Gilbert. He recalled a young man who had been beaten and mistreated by a negligent and alcoholic father. The administrator said that he'd actually had to take the kid out of school one day and pay for his haircut because Gil's parents had no regard for their child's health or appearance.

Through all of this, Gil was one of the best students in the school. He won awards and broke records in mathematics, but in the end he never finished school. "He got in with the wrong crowd," the vice principal said. "Do you see what I'm trying to say? *He is the wrong crowd,* and he can threaten your future. If he ever offers you anything, come back here and tell me."

I rode home from school that day and found Gil roaming through his backyard half dressed. The veins in his arms were thick. His skin was practically blue, and he had breasts almost like a woman's. (My mother later assessed that this may have been a symptom of severe alcohol abuse or malnutrition.) He walked slowly toward me and I told him about how I'd been pulled out of class and what for. "Gil, why would anyone want to warn me about you?"

His face fell. While he spoke, foggy and unclear, hanging on to a single thought that kept slipping his memory, I would follow the second hand of my wristwatch. He averaged something like a word a minute, but eventually he got his meaning across.

He shared with me how his father, a naval officer who'd fought in both the Korean and Vietnam Wars, had become an importer and was often overseas. He would cross the Atlantic with his own carrier ship. First he would dock in Spain, and then he would cruise up to Scandinavia, where he could carry aboard bags of pure, uncut heroin and bring them back to the United States. By the time his father died, Gil was only fifteen and he was hooked on junk.

Gil dropped out of school, leaving behind one of the best GPAs Thomas Jefferson Junior High had ever known, and began to support his mother. When his father's pension started coming in, he stopped working. Mother kept the house, Gil converted the garage, and they began to live like strangers. His face convulsed slowly, heaving dry tears. I stayed near him that day to keep him from swallowing his tongue as he had done in the past.

This was *my* America, a lost America where men were slaves to silence and inadequacy, where poverty was a condition of failure. My father, out of shame for our modest means, could hardly bring himself to talk to me. He hid away like a piece of furniture, watching the ball game on TV and eating Cheez-Its from the box. His problems seemed heavy and hard to bear. He never gave me the opportunity to understand. He was just looking in the other direction. And while he was, I was hanging with Gil.

Gil treated me with a man-to-man sense of respect. He gave me time out of his day to talk or to explain something about the world. The kind of conversations I should have had with my father I found

I could have more easily with a heroin addict who was feared, distrusted, *hated* by the entire community.

To me he was a teacher. He showed me how to respect the man with the clouded eyes and the crude speech. He showed me that I didn't have to be fearful or angry at him, because he, like all of us, has lived as honestly as he is able. With that, I forgave the man in the elevator his vile speech and watched the lights of the floor numbers fall.

SUDDENLY, AS DOORS OPENED on the second floor, the suspended car jarred in its place, stopping four inches below the line of the landing. The lights flashed off and a young woman with bright blond hair backed away from the doors to protect herself. We were all struck with a moment of terror, the kind of instant hopelessness that only gods and machines can offer. The speaker started to crackle, becoming the first groans of a human voice, preparing a script. *Breakdown! Dammit!* I had been in this situation before, and I did not have time for it.

I sprinted out the open elevator doors, found the fire stairs, and started to leap my way down them. The metal clips of my cycling shoes tapped and slid as I scurried down the flight of compounded-stone stairs to the lobby floor. I piled into the lobby door's crash bar with all my weight, but the door didn't open. I smashed into it again with no results. I stepped back to see that the door was locked by a thick chain swung many times around the crash bar's handle and bolted shut with a padlock. *Just my luck.* "Open this fucking door!" I shouted, beating the door with my fists. I got no response. The guard's desk was less than twenty feet from where I was pounding and shouting. How could he not hear me?

"Goddamn it! I need to get out of here! This is such a fucking fire hazard!" My voice echoed back into my face off the soundproof door. Then I realized that the guard had probably gone up to settle things on the second floor. There was another door, a black metal door off to my left. I swung it open so hard that the doorknob smacked into the scraped drywall behind it, revealing a stairwell that went farther down into a basement space. I didn't know if I wanted to push my luck by going into the basement. I might never get out. Or I could get arrested if they thought I came down here to steal something.

Run back upstairs. Cut your losses and get the hell out of here, I decided, but when I got back up the flight of stairs I found that those doors were locked too. "If anyone is out on the landing, could you open this door for me?" No response. I was panicked and furious. I felt my breath tight and quick, signifying seconds wasted. Each breath, another second would vanish, so I stopped myself.

"Think!" I shouted in the stairwell. The exit doors were one-way to the lobby door. The lobby door should always be open, but it wasn't. *Why would he or anyone have to lock a lobby door?* I understood locking it so that someone couldn't come in, but I didn't understand locking it so that someone couldn't come out.

Underground access, BINGO! I ran back downstairs, looked at the black door, and hesitated. If I called the guard to open the padlock, it would take forever. The lock was on my side, so the guard would be forced to go up to the second floor and then come down with the key. I would then have to have a meaningless and probably demeaning conversation with this guy, who would ask me questions that I didn't have time to answer. Then I realized, *He could still be smoking his cigarette for all I know—O the lords of oblivion! The black door. It is worth a try.*

Smashing open my only escape route, I began tip-tapping down the cement staircase into the basement. The radio, which had been turned low, began to call my number. By the sound of the dispatcher's voice, I could tell it was not the first time he'd tried to reach me.

At the bottom of the stairs a hallway continued, winding away. I pulled the radio up to my cheek and pressed the button to respond. The radio went numb with a single beep. This building was too thick to allow the little radio waves out. It was swallowing any kind of transmission, much as it was swallowing me.

"Thirty-nine? Thirty-nine? Thump thump, Thirty-nine!" I could hear the buttons of the telephone in the office as he paged me. "Where's my Energizer bunny?"

"Shut up, man! I'm trapped in a fucking basement!"

No response. My pager started buzzing: 911911911911911911. "Shit."

I ran down the unpainted hallway and came across a metal gate that swung wide open into some kind of underground garage hidden beneath the street. There was not a soul around. I tried the radio again and still I was in too deep to transmit. The radio looked back at me with a kind of electrical retardation. I was in a black cavern beneath the earth, a garage, with dim yellow lights that only further hid the distant access ramps. There were no cars in the garage; emptiness was very present.

AS I LOOKED into Gil's black eyes, the same was true. They were hollow—too empty to even look back at mine. Intoxication and insanity had muffled his sharp mind to dull sound, but in it I had no fear.

But then I was not your average kid. I'd always been attracted to breaking the rules and seeing the parts of the world that I was not supposed to see. And so I found Gil, a guide and a generous friend who helped shed a little light into the darkness. He introduced me to the attitudes, the people, and the habits I was never supposed to come into contact with.

In the period of our friendship, roughly from the ages of eight to fourteen, I had been offered marijuana on a weekly basis, I had been invited to threesomes and foursomes with his loosely labeled *friends.* I had learned how to shoot an AK-47, his father's trophy from Vietnam. I was given elaborate descriptions of the bent spoons and pipes that cluttered his coffee table. I was challenged constantly about whether it was right or wrong to commit a crime.

"The best way to change a law is to break it—again and again. Break it until it becomes absurd to everyone."

Gilbert was not a good man in any customary sense. He was a dealer and a liar. He was a thief and an addict. To me he was a friend and a guide, telling me in different ways all the time, even amid his delirium, that I should not judge him, though I should never imitate him, either. He was the first person who taught me to question. He would offer me ludicrous things so that I had to reject him or refuse him. He would trick me into saying no as often as possible. For example, when he asked me if I wanted to try his "red seed," or when he asked me if I wanted to take a drive, I said no. "Good. That's good" always followed.

"Do you know what these are?" he asked, holding a plate of needles out across his musty sofa.

"Yeah."

"Want some? I have a bunch."

"No thanks, Gil."

"Good. You should never do this shit. Do you know why I do it?"

"No."

"It is an addiction. Do you know why I am addicted?"

"No."

"I made a mistake. I am not proud of it, but I am not ashamed of it, either. Do you know why?"

"No, Gil. Why?"

"It is a mistake I think I have a *right* to make. Do you understand?"

We went through this ritual way out on the 144th block of North Miami Avenue, in a city grid that went over four hundred blocks north and south and some three hundred blocks into the Florida Everglades. I was in training for the real world, and I didn't have any idea of it. We went through ideas about "us and them," "institutionalization," "authority," and "the corporate machine." I would listen. "What are our rights, really?" "What do they mean by *disorderly conduct*?" "What is a free market when every transaction is taxed?" "What is a free country, Travis? What does it mean to be an American?"

"I don't know," I said.

"You have a right to take any path you choose. Follow your bliss. But you can't hurt other people. That is the only rule. You need to be able to have your bliss without keeping other people from their bliss. *That is a free country.* That is America. At least, that is what we meant when we signed the Declaration of Independence and told England to piss off.

46

"You *can* follow your bliss, whoever you are. *In a true democracy, you can be low and noble—and no one can judge you for it.*"

Now I just wanted to get the hell out of this garage. My pager was going off, reading 911, and my number was still being called over the air in vain. There was a second dock door farther east in the parking lot. I ran to it, hoping to find another guard. All I saw were cameras and another hallway. I ran along the hall, recognizing the industrial finishing that protects the building from heavy cargo. Instead of stairs, I saw steel ramps built to comply with current safety regulations. *There has to be a way out,* I thought.

My teeth clenched, I found the metal doors of the freight elevator and hit the call button. I could hear the chain coiling up beneath the cable car in the shaft and I began to calm down. The doors opened and I stepped in.

One of my last memories of Gil was finally seeing his collection of vinyl records. It was early in the morning when I found them scattered across his back lawn. The large, arching glass doors I had helped him install between the house and his garage were shattered and toppled over. His clothes were thrown about. His furniture was upturned, and shimmering ammunition sat in the corners of the cement floor. Blood-colored glass was embedded in the grass beneath my feet. His wooden door swung open as I stood above the wreckage in the cool November dew.

The doors opened to the lobby and I quietly stepped from them. I walked past the guard and pressed open the building's giant glass doors. The thick heat filled my lungs. I could feel the familiar burn of the bright sun on my forehead again.

My bike was still locked in the shade, leaning against the huge gray arches of the ADA. I forgot how I had gotten here, what streets I'd taken, where the police were, if I was in danger or if I was not. *I don't suppose I should remember,* I thought. *I don't suppose it mat-*

ters. I stood there twirling the U-lock open in my hand. My bike leaned into my right hip. An enormous panorama of motion and space surrounded me, and light seemed to penetrate into every crevice everywhere. There are many ugly things about our world today and there are many ugly things about the city I live in. The one defense that allows me to move easily through a society this diverse, that *force field* that I have, is respect. To move forward, to act upon my freedom, and to make a living, I must respect the things I don't understand.

CHAPTER THREE

TORSO: AN XER'S PATH TO POLITICS

Only he who can view his own past as an abortion sprung from compulsion and need can use it to his full advantage in the present. For what one has lived is at best comparable to a beautiful statue which has had all its limbs knocked off in transit, and now yields nothing but the precious block out of which the image of one's future must be hewn.

Walter Benjamin

It WAS NOT LOVE THAT MADE ME A CYCLIST, NOR WAS IT any kind of innate passion for alleyways, punk rock, political disenfranchisement, or any of these crude stereotypes that follow in the wake of the messengers' personae. My drive began more simply. I was a cyclist by default; I was broke.

It had been two years since I'd moved to Chicago after earning a degree in theater from an arts conservatory in downtown Miami. I was living a lighter life now, perhaps a more sober one as well. I had developed a few good friends and a few freelance jobs working as an art preparator in River North. In the evenings I wrote plays and enjoyed a quaint domestic life with Lenyr, my girlfriend *at the time* and a painter from the arts conservatory back home.

My days were spent in basements packing sculptures into crates or suspending gallery walls with airplane cable atop tottering ladders, and even though most of my work was really a glorified kind of manual labor, I could say, with a real sense of accomplishment, that art was paying the rent. Lenyr would temper my pride by reminding me, not with words but with a raised eyebrow or the shrug of a shoulder, that art was *hardly* paying the rent and, at that, only hardly paying *my half* of the rent. Cash was scarce. We barely had enough for a good dinner, so paying monthly rates on unreliable transit service didn't seem logical at all. The idea of buying a car and driving to work was totally absurd. So to protect my fragile niche in the gallery district and to stretch our resources, I decided, and soon preferred, to bike to work.

I would take Clark Street through the North Side into downtown. It held a diverse strip of ethnic enclaves laid out six miles long, like colored socks in a department store. I enjoyed the sunlight, the circulation, and that ineffable oozy-bouncy groove feeling that only a bike can provide. Wiping the beads of sweat from my brow, I was out there swerving around beer bottles in Wrigleyville and dodging whale-sized CTA buses that swam through the gutters, wagging their articulated extensions and spewing black froth. Even in June, brothas cruised the alleys wearing down coats, looking something like mutated inner tubes. Their black faces and gold teeth seemed to yawn condensed air from their evening revelries.

Long lines of cars would obstruct my path, sometimes violently, and I would timidly veer toward safety. People would shout crass comments out of their windows at me and I would just keep rolling without complaint. Occasionally someone would throw a Coke can into my path. Other times the drivers would bully their way between other cars and the curb and make it hard for me to pass. In stalled traffic I would sit behind their idle bumpers trying to avoid the clouds of carbon monoxide that pumped out of their exhaust pipes.

On a few stretches I would share the curb with a small line of other cyclists—bike commuters, really—who followed one another loosely like a line of orphaned ducklings. Many of them, covered with reflectors and safety gear, were average businesspeople with their pant legs carefully strapped to the ankle. Occasionally I would see a messenger, sprinting through the car traffic, weaving around cabs and buses as if they were little flags on a slalom course. They would cruise past me like I was dust in the road; in their cool arrogant way, they seemed to move with their eyes closed, as if the four-lane wall of traffic at the intersection of Wells and North Avenue was some kind of bluff that they saw right through.

I didn't try to compete. I simply enjoyed being in the public sphere, traveling through the cement canyons of city life. I celebrated my sense of freedom. Like a spy of the metropolis, carefree and car-free, blasé as a well-fed homeless man, I was in the arena where society lived up to all its best and worst reputations.

Chicago to me was raw, honest, unabashed, and profoundly graceful. I could see the choreography of motorists fighting for parking meters. I could watch the wall-sized ads pop up and down the billboards on train stations and get painted over the brickwork of warehouses. I could see fashionable people and audacious bums strolling down the centerline of a street as if it were their own. I could track the paths of green-coated meter maids, who dropped thirty-dollar parking tickets on the hoods of cars like orange flower petals.

I was feeling a kind of flirtation with the roots of trees growing out of their cast-iron collars in the sidewalk and the slow-moving black asphalt that buckled over curbs and tore down street signs. I watched the graceful lines where cement, like splashing water, had crushed into gray spots around the corner of a building. I was attracted to the human nature that I could read in the man-made landscape. I was falling in love with public space.

54   I once saw a garbage can lined with a black plastic bag launch a beer bottle under the pressure of gusting wind. The bag inverted, filling up like a hot-air balloon. The bottle flew ten feet into the air, smashed over a gridded strip of subway ventilation, and vanished into the underground without a trace.

When I arrived at an art gallery filled with these images, I would always wonder, *Which was the more honest arena? The street? Or the exhibition? And which was the more profound?* The street, of course, the street, in almost every case.

ON THE THIRTEENTH DAY of June, I was working alone in the Maya Polsky Gallery, straightening one side of a warped diptych and hanging it just out of a line of sunlight that came in through the loft's tall windows. The city had just begun to see the first signs of summer: 80 degrees Fahrenheit, and clean, dry air. Beams of white light reflected off windshields and wax jobs. Outside the gallery I could see the couriers hanging out on the steps of 212 West Superior. These tough-looking rebels with thick arms and heavy gestures were still pale from head to tail by the markings of their winter gear. They smoked cigarettes and looked up at a big sky and a few soft clouds that passed overhead.

Fuck it, I said to myself, letting a bad idea consume me. I stuffed away my paint-spilled work clothes in the back room of the gallery and rode off in shorts and a blue guayabera, leaving my checklist of odd jobs for another day.

Rolling through the crisp air, I felt like an angel. A cool draft of wind shook my hair into long gold ribbons. I sped around the buckled intersections of the gallery district, cutting off taxis, timing my way through the buzzing traffic and crosswalks filled with workers in gray suits sweating in their black leather shoes. I was heading to Oak Street Beach to enjoy Lake Michigan just before it got warm enough to be pissed in by the rest of city. I looked forward to hanging out with a group of funky jugglers and jumping into some kick circles with the Hacky Sack showmen who haunt the lakeshore there.

I flew through flush green parks, parting flocks of pigeons. I pulled up alongside a yellow bus, sharing smiles with kids on their way home from school. I sped ahead of its barreling engine as it forced its way through the narrow streets of the Gold Coast. On Oak, in a small strip between State and Rush, where the traffic is always backed up, I skimmed past idling cars that sat—*crack!*

Suddenly I was thrown, *good-bye,* into the clear blue sky, like a white egret launched from mangroves.

I wasn't quite sure what happened. Even midflight I was enjoying this clean, dreamlike high. The painted asphalt was still moving beneath me, but my motility had changed. I was less agile, more inert. I felt like a javelin whose only obstacle was the wind. I thought: *Maybe my bicycle has vanished. Maybe I don't need it anymore.* The street continued moving and I kept gliding along. Instinctively my arms crossed my chest. My back twisted and my shoulders came up to protect my head, curving me backward in a crescent shape. Then, in a wave of motion, the strip of black asphalt reached up and pulled me out of the sky. I heard a series of cracks and snaps ricochet through my torso as I absorbed the intersection and slid.

My right arm, braced by my left hand, went limp slapping the pavement as I collapsed around it. My left shoulder came to the street as my right bounced away, turning me in space like a skipped stone. My left shoulder was ground into the grain of the asphalt, which scraped off patches of blue cotton and flesh from my sides.

My legs, now twisted to the left, smacked the street and pulled me along behind them into the oncoming traffic of Rush Street.

As I fell, my head did not touch the ground. After my landing, it dropped to the earth, exhausted.

When I opened my eyes the street was hot against my face and cars were moving past. My arms were coiled under my body like thick rope. There was no pain and no sound. My knees and ankles throbbed from their impact against the street like steel tuning forks ringing dissonant tones. My neck was pinned into my right shoulder; I could see the open sky between the long skyscrapers. For one still moment, this landscape sat peacefully on its side.

I was alive, but doubted my prospects. I knew that taking a headfirst dive into the street without a helmet left me very poor odds for survival. The whole "I think, therefore I am" routine had suddenly developed an important flaw: *What if dead men think?* Existence may not actually mean survival. As much as I could cogitate, I couldn't move, and so I thought, *If I can't move, who is to acknowledge my living?*

I turned my neck to sigh, frustrated by the existential dilemma. That's when the relief kicked in: *I AM ALIVE! Halle-fuckin'-lujah!* In the end, Motion equals Life—*that* I could be sure of. Suddenly the skyline re-erected itself and the sound of passing traffic rushed back in. I rolled my shocked eyes back to the far right to see what act of god, what lightning bolt, had so swiftly struck me down.

The back door of cab Number 876, now over twenty feet behind me, was open, and beside it lay the pieces of my bike, twisted and bent into a pile of loose cables and tortured geometry. A young woman stood behind the cab's door, her mouth agape, her eyes red and frightened as they looked upon me, a motionless, tangled mess.

Doored. She had opened the door into my path. The timing was so perfect that I never even saw it happen.

A crowd gathered. The key witness, the chorus leader, was a day-time drunk talking crazily and walking with his feet too wide apart, keeping everyone on the sidewalk while I lay there like a petrified salamander.

"Don't move, don't move. Call an ambulance! *Not you.* You, you over there," he said, pointing to the store clerk of Bang & Olufsen, "you." A tall, well-dressed clerk disappeared into his shop on command while the clown bragged of his intelligent maneuver: "He pays real estate tax. See, *that's* how you get things done."

I planted my left hand on the asphalt and pushed myself back on my knees. "Wait! Don't move! You don't know what could be broken. Jesus, man, what the hell are you thinking!"

I tried to respond but I was nauseous; it hurt to breathe. I tried to stand because I had to know if I would ever walk away from this. Stacking myself up inch by inch, putting my weight on my right foot and pressing the street from beneath me, I found that the back of my left hand could be pulled from the ground. My left leg was not responding, but I forced it into place by tilting my hip. I could see that I was bleeding from my elbow, my left hand, and a line of road rash that trailed from my shoulder to my ankle. I straightened my back and looked up to see myself standing in the path of a mustard-yellow Crown Victoria.

The driver came out of the cab yelling. I heard his voice; he was Indian or Pakistani, and he was trying to blame the accident on the passenger. He insisted that he was not at fault for being a good eight feet from the curb. He said the woman had jumped out of the cab unpredictably.

When the cop arrived, he took a glance at me and proceeded to the passenger in question. She was a PYT half his age. She looked at me from the sidewalk and spoke. I hoped that her words would be meant for me. They weren't. She was looking at me but talking to the cop: "Can I go now?"

But the cop was just warming up to her, trying to get her number, talking about himself with these mellow Al Green tones. The crowd continued looking at me from the various corners of the street silently, shocked and amazed, much like me, hooked by the aesthetics of blood and injustice.

The injuries seemed to have come from every angle. I could track them, counting, noting each millisecond of my progress across the pavement. But then the injuries kept unfolding in the form of the insults and inadequacies of the surrounding crowd. The fool, the cop, the young woman, the taxi driver—all characters in a little play—spread the guilt among them. "What were you riding a bike for, anyhow?" the officer asked, looking back at his *sweet thang* for approval. Was this to be the moral for the audience and for me, the protagonist spared from certain death? Was I at fault for riding *a bicycle*? For *not* driving a car?

As I watched blood pool in my palm, I could see the captivated attention of the spectators. I closed my fist to keep from them the satisfaction, *the spectacle,* of my mortality. Arlequino walked me to the curb. This was not the theater I had come to Chicago for.

FOR MANY WEEKS following the accident with cab Number 876 the simplest of chores were agonizing. I would have to work as hard brushing my teeth as I'd once worked rigging a stage light during a performance in nearly total darkness. Dressing myself was equally problematic, but the worst part of recovery was the shame I felt at depending on someone else. Lenyr was graceful about the new obligations that my disability had foisted upon her. I was the one who found it hard to accept. For the first time in my so-called adult life, I couldn't feed myself and I couldn't work.

All of my installation jobs involved heavy lifting, hammering nails into walls, screwing eyebolts into ceilings, fixing electrical strips, crating and uncrating art objects, drilling holes, and painting rooms. I'd been rendered useless.

I called the galleries I had been working for and told them I would be out of touch for a few months. Upon explanation, I got little pity and certainly no compensation for my time out of work. I understood that; it wasn't their fault that I was an independent contractor working without insurance. Only one of the gallery managers showed concern about how I would manage. Even then, I am not sure if she, who had lived most of her life in the Soviet Union, was really concerned or if she was just curious to see how the disabled function in America.

"How are you going to get by?" Eva asked.

"I really don't know," I answered with some embarrassment. I had no plan of action, no guidance, and little rest from the injuries. I needed medical care, and so I opened the big book and started making calls.

"Do you have insurance?" the office jockeys would ask.

"Well, that's the problem, ma'am, I don't. But I can give you the insurance information of the responsible party. A guy named Mike Hensen from American Country said I would need a lien on the payments and that you can send all the—"

"But we don't do that, Mr. Culley. We need to have some form of insurance to offer you treatment."

"Well, American Country Insurance is *insurance*. Isn't it?"

"Is it *your* insurance?"

"No. It's the responsible party's insurance."

"Then we can't help you."

Every call I made was a refusal, except for one to an orthopedic surgeon whose office on the Northwest Side took me ninety minutes to reach by bus. Once there, I waited for four hours in a crowded lobby filled with families that spoke, or chose to speak, no English.

When the doctor finally saw me, he told me take off my shirt. I looked at him like he was a madman: had he no idea how long it had taken me to put this shirt on? He went to work probing my bruises, twisting my arm into positions that made me shout in pain. When he released me from his grip, he began dictating the torn ligaments, fractures, and hematomas into a telephone. Then he told me to make six follow-up appointments with the secretary and he shoved me out the door like I was a cheap whore.

The secretary handed me a bill for $195! I was reminded: *whores don't get billed after they are screwed, clients do.* I explained that I had only come to that office because the person I spoke with on the telephone had agreed to put a lien on the cab company for my payments.

"That's your lawyer's business," she replied. "Everyone who leaves here gets a bill."

I left more battered than when I'd come in, having learned nothing about my injuries and gotten no pain relief or even a recommendation about how to help heal the injuries. Then I spent the next two hours taking buses through the Northwest neighborhoods trying to cover the distance of a twelve-minute bike ride.

The next day I got back on the phone and continued lining up one doctor's refusal after another until, slowly, through the litany of rejections and the continued pain in my arms, back, hips, and knees, through the buckled vertebrae from leaning over the phone and the headache generated from the sound of dial tones and numbers bleeping off in tune, I began to smile. The impossibility of finding help had forced its way into my sense of humor: *So you want to play dirty? You want to treat me like I can just be pushed aside? You want to funnel me through your social sewage system and make me feel like I am of no worth to the world?* I grimaced. *Okay, we'll play dirty then.*

I knew that I could do it—I had been through worse. I had once been a sixteen-year-old runaway living in a gold Chevy Caprice Classic that I called Puke. That time in my life was not easy and it was not fun. But I survived. I finished high school by busing tables at a restaurant. I would run the half-eaten plates into the kitchen and chomp into discarded sandwiches, scraping the remaining food into the big rolling trash bins beneath the cook's window. One bite per plate—only one. That way I would never get caught. If the manager came in I could lower my head and run out to clean off the sloppy dishes on the outdoor patio. A tomato, a handful of french fries, a margarita, a fish filet, a tuft of turkey covered in mayonnaise and pulled from an inedible baguette—this was how I made it through high school. I would eat whatever I could sneak and I would wash it back with eighty-proof swill: rum, vodka, a fruity daiquiri or a shot of Jameson that was left unemptied.

In these hard times, I had to give up the amenities of my youth and focus. I dedicated myself to the theater and to school. Before I knew it, four years had passed and I had earned a BFA. When it was all over, I had what looked like a golden future and a world of promise. My degree, my talent, and my education made me feel that I was part of the world, that I was useful, even *necessary.* I had lost that feeling somewhere in my move to Chicago, and at this moment, handicapped and unemployed, I missed that sense of promise. I'd veered from my path, and I wasn't even quite sure how it had happened.

By the time I was well enough to work again, I had opened a theater company, booked a space at the cheapest theater I could rent, cast it with a handful of young actors, and dressed the scene with the work of artists who were making a living as waiters, students, café baristas, or retail salesclerks. As a group, but mostly on my credit card, we mounted an elaborate production at a little space in Bucktown. I thought I could rebuild my bright future by doing what I had been trained for. The whole world had seemed to applaud my work before. Why would they not applaud now when I was using *real* actors and a difficult play in a *true-to-life* Chicago theater?

The opening weeks of the show were exciting. Community interest was high, reviews were fair, but by the third week of the production we were playing to one or two shadows in an otherwise empty theater, having long lunches because our matinees had been called off. The applause, and the sense of promise with it, did not come.

Soon I was working on the next project, trying to find the resources to continue. I would make any sacrifice, working twenty-

63

hour days, storing lumber in the dining room, turning the apartment into a rehearsal space. Props, lighting instruments, stage pieces, and new plays organized my weeks, but my life only seemed to be spiraling more and more out of control. Under all the stress and confusion, Lenyr and I decided to call it off. I didn't grieve. I just kept working, thinking that it would all pay off soon. I found myself instead selling my used books and CDs so that I could eat and avoiding bills so that I could take out ads in the audition section of the local papers.

Eventually, I went back to work, putting in hours at bookstores, retail shops, and galleries. I found work as a carpenter's assistant, a mover, a handyman, and the more I wanted to create, the more resources I needed to accomplish it. I teamed up with other local artists and continued directing and producing whatever I could, keeping the faith that one day I was going to be able to survive as an artist. Yes, one day I was going to *make it.* In the meantime I would be a wage slave, a failing member of the working class, wondering how in the hell I could ever make an important contribution from down here.

ONE OF THE better jobs I found was at a warehouse in the East Bank area, not far from the Merchandise Mart. I worked with Bosnian immigrants, veterans from their recent civil war. In the American workforce their education was nullified, their credentials shredded, and to pay the bills they were forced to work sixty hours a week delivering heavy boxes, loading storage bins, and dividing the floors of a warehouse into miles of six-foot rooms that would be leased out monthly to yuppies in need of a place to put their skis for summer.

I was a leasing agent for this warehouse, but when I worked with the Bosnians, I was a go-between, a translator, telling them where to put their labor. These guys were the one reason that I didn't just quit in three weeks and move on to the next job. With them, I could get out of the dusty office and help load kitchen appliances or un-load banking boxes or maneuver heavy crates. I could have sat in the truck with the paperwork while the guys did the grunt work, but I had too much fun maneuvering couches through tight hall-ways and climbing over furniture to unload boxes from the deep re-cesses of an old truck. I wanted to be part of the team because I respected the hard work they were doing.

That respect was magnified when, unloading records at the Chicago Sun-Times Building, Dzevade and I were moving like a single machine, schlepping copy boxes two at a time like we were a human conveyor belt. When one skid was clear, Dzevade would up-turn the pallet, smacking the wooden flat against the inside wall of the truck like a wrestler. Then he would dig his claws into the new pile and emerge with two new boxes. Work was his life—I could see it in every move he made, in every assignment he took, and in every box he stacked onto our dollies.

Going in for the last armload, Dzevade slipped and fell between the truck and the loading dock, slamming his right knee into the iron liftgate. He looked up at me, sweating. His face was rigid and white, shaking with pain. For a moment he forgot how to speak En-glish. We interlocked our elbows and I helped pull him from the hole. He collapsed onto the cold dock floor and his eyes rolled up toward a line of yellowed fluorescent lights in prayer. When he could sit up he began to pull his pant leg to his thigh. A lump of flesh the size of a tennis ball was swelling up around his kneecap and leaking a mixture of blood and clear fluid. He told me to fetch a roll of packing tape and to get the napkins from under his coffee cup in the truck's dashboard.

He stuck the coffee-tinted paper to his swelling wound and wrapped it with the brown tape, cutting it from the roll with his teeth. "Help me stand," he said. We interlocked our elbows again and I leaned back, way back. With his arms he climbed his way up my shoulders so that, by the time he was standing, we were in a close embrace.

It was strange to carry the weight of a man I worked with. That weight signified the break between life and labor that many people will never know. His smell was thick and his arms were tinted black from dust. His sweat had fallen onto my brow and had slapped the inside of my forearm. This closeness, I understood, was part of being a soldier. It was the realm that these veterans shared and understood implicitly. It was not their nationality or their language that made them all appear to come from the same spirit; it was their trust.

"Travis. Don't tell Vanya, please," Dzevade whispered. "I cannot afford to be out of work. You understand?"

"Yes, I do. Yes, I do," I consoled him. Our contact broke and Dzevade climbed his way off the dock and pulled himself into the cab in silence.

Dzevade told me as we drove back toward the warehouse, shaking and rattling down Union Street, that he just wanted his kids to be citizens who could speak the language, choose their work, and live with security and confidence.

"I have bad news, Dzevade. I was born a citizen. I have a relative who signed the Declaration of Independence. My blood has been in this country for eleven generations, and I struggle. I struggle, Dzevade, or I would never be working with you."

He laughed. "But you will do something? Something great?"

"Shit, I don't know."

"The theater! Yes? I know. You do the theater, won't you!"

"It doesn't look good."

"You're telling me!" The two of us, nearly crying, found ourselves laughing hysterically as we acknowledged the gap between the hard realities of life and the dreams we had concocted of being American.

ONE FRIDAY AFTERNOON I found myself working alone. John, the kid who would usually close the office with me, was taking the opportunity to get high and get laid. He'd hopped over the counter, given me a big bright smile, and jingled his keys at me as he'd run out.

A few minutes before I could lock up for the day, the phone rang. It was Julie, a dancer and choreographer who was also my girlfriend *at the time*. (I seem to have girlfriends only *at times*. I am not quite sure why, but for me, love never seems to stick.) Anyway, she asked if I was going to the bike rally that she'd seen mentioned in the *Chicago Reader*.

Bike rally? I thought about the accident. I suddenly remembered the cop who'd asked me *why I was riding a bike*—as if there was some other way for me to get around a city! *That's right!* I thought. *Just because I don't have an automobile doesn't mean I have to suffer the arrogant disregard of every four-wheeled prick who thinks he owns the road! Just because I am poor doesn't mean I am without my rights! Does it?*

A thing called *bike activism* suddenly made perfect sense to me. It would be a call in support of a forgotten constituency: those who, for whatever reason, don't drive. I could hear the cars roar in the distance and I could see the yellowed sky out of the big warehouse windows. I remembered the dark headlights of cab Number 876 and the black splash marks on its open door. *"Can I go now?"*

"Of course," I said into the telephone with the sound of eureka in my voice. "Of course I'm going to the bike rally."

"Oh, so you know about it?"

"No, I don't know anything about it. But if there is a bike rally I am going to be there." She gave me the specifics while my eyes, almost naturally, drifted up at the highway shadowing Ohio Street in front of the warehouse. *Just because I don't drive doesn't mean I don't pay taxes. Just because I don't subscribe to OPEC doesn't mean I have no right to the place I fucking call my home! Does it?*

I shut down the building, running through the warehouse's wooden halls, heaving on the heavy dock doors until they closed, and slapping padlocks on their steel latches until they snapped shut. I set the alarm, hopped over the gray countertop, hoisted my bike onto my shoulder with a "By this, ye shall conquer" kind of valor, and clamored out the front door, fully prepared, once again, to make my contribution to the world.

I had seven minutes.

PULLING INTO DALEY PLAZA I came upon a motley crowd. Bike messengers who looked like tired camels sat on their bikes, laughing and talking with riders dressed in suits who wore small Velcro straps around their ankles. Some guys with long beards and knitted hats wore signs with slogans like ONE LESS CAR and FUELED BY POTA-TOES. These greenies rode in harmony with young executives, schoolteachers, business owners, lawyers, stockbrokers. Many ages were represented. Children sat comfortably in plastic pannier seats, their round helmets tipping to one side.

There were a few older people there as well. There was Bill, on his 1960s steel clunker, who had kept his 1960s sense of social responsibility rolling smooth. There was a woman my grandmother's age, still working as a teacher in Hyde Park. In her late seventies, she'd ridden eight miles just to get to the Loop, and she had at least fifteen more miles to go before she'd make it home again. Then there was Jim Redd, a man in his fifties whose white hair and leathered hands could not conceal his youthfulness. He was strong and tall and he glowed with joviality. He stood on the stone pediment that footed Chicago's famous Picasso sculpture, throwing rolls of blue crepe paper into a crowd of hundreds. People in the crowd scooped up the flying tape and began to tie it around their bars or lace it into the spokes of their bicycles.

I set my bike down, wondering for a moment if I should lock it up. Around me, sitting on their sides or in piles, were hundreds of bikes, twenty-dollar beaters, two-thousand-dollar road bikes, and four-thousand-dollar Y-frame mountain bikes left upturned on their seat and handlebars. None of them were locked. In a rare act of conformity I dropped my old machine in the granite courtyard and stepped up to the white-haired guy and asked if he was the one in charge.

"No one is in charge! Are you kidding? That would spoil all the fun." Redd laughed, turning away to toss more decorations.

A clean-cut man with red cheeks and bright blue eyes handed me a route map that would steer the demonstration through the city and lead us to the intersection of Clark and Belmont—an intersection on Chicago's hip North Side. His only words to me were "This'll wake 'em up." I found out that his name was Michael Burton; he'd once been a bike messenger but now he was working for the Statewide Housing Action Coalition.

I saw a man with long silky brown hair and a thick beard. He had a boyish, saintly face and a helmet painted like a walnut. "Jimbo," he said outright, shaking my hand. I gave him my name and in exchange I got a little orange flyer advertising the next Critical Mass ride.

"Critical Mass?" I asked. "Is that what they call this?"

"Uh, yep," he said simply as he walked away.

In the next instant I received a flyer for the A-zone, an anarchists and activists network. Then I received an invitation to a party that was being thrown by D.J. Esperanto. I received a flyer advocating a big presence at the demonstration against police brutality in October. Then I received literature about Rolando Cruz, Mumia Abu-Jamal, and an underground film project. The offerings went on and on, until my hands were filled with colored paper. I balled it all up, looked at a young woman with shining curly hair who was straddling a mountain bike. "What the hell is this about?" I asked her, shoving all the flyers in my bag, overwhelmed.

She looked back with a big smile, held up a pack of flyers cut vertically that were tied together with a zip cord: "Did you get one of these?"

"What can it possibly be that I don't already have!"

She laughed, scooted her bike closer, and handed me the whole pack of flyers. "These are for the people we'll see. It just tells them what the ride is about."

"Now, that's what I need. I have no idea what this is about."

The young woman, whose name was Katherine, said, pondering a little, "I think it's about bikers who are tired of getting run over."

"I can relate," I replied.

Cheers from the crowd greeted one special guest. He rode a big Schwinn cruiser from the fifties with an old leather springy seat, wide handlebars, and fat tires. Mounted on his bars was an old brass horn with a big black rubber bulb. He wheeled around the massive sculpture, squeezing the fat bulb, making the horn sing over the crowd. Katherine called him BigHorn and said she thought his name was Eric.

"Okay. BigHorn it is."

Other instruments came to life, accompanying the tooting trumpet that circled the crowd. There were tambourines, bike bells, and ear-piercing air horns. One guy had a collage of cowbells attached to his bars, and another had drum cymbals delicately straddling his front tire. He held a drumstick and could reach down and crash the cymbals as he rode. One biker played a mounted conga with his right hand while he steered with the other. For a moment I couldn't stop laughing. I was entranced by the inventiveness of these demonstrators and their demeanor. They were serious, but they were not angry. They were just having a good time working to make important local changes in urban life and city management. I told Katherine how impressed I was, but she interrupted to say emphatically that this was not just a *local* thing. Apparently it happened all over the world, though it had only recently caught on in Chicago.

"All over the world?"

"Yes, simultaneously, the last Friday of the month, all over the world." She clarified that dates changed a little bit here and there, but basically it was the same. She listed cities like Sydney, Berlin, Zurich, Paris, London, Tokyo, Kyoto, Austin, Phoenix, Seattle, New York, Philadelphia, Portland, and Atlanta. The movement started in San Francisco, where they have gotten over ten thousand people in their rides, completely dominating the city traffic. "It is local, but it is a different kind of local. It is everywhere, *locally.*"

I introduced myself to a couple of guys who appeared to be near the core of the activist group. I was surprised to find that they were not throwback radicals simply trying to eradicate the automobile from the world. This core group, as radical as some of their ideas seemed, were talking, arguing, and then agreeing upon safe and conservative ideas for the mass.

Amid this group was a conservative-looking guy named Gareth. He wore a tie, spoke with clarity, and advocated his ideas with an acute appeal to reason. "If you ask me, I would say let's get the mass on the highway and head out toward the airport. That's where our audience spends most of their time in transit," he reasoned. "For a stretch of a mile or two, what could they do? Come after us? I don't think so. They would just see us zipping past and they would get a flyer jammed in their wipers, big deal."

Gregg Gunther, a tall and serious-looking cyclist who wore a bright pink jersey covered with yellow happy faces, tempered Gareth's idea. "First things first," he said. "We need to take back the streets we have a right to: Logan, Clybourn, Clark—*city streets.* The people who are using these local streets might not be the sub-urban conservatives we love to hate, but these people *can* bike to work. They just don't know that they can."

"I don't see what's so *conservative* about suburbanites," Gareth interjected.

"That's where there are whole closed-off neighborhoods of white Republicans with two point five kids and all that."

"Suburban may be traditional, but traditional is not conservative. The conservatives are right here *conserving*. That's why I say we need to have some suburban influence. But you make a good point: if city people can bike or access a train, you're right, we should encourage them to do that."

"Not that the highway is a bad idea," a guy named Miles asserted.

"But it's too involved," Gareth agreed.

"Right. You're not asking those people to bike, you're asking them to sell the car and move and change their whole lives—and that's a tough pull."

A horn sounded through the square like a trumpet. BigHorn was circling the sculpture blowing on a little plastic bugle. In minutes there were hundreds of cyclists following him, giving catcalls and weaving in and out of one another. For a moment I stood up on the sculpture's steplike platform. The sea of riders moving in circles was momentarily overwhelming, like seeing the swell of waves rise above the bow of a ship. From the ledge of the Picasso, I mounted my bike, pulling into the current of moving bicycles, becoming swarmed by the sound of their bike bells and air horns. The ride had begun.

CYCLING IN A GROUP of three hundred people is an incredible feeling, but the first time, it was a little weird. I was used to biking hunched down in a posture of perpetual defense. But now there were all these people around me to talk to. It turned out that

BigHorn and I had put in hours at some of the same stores to fund our creative endeavors.

"You got to make a living." He laughed, recognizing a curious social paradox. "If you can't make a living, how can you get any work done?" We compared notes about the ways we had to work to support our careers. "And everything you earn goes right back to the world in materials, in time, in labor. You work to give it all away again," he said.

"Yeah, you have to sacrifice everything to contribute anything at all," I agreed.

"Totally! You've got to have a suicide reflex, a will to sacrifice all of your harvest, all of the time. If you don't, you won't ever have a chance to succeed. If you are not out there spending everything, how can you possibly earn anything?"

"I think I am going to throw myself in the fire and get it over with," I said lightly, thinking little of my own comment.

His laugh ripped through me, a laugh that was neither an agreement nor a disagreement. He had a fuzzy goatee and a boyish face, and he smiled as his knees rose and fell smoothly with the traffic. He stretched his fingers out across the plastic handgrips of his old cruiser and extended his right palm to me. Our fingers met gently in a slow-motion high five that rolled smoothly from palm to palm. "Rock on," BigHorn said slyly.

A black kid with short hair and a blond beard rode up and piped in, "It's like we're being told you can be anything in this country *but* creative, anything *but* different, anything *but* genuine. We are not forced into slavery. We're forced into minimum wage and we live in ghettos, left to fight over little pieces that are left for us like rats in a can. That's why the middle class drives cars and lives in the 'burbs. It's protection from the dirty and the poor and the people that are different. They put sanctions on the city, man!"

Soon there were at least ten people supporting his speech by listening closely. "Do you know how many people are struggling just to make their own work come alive? Their life's work? Fuck music, fuck art. I'm talking about raising a child!" He started riding with both fists in the air. "I'm going to take this country, man! I'm going to take it back!" Then he hurried off toward an oncoming taxicab and slipped one of those vertical flyers through its half-open back window. "The power is here, brotha," he told a passenger as the mass carried on.

The women on the ride seemed especially excited. They smiled brightly and sat upright. Adrianna, a former courier who had horns coming out of her silver helmet, exulted that it was great to ride in this kind of group. She complained that she was so used to being honked at, touched, and told to get off the road that it made her sometimes hate riding. She told me about an incident that had taken place only a week back. A woman came up behind her in a car, hit her back tire, and knocked her off the road. If Adrianna hadn't shouted at the driver, she would not have even stopped! When she did stop, Adrianna found that she could actually have a rational conversation with her.

The motorist's testimony was that she just didn't know what else to do. "You were on the road. How *should* I get past you?" the driver asked. "What am I supposed to do?"

"Finally!" Adrianna said about the demonstration, someone was speaking out to protect *her* rights on the road, and to teach drivers how to *share space*. "I am not stuck in the sixties, but I am not necessarily stuck in the twentieth century, either. Roads were not made for automobiles!" A group of cyclists cheered her protest, and she shook her head, trying to hide her blushing cheeks.

At this point, the mass was moving only about seven miles an hour. We were trying to stay together because in demonstrations like these, strange things are known to happen. If the density of the group ever got too drawn out or diminished, I was warned, motorists would be tempted to push holes through the crowd. In other cities, cars had charged through the mass at the expense of the two or three bikers who were in their way. At one point in a Philadelphia mass, a courier was run over and dragged about a hundred feet along the South Street Bridge. When his bike disconnected from beneath the car, the motorist just drove away.

Shocked by stories like this, I began to ride a few blocks up ahead of the mass, wondering how it is we let such hatred grow in our own cities. Roaming through my mind to find a suitable explanation, I noticed that I had traveled nearly seven blocks ahead of the mass. A little shocked by having so mindlessly ridden ahead, I decided to stop and let the group catch up with me. It was then that I realized I was standing in the middle of an intersection.

Lines and signs marked the street lanes explicitly for automobiles. The pedestrians were sanctioned to cross inside carefully drawn white lines. I was somewhere in between, unsure of which directions to follow.

Traffic going north and south was thick and aggressive. Cars were speeding around me at thirty or more miles an hour. Contact with any one of them could have been fatal. A truck, flashing a left blinker, stopped and sat on his horn. He looked at me through a dirty windshield and yelled something. I knew that three hundred cyclists were a few blocks back and gaining. I thought, *What if I don't respond? What would that make me? Some kind of engineering obstruction? A malfunction? Would the driver get out and hunt me down or seek to punish me for assaulting his schedule? For tying up the tracks? Would he take or destroy my property? Would he kill me?*

I am a human being. I am not some machinist's error. Let him do what he's got to do.

With that, I dumped my bike, lay down in the street with my arms spread wide, and looked up at the miracle of life as seen in the reflection of a blue sky. At a café on the corner I saw two women hiding behind the thick plate glass stand up, excited and curious. They had no idea what was going to happen here, and neither did I.

The trucker was cursing at me through his closed window, revving his engine. Other cars approached, one going south and one going north. They both came to a stop, clogging all the traffic behind them. I could hear the truck's wheels turn toward me. Then I began to hear the approaching cries and cheers from the bike parade as they approached the unsuspecting audience. As I looked up at the small clouds rolling past, the first few bikers started passing through them, shouting, "Yeah, dude!" and "Go for it, man!" I pressed my ankles together to be narrow as possible, lifted my hands up in the air, and shouted back in full voice—no words, just sheer celebration.

One after another, flying overhead, passing through the blue sky, bikers leaned down and started slapping hands with me. Some of the skin was soft, some of it hard. Some of the hands were white, and some of them black. Some were the hands of men, some were of women—but none of that mattered. Everyone the same touched my palms and fingers, shouting and celebrating to reclaim the street, to make it human again.

I lay there beneath the mass utterly amazed, watching the shadows pass overhead. I could hear the freewheels spin and the whirl of rubber traction hissing in the air as they passed. I shut my eyes while the last hundred bikers flew past and touched my upraised hands. When the storm passed, I found myself at the back of the pack. My palms tingled. My fingertips were sore. Digital Dan Kopald hung back to make sure I got up okay and that *I* was in order. He proved to me that these were not just weirdos letting weirdo people do weirdo things. These people cared.

I leapt to my feet, my eyes wide open with excitement. He laughed at my stunt and uprighted my bike for me. I climbed back onto my pedals and sprinted into the crowd again.

At the next intersection I did a headstand, and as the bikers passed again I shook my legs around crazily. This time someone else was at the back of the crowd to stay with me. I thanked him, mounted up, and sprinted off ahead of the group again. At Wellington Avenue, I grabbed the seat of my bike and held the entire thing in the air with one hand. The front wheel leaned to one side in a soft repose. The handlebars twisted high above my head like the arrogant posture of a Civil War monument. Beyond the spokes and thin pipes of my simple instrument I could see that perfect blue sky. Lines of white clouds were drawn softly overhead as if they were carried by cherubs, and hundreds of cyclists passed this time in a blur of color beneath the bicycle, as if it were a flag in a battlefront.

At Belmont, where the rolling demonstration came to an end, I was walking in circles with my bike still held in the air. Around me in every direction, crowds of other bikers held their rides up triumphantly. The demonstrators were circling and shouting, using the street as a stage. None of the traffic disturbed us. Cars, pedestrians, and cyclists stood in amazement as far as the eye could see.

This was the theater I had come to Chicago for. *This* was the point where theater could change the way people think and live. This was a mission achieved, a performance worthy of its acclaim—and I was only one small part of its whole.

CHAPTER FOUR

THE RUN OF THE BULL

From high in the sky a man is falling. His speed is accelerating, speed for which he has no brake whatsoever. The time he has left dribbles away in silence . . . The ground—oh, how much in a hurry the ground suddenly is—to meet a man, just one, since there isn't another in the air right now, at least not one in sight.

Henri Michaux,
Tent Posts

VISITING MY FAMILY IN SOUTHERN FLORIDA FOR THE holidays, I was feeling better than I ever had before. My life had just hit this new kind of ecstatic completion. I had been working on an anti-car art exhibition with many of the people I'd met in Critical Mass. Once we'd agreed upon the title—*Autogeddon: A Critical Response to Car Culture*—I put the call out to anyone who would be interested. By the time of the opening, sculptors were giving me paintings and painters were giving me sculptures. Most of the artists were encountering the theme with creative tools they had never used before.

There were pieces that represented car-centered children's toys as budding ecological atrocities. There were paintings that showed the monstrous underside of the car as a fetish or a sex object. There were conceptual pieces that analyzed the many pollutants that the automobile creates, and there were numerous hanging or free-standing drumming devices made of brake drums, bumpers, springs, and empty Pennzoil cans. On these contraptions bikers and gallery-goers could get out all their urban animosities.

Having organized the show, hung it, and lived with it for a few weeks, I found myself riding this highly creative wave all the way into the holiday season and back to Florida, where I would be visiting my family. There, my imagination would still spin its way into wild and original ideas about the automobile and its effect on the earth, about racism and the development of the suburban state—evils of the industrial age.

This line of inquiry didn't get me cynical. It made me feel excited and a little embarrassed. When I first saw how much work we bike advocates had on our platter, I got that crazy blush you get when you smash a vase in a department store and all heads turn your way. I was giggling at the scale of a problem I had never before seen the extent of. Forget cynical—I was almost *apologetic.*

At this level of excitement, when I should have been spending time with my family, I was writing and turning big ideas into little projects. I was inspired to the point that I couldn't sit still. I would pick up crushed pens from the street and take philosophical notes on my forearms. They seemed to tell me something about the point of America, and what a good business it had become. I would leave the house excited to do nothing but stand on corners, watch the traffic flow, and write something about the tacky South Florida architecture and how all of its flamboyant colors would disappear the moment you could see them from a higher perspective. At the right altitude the entire city would look like a single sheet of cement for automobiles and air conditioners. *What would the city be shaped like,* I wondered, *without the car in its way? What would the city feel like?* I really had no idea.

One night I arranged a seven-foot sculpture of cleanly cut tree branches and a stack of abandoned car tires. I left it where it would obstruct and bewilder the morning manager of a convenience store as he drove up to the shop. The title, *The Cost of Living*, was etched into the black asphalt with the chipped corner of a cinder block.

I shared with my mother and grandmother a press clipping that showcased a sculpture I had made for the anti-car show. It was a male figure that stood about ten feet tall on a set of stolen traffic cones. It was made out of license plates, hubcaps, reflectors, and black hoses. A rusted tailpipe stood erect, parting the figure's brown fly. I called him the *Polutician*, and I thought he would make my grandmother proud.

One afternoon I found myself looking at the sky in the quiet five-by-five-foot backyard of my mother's community development that overlooked a massive rectangular lake. Across the water's surface I could see five or six enormous radio towers reflecting down into a stirring gray sky like the antennae of the Death Star— very bizarre, very bum-fuck Florida, really.

"Trav, are you working?" I heard my mother ask from her chair in the dining room.

A weighted question, I thought, but the answer was a simple "No. I'm not working," and I stepped inside to tell her my very rational reasons for being unemployed.

See, in my social sphere of twentysomething dropouts, I had seen so many young people trying to live a good life, coasting down sidewalks on slowly swaying skateboards, pounding out high-speed chess games with green-painted fingernails and untamed beards. *How do these people make it?* I'd wondered. *How can they live such pure lives and yet never seem to be in need? Do they land record deals or stock jobs at record stores? What world are they in that they don't have to make any pretenses or compromises? Or apologies about their lifestyle?* I had envied their freedom for too long, and so that fall, I'd

84

caved in and told myself that I wanted a better life and that I didn't want to pay for it by working, by making someone else rich. After all, I was an artist, a playwright, not a fucking leasing agent! I had rehearsals to go to, exhibitions to organize, sculptures that I had to move across town. I had countless things to do in the art community, and none of it required cash.

In fact, it seemed to me as if I had reached a social plateau in which I would no longer need to buy anything. I was getting free food at restaurants, free passes to theaters and movie houses; anywhere a friend worked, I was a VIP. I could get supplies with the connections I had in photo stores, art-supply stores, and hardware and lumber outlets. I had transcended commerce and found myself living in abundance, if not excess. So the question arose: if I don't need to spend money, what would be the point of making it? I could just raise my arms in the air and say, *Fuck you all!*

I did just that. I walked out of the warehouse one afternoon and spent the rest of the day writing with colored chalk on the steps of the Adler Planetarium: *I am as I am as I am as I am as I am as I am as I am.* This memory brought on a big smile.

"How much money do you have?" My mother followed, understanding my line of argument.

"Thirty-two dollars," I said, unable to hold back my laughter.

Her head turned sharply and her eyes seemed to grab mine right out of space, the way they did when I'd once told her I'd skipped school. *I was in trouble.* "So I don't suppose our Christmas is . . ."

"No. I don't have anything, Mom."

"You mean, your grandmother comes all this way to see you and you don't have a gift to give her for Christmas?"

"Something like that."

"Have you paid rent for January yet?"

"Good question."

"Have you?" When I didn't answer, she stood up from behind the table littered with little envelopes with cellophane windows. She turned on the light above us: *No. It was true.* She had never seen my face so tired and thin.

"Have you been eating?"

My eyes burned. It was amazing to me that by some hidden command my head could just fill with all this heat. The heat turned into these soft beads of liquid in my eyes. My mother stood in the doorway of the small kitchen with her arms crossed.

I started calmly. "Mother, why do we live here on this earth? We live to find a reason to live. That's all! We live to find something to be a part of. Who cares about all the rest? I have never been happier in all my life than right now! I have never been more proud of what I am doing." She turned away. "Mother, don't you see? I am doing exactly what I want with my life! To hell with the world if it doesn't want to take interest! I am not here to make other people happy. I am not here to make other people *like me.* I am going to win the top prize. The prize that says I LOVE WHAT I DO! I don't want the other prizes. You can keep the award that says *I make a good living.* You can keep the bronze medal that says *I have done what was expected.* That is not what I am here for.

"I will love what I do, and so I will do what I love—*and that's final.* I am fed up with having to live my life to somebody else's standards. Fuck everyone's version of a good life. What do they know? I have nothing to give for the holidays but a fuck-all happy son, a son who has never been more proud of himself and more important to the world around him. I think that is a blessing; count it!"

My mother sat down in her chair and held my hand. She had seen me in trouble before. She knew the rings beneath my eyes and the high pitch of my voice, but she had never seen my face so wrought, so tight and gray. She knew that the lines on the back of my neck were not those of *her child*. The rough skin of my fingers, the veins that ran over the bones of my hands, they were new. I went into the kitchen to wash my face.

"How long do you think you can do this?"

"Until the world matures. Until they figure it out."

"Figure what out?"

"They can't stop me."

"Why would they want to stop you?"

"I am going to win the top prize."

She took a deep breath and chuckled. "You'll need to eat first."

THAT CHRISTMAS I was given a dress shirt, a pair of sneakers, and a wristwatch from a sporting goods chain. Flying back into the gusting city of Chicago, I returned that watch for forty-five dollars plus tax. *I would need to eat first.*

I walked home from the Foster Avenue El station, sat down at my desk, crunched some numbers (very few), and realized that outside of a two-week installation gig at the Mexican Fine Arts Center Museum I had no income and no future. Regardless of how many miracles might fall in my favor, even if I could return my sneakers, I would soon be homeless.

Working at the museum was still helpful. Not only did it pay well but I was free to dress in my thrift-grade rags, and because I didn't have to work with the public, I didn't have to smile for anyone. If I was ecstatic, I was ecstatic. If I was pissed, I was pissed and everyone knew it. This was all that I needed, a chance to be *as I am* instead of *as I should be.* I just wanted to be real, proud, and as honest as the world around me. There, I could be comfortable. I could enjoy my work and be judged by the quality of it. I could hang art and help design spaces. I could see the ideas of the visual arts director and help him achieve his creative vision. I was in my element, using the skills I had learned from doing what it was I loved.

When those two weeks passed, I actually succeeded in landing some continuing work there. I would earn nine dollars an hour for eight hours every Monday to touch up the gallery space. These Mondays went by light as pigeon feathers in the industrial alcoves of Union Station. The rest of the week just sat there like the empty underside of a bridge. I would sit in a small swivel chair, writing and thinking up new artistic ideas. I would turn off the heat and bundle up next to a small space heater with buzzing orange coils. By now, the sums on all my utilities had risen beyond recognition. I had heat and electricity only because it was illegal for the utility companies to shut them off in the winter months. I could not make long-distance phone calls. I was lucky to have a dial tone.

I ate only canned food and rice. I would spend hours every day combing through the help-wanted section of various periodicals, trying to find work that I would be able to enjoy, even just work that I wouldn't have to hate. The galleries that I once knew were suddenly crippled by public disinterest. The gallery that I'd hung the anti-car show in was one of a few galleries that had actually had to close its doors for good. Outside of the few occupations I knew I could never enjoy doing, like waiting tables, washing cars, and sitting children, very few opportunities seemed to apply to me.

I tried. I tried scraping off the gummy stickers of used texts at a university bookstore. I did some light construction, where I could, installing insulation in the walls of a basement space a friend was building out. I shelved books at a big corporate bookstore on off-hours so that the general public wouldn't see my ragged clothes and oily hair. One night as I was leaving, the general manager offered to give me back a full-time job that I'd once held there.

"Would I have to wear a tie?" I asked her.

"I'll bring one from home if you want me to."

"Thanks, but I can't do it."

"Oh, Travis . . ." she said, seeing me look so much harder and hungrier than when we'd first met. "You make your destiny."

"I suppose," I said arrogantly. A few days later, I stopped showing up for work.

One day, now completely unemployed, I found a three-day notice from my landlord slipped under my door. It was demanding two and half months of unpaid rent. My time had come, I had failed—so I sat down to write about it. I thought about the light-bulb under the lamp. If the city wanted to shut it off, to pull the plug and make it all go black, who would I be to stop them? As I wrote, between thoughts, scribbling in a sadly worn-out sketch-book, I would look at the light and consider that at any minute it could all just go away, *snap:* blackness. But the city didn't pull the plug, and so the lights stayed on.

I kept writing. What else could I do? Living is hard, god knows, and one day someone will just pull the plug. *It could be today,* I thought. *It could be tomorrow. What would really be the difference?*

AT A SANDWICH shop the next day, I sat down with a ninety-nine-cent meatball sub, a stolen bag of chips, and a stack of help-wanted pulp. Thumbing through the papers, I focused hard, thinking, *Any job. This time, any job.* My eyes began to object. They were watering and drying out, stinging, turning red, fighting me all the way. As I went through, circling possible work, I saw a bike delivery job with an 800 number. Hoping to save the change in my pocket, I made the call.

The woman on the phone said that they needed couriers immediately. All of their three full-time bikers had been canned last week. I asked why and she said they were taking advantage of the company's $250 per week *guarantee pay.* I didn't know her terminology. I proposed an interview and she gave me the address where I would meet Ken, the downtown branch manager—in twelve minutes.

As I rode, the sky was high and bright above the high-rises, but the wind tunneling through them had a merciless 20-degree bite. I tucked my thumbs beneath my palms as I rode to keep my fingertips from freezing. The rest of me was warm, even excited. I was about to get a job riding my bicycle. It sounded fun, adventurous, even absurd.

I swung in and locked up next to the run-down building at 400 North Wells tucked awkwardly up against the Merchandise Mart El tracks. The place was a little creepy. I hadn't expected that. Arriving on the third floor through a natty carpeted elevator, I stepped into a dim hallway. The dark brown carpet and yellow lights created a dank, closetlike atmosphere. The doors in the hall were frosted glass, like in the old detective movies. Did I really belong here?

There was only one long hallway, extending in two directions from the elevator landing. I didn't know which direction would take me to Joey's Movers. I walked to the right and looked at all the doors. Most of the dim windows revealed shadows of empty rooms. There was an obese woman with thick black hair sitting at a little desk by the door of her office so that she could get whatever fresh air there was in the hallway. She was gasping for oxygen like a lab rat that had outgrown its jar. Before I could ask her where the courier company was, a large black man appeared, walking from the other end of the hall. His hair was dirty and thick and he dragged an old mountain bike along beside him. His brown jacket's seams were frayed and open to the wind. He carried a black garbage bag filled with small, heavy objects—bike parts, I assumed.

This man was of another world than I. He'd clearly seen more struggle, more poverty, more crime, more hopelessness. He was my age, about twenty-four, but he seemed so much bigger and rougher than I.

"Is that the delivery office, where you came from?"

"Yeah, it's open. Just go right in," he said in a low voice.

"Do you work there?"

"I did."

"Could you tell me a little about the job? I've got an interview in a few minutes."

"I got fired. No notice. There ain't much to say."

"Is that how they work?" I asked stupidly.

"Work? Is that work? I don't know if I can call that work because I don't think this place *does work*. But you'll figure that out." I didn't respond. I just watched him, hoping he would continue. "Listen, they don't give a shit about you. They'll work you for a few months and then they'll stiff you your last check just like they did me. Take their guarantee as long as they'll offer it and have something to fall back on."

Guarantee? *What the hell was he talking about?* I pretended to understand. While nodding meaninglessly, I noticed that his thick black hair was bleached from the salt that the city dumps on the street to melt snow. I could see from his thick black Reebok high-tops that posed as boots that he had been living in the same kind of failure that I had only recently come to know. "Do you have something to fall back on?" I asked him, honestly concerned.

He looked at me pissed, like I was making it harder, like I was only trying to rub the shit in deeper. As he stepped into the elevator with his bike, he looked back at me blandly, stuffing his plastic bag into his torn-up backpack. "Jesus Christ is my Lord and savior."

"Right. Well, good luck then," I responded awkwardly.

He hit the button for the lobby and the thick door slid shut. As the elevator descended I heard him say, "I don't need your luck. That's the whole point."

How far was I falling? Was I now part of a world where every day that the sun rises would be a blessing, every waking minute would be a miracle? Had my basic human sustenance fallen below the realm of being manageable? I think many people in poverty have a resilient faith because nothing else seems to step up and support them. If they lose that faith, they lose hope, and when they lose hope, not even God can help them. In real poverty, the goal is singular: tomorrow. If tomorrow comes, then there is still a chance that our human prayers will be answered, that an angel can come and bring with it a little taste of justice.

Were he and I now in the same place, trying to work through

equally unmanageable situations? Not quite. He was a black man, and no matter how hard it would be for me to find sufficient work, for him it would be harder. His cheap mountain bike, his thin sneakers, his untamed hair spoke of the years he'd spent struggling and surviving. It was sad to know that his struggle would continue. It was sadder still to know that I would take up the struggle that he had left behind.

I WALKED TOWARD that lit door at the end of the hall, my face now pale and resilient: I was angry, as would be appropriate for a poor man or the black man who had just stepped from it. My heart had changed from naive excitement to a grave sense of caution.

I swung the door open too forcefully, into a single bone-white room with one window. A guy named Ken introduced himself from behind a desk and began a little monologue. He told me how the job worked. I would be picking up envelopes either from this office, known as Hub 1, or from various addresses downtown. At the Hub, I would find packages coming from various suburbs and I would deliver them to their destinations either in the Loop itself, an area marked by a line of circling elevated trains, or in the nearby areas that surrounded this central business district. When I was called to pick up these suburban runs from downtown addresses, I would deliver them to this office, where they would, in turn, be delivered by car. I would be managing the denser half of a city-to-suburb orbit.

"Am I paid per package?" I asked.

"About sixty cents each if they're coming to or going from the Hub. But then there are also locals."

Locals were jobs that were both picked up from and delivered to addresses across town. I would be called on all of these as long as I could carry them. A local drop paid a full 50 percent commission on the billing cost to the client. If the package was in a rush, the billing price would increase. If the package was long-distance, the billing price would again increase. This, according to Ken, was where the money was: long, fast, crosstown commissions.

I would get all of my jobs sent to me on an alphanumeric pager, and I would confirm them via a two-way radio that I would lease from the company and attach to the strap of my messenger bag (luckily, I had one). He advised that in cases when there was a lot of work to do, I should go around picking up packages, so that they got out of their clients' faces; then I could run around and drop them all at once.

"And when there's no work?" I asked.

"That's why we have a guarantee. If your commission doesn't surpass the guarantee, you will at least earn, every week, a specified minimum. If your commission is better than the minimum, you keep the commission."

"And what's my guarantee?"

Ken suggested three hundred dollars a week because I was going to be the only biker on the board, replacing *three* people. I think it was because I looked like I had a head on my shoulders, like I could read, like I was white—I'm not sure. I was a little offended by the special treatment, but naturally I agreed. In the game of survival, you take the opportunities as they come. You don't question unless you have to. He showed me the pager and the radio that I would have to pick up every morning, and he told me that I was responsible for any other gear that I needed or chose to use—"bicycles, helmets, handguns, whatever." We beat through a 1099 independent-contractor tax form and we set a date: tomorrow, 8:00 A.M.

THAT NIGHT, I FILLED my tires to maximum capacity. I replaced the toe straps on the twirling clip pedals that my sneakers had worn down. I dumped all of the paper clips and highlighters out of my saddlebag, replacing them with bike tools and an extra layer of clothes.

I wore a tight wool sweater and thick orange gardening gloves with a few fingers cut off them so that I could handle a pen and shift gears easily. I wore two pairs of socks and my new pair of sneakers, which, aside from my snow boots, were now the only pair of shoes I owned. I packed a journal and an extra pen, so that I wouldn't feel alone.

I wore my white helmet and a pair of mean-looking pants cut off at the knee with a pair of tights beneath, pink-and-purple tights with little colorful drawings that translated ballet terms like *la scène, en point, la costume,* and *la couronne.* I thought the girly tights would create an interesting juxtaposition with the hard-core facade of being a messenger.

I had seen guys with green goatees, fat polyester ties, and cowboy hats—appearance meant nothing. One Chicago phenomenon, Joey Love, a little Puerto Rican guy from New York, was known for dressing in complete hockey gear and skitching the city on a mini BMXer. Other times, I had seen him in a fully enclosed football helmet and a black leather jacket that was lined with flashing chaser lights. The tights were tame in comparison; besides, they kept my legs warm without getting the pant legs snagged in my chain ring. Function determined all of my decisions.

As I headed into work the next morning I had this strange feeling of being a decorated bull, an animal thrust into a macabre arena, half sport, half ancient sacrifice. Soon the doors would be swung open and I would have to charge forward at the unknown. I was nervous. I felt caged, enslaved, as if the gate would be opened and I would be chased down and killed by a pack of Indian men on some kind of weird British hunt. I figured that I would fight as hard as I could, but eventually I would just break down from exhaustion or be thrown over a taxicab and slaughtered to the sound of light applause.

Mentally I was preparing myself for the worst as, perhaps, even the bull does. Knowing that he is powerless in the arena, he wastes no energy trying to prove it. He doesn't feign weakness. He doesn't give in or beg for mercy. The bull has no escape and, appropriately, no escape reflex. He charges. He uses horns. They are his one defense.

After I got the radio and the first few packages from Hub 1, I started riding into the Loop area from the Wells Street Bridge, trying to match addresses to buildings. I was terrified and disoriented.

I began moving slowly, knowing that I would soon be running at full speed with my head down and my horns up. My face felt heavy and muscular. The hair on my head was for the first time in my life the hair of an animal, a long, protective fur that would keep me warm. My hands were now merely tools, meant to grip, to scratch, to clean, to hammer, to feed. In my face and how I held my jaw, I was a bull breathing heavily, preparing to stampede through what seemed complete chaos.

The work would either kill me or keep me. This had become the test. Either way I would be riding my bicycle, kissing no one's ass, doing what it was I loved. Charging the conflict head-on with only handlebars to hold on to, I knew only that whatever the outcome, an important understanding would follow. Either I would fail, proving that I was perfectly meaningless and without value to the world, or I would succeed. And success would mean that I, the *low and noble,* was still free to determine his own end and love his work.

By the end of my first day I'd made eighteen deliveries. Many of them came from or went to Hub 1, where I would connect with the drivers who would take them up to Evanston or Northbrook. I found out later that only two of the local deliveries would pay me more than one dollar. In fact, by the end of the first week I'd earned barely one hundred dollars on commission, though I took home three hundred thanks to the guarantee.

I think Ken had the idea that this was a good deal for me. I could sit around and get paid for work that I was not doing! It seemed like a bargain at first, but then I wondered, *Is it sane to risk your ass like this to just barely get by, suckling a minimum?* In this situation the low and noble could never be anything more than a weight on the world, because he'd be dependent on a subsidy, fixed to a path of taking more than he earned, "winning by losing," as my father would say. I could not love that kind of work because I could not respect it.

Sure I was riding my bike, sure I was free to navigate my own way through the city without any boss or manager telling me how to do my job, but I didn't feel that I had a chance to succeed. No matter how hard I worked, I could never significantly compete with their guarantee pay. Every check would be a statement of what I couldn't accomplish. I could still lose by being run down, and I could still survive by being able to pay my rent, but I could never pass the test.

For a few weeks while working at Joey's I did nothing but drag-ass, sixty-cent runs. Some days I would ride around in circles with nothing in my bag, taking the time to assimilate the visual experience of the metropolis. There were no long, fast, crosstown commissions.

I would sit around watching the cars go by, making notes in my journal. I would pay attention to the other messengers on the street, giving them casual noddings of the head to say "Wha's up?" with a cool kind of disinterest. For a while, all the bikers looked the same, and they all gave me the same kind of "Wha's up?" in return. Sometimes I would hang out with other rookies, listening to them talk about gear and components. But I was watching the crowds, asking questions like, Why do people look defeated on the sidewalks of Jackson when the people on Plymouth walk in the center of the street and smile? I would stand where Plymouth met Jackson and try to work out the dynamics. I sat at this intersection contemplating: If the city was the high form of art, then the street would have to be the high form of theater. And if they combined in the careful and spontaneous navigation of a human life, who would be in charge of the artist's statement? The pedestrian? The city planner? Or someone still higher?

When the work did come, it would come on the pager in a series of letters and numbers that I would have to translate. I would run the work and then call in "all cleaned up." Cleon, the dispatcher, whom I never saw in person, would give me a confirmation. Then I would sit around waiting for the next >>PU 500 MAD TEL3700 DEL BUR20N 1143 REG<< or the next >>PU 175 FRANKLIN ANDERS DEL HUB 1 1150 DIF<< to energize me for the next few minutes.

I tried to learn the city. I tried to figure out all the details, like which streets went one-way west and which one-way east, which streets had metal bridges and which ones had cement, which buildings had bag policies and which did not. I learned the shortcuts to the Standard Oil Building and 333 Wacker. I did the work but I remained just as poor, just as hungry, and just as cold—maybe more cold.

Even though it had been a light winter, the below-freezing winds had burned my wrists and forearms, leaving them bruised and red, weakening all the muscles and tendons in my arms. The skin was raw from the hard wind and the cold pipes of my handlebars. I found it difficult to write, to open and close my hands. My fingers were white and rough like unpolished marble. Little pieces of skin hung off the edges of my hands, making them feel like the coarse end of a steel brush. While I worked, thick bloodless cuts would open up along the lines of my fingerprints. But most of my bleeding was done at home, when my fluids would carefully thaw out my fingertips again.

My long hair and a knit cap kept my ears warm enough, but my nostrils were always skinless and irritated. Occasionally a piece of an earlobe would sting for two weeks or so; then the piece would come off in my hand like the edge of a potato chip. My lips were so often numb that I could hardly speak into the radio without sounding like a drunk. My jaw felt like cement on the outside, and from the inside like cold rubber. And for all of this I would get this meaningless three-hundred-dollar check, none of which I could hold on to and most of which I didn't even earn. I understood what that other courier meant when he questioned if this was work. For both the company and for me, the subsidy wasn't working.

But there are many competing messenger companies in a city like Chicago. There are some that work and some that don't. Some are loaded with flashy bikers, like Eric from On The Fly or George from Velocity, and it is often hard to find work with them. They seem too choosy or arrogant to take you on board without a special recommendation. Even if they did hire you, some of these companies are too big or too corrupt or too run-down to trust. As I thought about quitting Joey's, which was hardly a company at all, I looked at the more reputable couriers in the city, to see what I might be capable of.

When I first met Pat, Number Thirty-four, in the lobby of 980 North Michigan, it seemed that he was working in a fair and friendly environment. He was being paid well for the work he did and *he was fast.* He looked fast. He felt fast. He talked fast and, based on an invitation to a party he got over his radio, he was also enjoying a healthy life outside of work. Maybe he was a painter, maybe he was a musician, but he wasn't starving—that was, to me, something to admire.

We had a small exchange on the escalator. I asked him if his company was in need of new bikers. He wasn't sure, but he told me who to talk to at Service First Courier (62 West Huron).

After a few drops on the North Side I found time to sneak into their basement-level office to get an interview. "I'm looking for Chris," I said to a tall woman with a feathered, blond, Fleetwood Mac–era hairdo. "Pat, Number Thirty-four, sent me."

"Chris? Sure. He's in the dispatch room." She sparkled with a big smile. Then she stepped into an office and got me an application. "Fill this out and give it to Chris in the dispatch room. You can go get his attention, but he might be a little busy. Just be patient."

In the dispatch room there were three people: a lanky guy with a trimmed beard and an alert posture, up to his elbows in tiny little white and yellow slips; a guy in his late forties with shoulder-length gray hair and a folksy, 1970s mustache sitting behind a stack of paper; and a punked-out kid who looked about eighteen and wore a baseball cap backward, hiding a clump of blond dreadlocks.

The kid was leaning forward over a microphone insulting someone. "Number Thirty-six, which is it? Are you east or west? Alicia, that is, are you in *the lake* or are you *on pavement*? Just answer that." He sat back in his swivel chair and started to do pirouettes, kicking himself around in circles with one foot.

From a speaker, a voice retorted, "Dammit, dispatch, listen for a moment. The entrance to the building on West Jackson is on the *east* side of Green Street. The names match. No one is here. Do-you-copy-that? And will-you-stop-being-a-pain-in-my . . ."

"10-9? 10-9? In your *what,* Alicia? Come back?" the dispatcher dared.

"I'll toss this goddamn package in the street and get on with my West Side if you want me to."

"Nah, that's okay. Clock your waiting time, I'll get on the phone." The kid leaned over to the older guy. "Goldberg, would you?"

Goldberg was fingering seven or eight little four-inch pieces of paper on his side of the desk. "Who is it?"

"Sanchez and Daniels. They gave us a bad address, and when we got the right address no one is there. We need a phone call to the re-

cipient and we need a book adjustment, 'cause if Number Thirty-six wasn't on this, the package would never get off."

"10-4." He got on the phone.

The kid stood up and looked at me. "What do you need?"

"A job. I'm looking for Chris."

He rolled his eyes. "One minute." I still didn't know who the hell Chris was. But I waited.

The kid, who seemed the only one in charge, leapt back into the chair, spun a one-eighty, leaned up, and grabbed the transmitter: "Did you hear that, Alicia? I wish you heard that. I said that if you weren't on this, the package would never get off. That was a *com-pli-ment,* in case you've never had one. You are still standing by but you are also *add-stopping.* Do you copy?"

"10-4 on the add stop. 10-9 on the . . . *com-pli-ment*? Umm, 10-9?"

"You wish I'd repeat that. She's crafty, and she's just my style."

"Yeah, 10-4 on the outdated music."

The paper pusher with the thin beard gave a broad Germanic laugh, loud enough to be heard over the airwaves, as the little guy mumbled something in response. Then he leapt away from the microphone and looked me square in the face. "I'm Chris."

"Travis." We shook hands.

"Do you have experience?"

"Some."

"Where?"

"Joey's."

"Oh, I've heard of those guys. How long?"

102   "At Joey's?" He nodded. "As short a time as I can possibly make it."

"10-4. What kind of bike you ride?"

"Diamondback Topanga, ninety-four."

"Mountain bike?"

"Sort of. Frame is. Everything else is roadie. It is a monster, but it will get me there."

"Break down a lot?"

"If it does, I'll fix it."

"Know the city?"

"Well enough."

"How long would it take you to get from 525 Monroe to 303 Wacker?"

"Pick to drop? Seven minutes."

Goldberg, having overheard our conversation from his chair, piped up: "But isn't that . . . ?" He stopped himself, having twisted two thoughts in his head until they canceled.

"No. That is about right. How many do you do a day?"

"About twenty-five, these days."

"Is that all you can do, or is it just slow?"

"I'm their only biker. That's *all* the work there is."

"But you could do more?"

"I'm hanging all over the place."

"10-4. Can you start today?"

"Monday, earliest."

"You can't start now?"

"No. I'm still at Joey's." I showed him my radio.

The gray-haired guy, who I knew only as Goldberg, stood up to get the gist of me. "But it's Friday now."

"Exactly. I'm going to close out the day, turn in the radio, and walk. I am not going to bounce on a Friday." Chris took the application from me and started looking it over.

"But *we* need someone now, like *right now*. If you could do it now, you're on. But Monday?" Goldberg shook his head. "I don't know."

"What is the difference? You need someone or you don't," I said outright.

"We need someone *now*."

"Then too bad. I don't work that way. You wouldn't want one of your bikers to bounce on you on a Friday, would you?"

Chris interrupted, "Why are you quitting?"

"I am 1099. I want to be a W-4. I think it is criminal to hire bikers 1099."

"He's right," Goldberg admitted. Chris looked puzzled. "1099 is the tax code for an independent contractor, Chris. It's like how the drivers are hired. Taxes aren't withheld, but there is no workman's comp if you're injured on the job. If a biker who's 1099 gets hurt, a company can sometimes just wash its hands of him."

"So hire me. I'll start Monday."

"Well . . ."

Chris objected, saying that they didn't want to "overhire." "I got to keep my bikers happy," he said and ran back to the microphone to respond to something he'd heard on the radio.

To Goldberg I put it simply: "You've got my number. Call me this weekend when you figure it out. I've already got a job. I can continue running circles for this stupid company, or you can put me to work. If I don't hear from you by Monday, I'll just look somewhere else."

"Where's your number?" Goldberg asked.

104   "It's on the application. I got to roll."

"Okay, you'll hear from me," he called out as I left.

"10-4," I replied as the door shut behind me. Even though I may have sounded a little testy or sharp, I really wanted this job. The management seemed fair; the work seemed steady. I would actually be hired on a W-4, where I would be assured a little security and I would have my taxes withheld. These bikers were still paid by commission, but the jobs would pay an average of three dollars each, which meant that earning a hundred dollars a day was almost standard.

THE PHONE CALL CAME that Sunday morning; it was a new voice. "Tom," he said. I couldn't say that it was a job he was offering me. It was just an opportunity. He couldn't care less if I worked out or not. If I were to give him an afternoon, a week, or a year of my life, they would just move on. If I was not strong enough to carry the weight, I'd be cut. To the company, it seemed, bikers didn't matter.

And to the bikers, companies didn't matter. If canned, they could just move on to another company. Guys would get fired after breakfast and hired again by noon. I had seen guys working in a company shirt from Velocity, carrying a bag from Cannonball, and wearing a yellow helmet from Arrow Messengers—all while working for a smaller company, like On Time or KDR. Independent contractors at their very core, they didn't care who paid them. They were 1099, independent to a dangerous extent.

One problem I saw was that working freelance transferred accountability away from the messenger company and made the couriers themselves personally responsible for their own insurance and their own delivery. Couriers in this situation, acting essentially as independent companies, are sometimes right out of high school or between years in college. They don't know how hard it can be to work around the problem of disability. They don't seem to care. This fantasy of being utterly autonomous contributes to the determined sense of righteous disregard that the messenger has become, quite unfortunately, famous for. I thought about them compassionately. What if a serious injury comes? Would they have the resources to manage it?

During a spontaneous trip to visit friends in New York City, I had the idea of hanging out for the summer and finding a little work to bide my time. Walking through Hell's Kitchen, I saw a for-hire sign at a storefront. Ratty bikers sat around outside, smoking and looking tough. Their scraped-up bikes were tied to the fence of a garden apartment's fire escape with bare metal chains. The couriers looked at me like I was a traveling salesman. I just wasn't in their league of fashionable filth and arrogance. I walked past them and stepped into the small building. The foyer had dark wooden walls filled with staples and flyers and names carved into the wood. There was one door with a thick computerized doorknob, and there was a window made of inch-thick Plexiglas that would stop bullets. In front of the plate of glass was a small shelf with two phones and a stack of the company's manifests. I looked into the window to see a weathered black man looking back at me. The coarseness in his face let me know immediately that if I were bleeding to death on this side of the glass, he would not be the man to help me. He would probably order some rookie to drag me out of the doorway. He pointed to a sign in the corner of the window:

IF YOU *WORK* HERE, PICK UP THE WHITE PHONE.

IF YOU *WANT* TO WORK HERE, PICK UP THE RED PHONE.

IF YOU *DON'T* WANT TO WORK HERE, YOU HAVE NO BUSINESS BEING HERE.

I picked up the red phone and had a very short conversation. I told him I was here from Chicago and I wanted to stay in New York for the summer. He was not impressed.

"Do you know the city?"

"Not yet."

He rolled his eyes with intense drama. I felt instantly that I was wasting his time. "Do you have a bike?" he asked unwillingly, like this conversation was causing him a severe pain. I thought about answering his question, but I didn't. I was wasting his time. So I just hung up and walked out.

Looking back, I'm glad I didn't make that my first courier gig. I would have been even more disenchanted than I was at Joey's. They weren't hiring at all. They were just putting out enough cash per package for the hungry to hang on to. There are many such miniature companies tucked into storefronts and lofts, fighting for any kind of business. They have very little organization, almost no accountability, and they are governed by very few basic regulations. Small courier companies like these are pirates, surviving on scrub work from stingy corporations who run from messenger service to messenger service for the lowest rates and get shady, unreliable service in exchange.

It was Captain Jack who solidified this impression for me. He was one of the organizing members of the Windy City Bike Messenger Association and an editor of the local messenger 'zine *Dead Air*. I told him about my New York experience while talking over a fourth beer at the Fireside Bowl, a few days before his move to New York. He said that his friend had found a job with a similar company in Manhattan. The manager, behind the thick window, had asked his name.

"Rob," the friend had said.

"Rob? We've already got a Rob. What's your name?"

"Something different?"

"Yes."

"Robert."

"No. We've got a Robert."

"Do you have a *Zed*?"

He checked his list. "No."

"Okay then, I'm Zed."

For the next two years Rob, a.k.a. Zed, lived in an apartment with five other couriers, each paying two hundred dollars a month. None of the roommates even knew the guy on the lease. Rob had no driver's license or identification, no bills to pay in his own name. He took home cash every day under the table, having filled out no employee paperwork. He was known only as Zed.

"You can be no one," Jack said excitedly. "You can disappear off the face of the earth living and working in those companies."

He liked the story of Zed and, in part, I couldn't blame him, but I had to object, personally. Fighting to stay alive on these streets without even a name would be, to me, a very sad life. "I can deal with the streets and the struggle, but I could never do the job nameless. I refuse to let myself be just a number or an alias, because I am not a slave," I said. "I want people to remember that."

Jack, probably the most experienced messenger I have ever met, a rider whose eight-year stop in Chicago was only part of his path from San Francisco to New York City, understood my sentiment.

"Well . . ." He was tired. Finishing a beer and ordering another, he blushed slightly, gleaming at the idea that he too could disappear. His eyes were dilated and wide. It seemed that he was looking at the bliss of nonexistence, the darkness and peace of the other side. "It's your world. You do what you want with it. Right?"

"I suppose."

CHAPTER FIVE

THE EXPOSURE PRINCIPLE

The ancient private/public occultation and the
distinction between housing and traffic are replaced by
an overexposure in which the differences between "near"
and "far" simply cease to exist.

Paul Virilio,
Lost Dimensions

Everything excessive is white.

Antonin Artaud,
The Theater and Its Double

The moon was high over Grant Park as a man with a thick red beard, known as Superdave, lined up the twelve competitors along a broad sidewalk. Their front wheels were drawn carefully along a thin outer edge of the park's poured-cement slabs. Superdave called this thin groove "the line." Behind it, each biker had one foot on the sidewalk and one on a pedal, cocked like the paws of cheetahs ready to sprint.

Superdave watched all the bikers closely. "You know the rules. If you're out, you're out. If someone takes you out, try to just get up and keep going. You will not be disqualified."

"Yeah, um, we've like done this before," Pee Wee complained. "Are we going to get started or what?"

"Okay, okay. We're moving. Are you ready?" Superdave asked in a strong voice, focusing on the face of the digital watch turned inward on his wrist. Then, more quietly, "Are you set?" Finally, now almost in a whisper, "Go."

All the feet went up in the air in unison, and yet the bikes remained perfectly still. Along the entire line, the cyclists were balancing with tiny tilts and adjustments as the frames leaned from side to side almost imperceptibly. This was called a track stand, a race against gravity by guys who ride fixed gears, minimalized bikes that lack freewheels and brakes. If the pedals move forward or back, the wheels follow. If the wheels move forward or back, the pedals follow. The simple engineering optimizes a rider's control of the bike by reducing it to its most basic principles. Such bikes are usually used for professional racing, but because they can be so carefully handled they are also used for small-parcel deliveries, skid competitions, and track stands like these, where the last one to fall wins the small pot of cash made up of what each of the competitors had slapped into Superdave's hand.

"Are we going yet?" Bones asked, concentrating on his front wheel as it slid forward two inches and back two inches and forward two inches again, his front tire tilted slightly, his long fingers lightly coaxing the aluminum drop bars to keep their angle. His lanky six-foot-four figure arched over the bike frame possessively.

"Yes, you moron," Superdave snapped back lightly.

Jerry giggled once for no reason. He wore a loud Hawaiian shirt. His light brown curls seemed to hover over his head. In his right hand, held between his fingertips, was a can of Old Style. While keeping control of the balanced fixed gear, he swirled the last gulp of warm beer in the circles of the aluminum can.

Sitting with a group of messengers on a nearby bench, I could hear guys laughing about how Superdave's black leather pants and yellow jersey flashed in the moonlight. These guys were covering their eyes as if blinded. Superdave continued to pace, his thick neck and wide shoulders aggressively presiding over the event. To the bikers he warned, holding his wristwatch in the air, "One minute."

For a moment I could hear only the measured breathing of the bikers and the tread of their tires twisting into the cement at careful angles.

"Wouldn't this be easier on bare rims, like without tires?" Ken, Number Seventy-nine, speculated.

"I suppose, if you're into folding rims," U.V. answered.

Then silence.

Pork Chop broke out, "Don't sneeze, James! Don't sneeze. You'll take us all out."

"You wish," he said flatly, sucking up a head cold, taking his track stand very seriously.

The whole group sat in place, jiggling lightly.

"Has anyone fallen yet?" Bobcat asked. At that moment Bones fell from the end of the line, landing on one foot with a slap. Then Ken tipped over from the middle of the line. He rolled his bike out quietly.

"Yes," Superdave whispered to Bobcat, "two down."

"Thank you, Superdave. Such a helpful person," the stone-faced courier whispered back.

"Two minutes."

The bikes remained still, once or twice impulsively tipping or rolling forward. Eric's bike showed the only bit of instability. He was a tall, fair-haired man with gentle features riding a beautiful, sparkling Klein he'd just built up from the bike shop where he worked. His wheels started jerking forward until the front tire crossed the line of the sidewalk. He kept his balance, trying to pull the bike back in line, but Superdave pounced up to him. "Here, let me help you," he said, pushing Eric's shoulder until he and his bike toppled over. "Disqualified!" Superdave announced over a small swell of laughter.

"Ouch, man. Like, that hurt my . . . *feelings,*" Eric whined while picking up his machine and pulling it away from the group.

Jimbo sighed with pseudosympathy and Superdave trotted on, watching all the bikes, seeing the spokes inch forward and back around the balancing rims.

"Thirty seconds and we are going to one hand."

Pork Chop started to lose his balance. "It's going to be a long thirty seconds! Man! Shit!" He had rocked forward and back enough that he was at a right angle to the rest of the bikes, his front wheel zigzagging back and forth, the back tire almost running into Marcus, who stood carefully over his seat post, a little worried.

"One hand!" Superdave demanded.

The bikers adjusted in line, losing a little control, pulling one hand off the bars and resting it gently behind their backs. Jerry took a last swig from the beer can and tossed it into the grass behind him. Pork Chop kept sliding backward, then sideways in the line until he pressed into Marcus's back wheel and both bikers fell. Pork Chop pulled his bike out of the line apologetically, while Marcus jumped back on his black track bike and tried to regain control using only one hand. He was too flustered. He tipped again and again, until finally he dropped his head and walked his bike to the benches near where I was sitting.

Uval Awazu (a.k.a. U.V.) came and joined us, letting his bike fall out from beneath him on a dismount. He shook his head lightly, complaining about his right knee, which had gotten banged up while he was finishing a relay race earlier that evening.

Now only five bikers were left. They balanced comfortably, concentrating, watching the fourth and the fifth minute pass easily. Five minutes is a long time to balance on a one-inch tire filled to

120 psi, but they made it look easy. Jimbo seemed to have the most grace about him; I could see that he was concentrating on the center of the earth. With the angles of his curved back, he seemed to be watching the moon rising up behind him.

James had a Zen-like meditation going on, his eyes nearly closed, his face serene, his bald scalp rising up like a second moon reflecting over the lake. With one hand he continued to wipe his nose.

Pee Wee was breathing carefully, his high-tech gear making him as iridescent as a firefly, his long, straight hair meticulously combed back and shining from a thick layer of gel. He and his bike were as static as an insect.

Bobcat, the one biker everyone seemed cautious of, was looking down at his bike as if it were a wild red animal that he was challenging. Who would strike first? Bobcat or his bicycle? Together they were a rendering of some mythic battle, held in that crucial moment when the dualities of the universe meet—fully armed.

Jerry in the Hawaiian shirt swerved and giggled at irregular times. He started to hum, scatting to the rhythm of falling forward and falling back; he was playful and reckless—always on the verge of disaster.

Despite their differences, these messengers were not the disorderly crew I had come to expect. They were ancient astronomers proving the roundness of the earth without the windy rhetoric or the arcane formulas. These men were not anarchists and radicals; they were the hidden explorers of a small handful of god's secrets, reaching toward some personal sense of perfection.

The fallen bikers sat with the rest of the crowd, watched carefully, and considered the playfully impossible idea of being vertical. It can't be done forever, not for any of us. But the idea of it was truly hypnotic, and Superdave's simple instructions took us all one stage deeper into its spell.

"Six minutes. *Both hands up.*"

Silhouetted by the full moon, the five bikers then slowly lifted their arms into the air like libation bearers, giving prayer, physically connecting themselves to the heavens. They were perfecting some primal desire to float above the earth, to levitate, to ascend beyond all the hell they'd each been through.

"SOME PIECE OF EVERYONE who ever comes into this business never really makes it out," Goldberg said that Monday morning, opening the door of his cluttered office while trying to control a pile of papers. "The question becomes not if you'll change or how you'll change but if you'll change for the better."

I stood at the doorway, adjusting the radio on the strap of my bag so that it wouldn't fall off while I was riding.

"I have seen a lot of kids come through here," he continued. "They all come in, young and eager, and they all leave—eventually. But some of them, only some of them, leave better off than when they came—leave as men, you know: mature, honest, disciplined: *men.* So just be careful, 'cause I am not paying you enough money for you to, like, jump in front of a bus to get a package off. That's just stupid. I depend on your judgment, not your speed. I want you to understand that. Work smart and work steady, because then you might be able to use this job for something deeper than—"

"Is this the speech all your rookies get?" I asked, a little suspicious of the intent of his lecture.

"No. In fact, I don't think I've ever said this before and, knowing my luck, I probably won't ever find the words to do it again. But I know what I'm talking about. I've been doing this a long time."

"Yeah, I hear you," I tried to say over his telephone, which had started ringing.

"Yeah, yeah. Go to work. But be careful. We just had a biker die in an accident. Charles Williams, you've probably seen him out biking. He was driving in to work. He wasn't *at work,* so I don't have any legal responsibility, but it's killing me all the same and I got to get this damn phone! Shut up!" he commanded the phone, though it continued to ring. "Nothing listens to a fucking word I say."

For a moment he cringed, reminding himself that he shouldn't curse, and then he picked up the phone: "Service First. I mean, yeah, this is Dave Goldberg. What can I do for you?"

I took a breath and went for my bike. It was leaning up against a tired ten-speed that had been ridden into the ground. I wondered whose bike it was and if it would ever find its owner. Yes, I think I was looking at a dead man's bicycle. Chris was standing at the dispatch desk, scratching his dreads and shouting over the airwaves, "I just want to know if you've dropped the *Rudnick*! Yes or no?"

As I rolled away from base, the traffic on Clark was overwhelming. Four lanes of cars and cabs and small police paddy wagons were cruising or sitting illegally along the street. The whole environment was disorienting and chaotic. As I rode into the street's furious current, the radio lashed out bits of conversation. An argument between bikers and drivers and the office staff turned into senseless shouting in my radio's makeshift holster. I couldn't tell the voices apart, and I couldn't understand what people were saying, so when Chris called my number, I was justifiably nervous. My heart rode up into my throat as I replied.

"Um, Thirty-nine to base."

"Yeah, Thirty-nine, meet up with Pat, Number Thirty-four, on City Front Plaza. He'll get you started."

"10-4."

Chris gave me the longitude and latitude of City Front Plaza and I rode toward the landmark carefully, preparing my heart for the most disorienting and frightful weeks of work I'd ever experienced.

Riding on streets I hadn't used, finding buildings I'd never seen, I felt like I was walking a tightrope. Trillions of tiny movements accompanied every pickup and every delivery. I felt lost trying to decipher a radio lingo I had never heard, following directions that would send me to mailrooms I'd never needed, trailing other couriers through alleyways and loading zones to find hidden entrances, and making deliveries to parts of the city I had never ventured into. As a truck passed me and its wind pulled my hair, shook my cheeks, and rattled the ribs in my chest, I turned on myself and said, *You don't belong here! No one does! This landscape is not human.*

That day I ran thirty-five packages, and that night my head felt like a cracked lightbulb that was drying the electrodes right out of my spinal column. I paced for an hour trying to describe the work to Haewon, my girlfriend *at the time,* and then I collapsed on the sofa like an unstrung marionette. I didn't know what had hit me, but I liked it. For some reason, I liked it.

That next morning I pushed out like a force of nature, a tornado, jumping rivers and canyons and then piling through the thick. I would wave vehicles out of my way and press on mile after mile, despite my weakening quadriceps and tired calves. My hands would hurt from holding up my weight and absorbing the vibrations of the city's potholes and construction sites.

Then Number Thirty-three, Sam, the blond skater-punk with the mind of a truck-stop prostitute, called in saying that he had just lost a tooth. He said that it had just come out in his mouth like a half-cracked pistachio nut. Chris offered to let him sit out until the bleeding stopped, but Sam wasn't interested. "That's life," he said. "One day you've got 'em and one day you don't."

My respect for Sam tripled though, at the same time, I thought he'd lost his mind—or at least surrendered it. Like a sacrificial offering, he'd given himself up to his mechanical environment. If the machine kept going, then so would Sam. Of course, between the perpetual displays of human contempt, and the relentless height and velocity of these steel towers that rise and fall like pistons in an engine, that sense of responsibility is not often envied. *This is what success avoids,* I had to recognize with an awestruck, deflating grimace. The soot and the smells of the alleys, the potholes that seemed always filled with water, the glimpses of faces twisted with contempt, cursing the traffic lights and the old men trying to cross the street. Wealthy businesspeople were stepping over the blankets of the homeless. *Please, let this not be happening,* I prayed, but every day it got more real and somehow more amazing.

I saw a woman mug another woman outside of 205 North Michigan. She leapt into the passenger side of a massive black truck that peeled out of a parking space and disappeared around buildings and highway ramps. I saw a pool of blood at the intersection of Damen and Clybourn. There was a glove in the blood and a little broken glass. Later, I saw a young man with a shirt wrapped around his head holding a sign that said I READ OUT LOUD FOR MONEY. He was sitting in a grassy median ranting prose. His pants were rolled up to his shins, and the afternoon crowds walked past him like he was some kind of discarded paper bag, or a dime novel whose spine had been snapped in the street.

I began to feel uncomfortable. In the crowds and in the eyes of the motorists stacked four blocks thick in front of red lights on Congress, no one seemed to notice the world around them or recognize the impact they had on it. It was this overwhelming sense of disregard that I really began to fear. I knew how easy it would be to make the wrong turn, to swerve in the road and be picked up into the air by the hood of a car and put back down, a dead man. If that were to happen someone would scrape me off the street. Someone else would grab the packages out of my bag. Life would resume. In fact, the packages in my bag would still reach their destinations. I felt so vulnerable knowing that one driver could run me down and another biker would continue forward, picking up my jobs right where I'd left off. My life would be no more than a snag in the regular and ruthless operations of the metropolis.

I began crawling my bike into furious intersections, crippled with uncertainty. *What would happen if I were to be hit or disabled again? Having nothing, how could I recuperate? Is this what it feels like to have nothing left in the world? Is freedom the feeling of being prey to other people's negligence? From the worker's perspective, is freedom not failure?* All this thinking; I had not yet surrendered.

Base keyed up and started listing pickups, obscuring the clients' names with slang. "Number Thirty-nine, grab a stack of Genocide. I've got six destinations. Drop the Tower first because Nancy Coffin's Meckler Bating a 230 West Adams."

"10-4, Genesis Travel to the Tower. The Tower to Adams Street."

"Drop the Bates Meckler—it's legal, so check for a round trip— and call me out of Adams, holding four or more."

Instead of unraveling those ideas, I just tried to keep moving. With every delivery I had to negotiate the erratic decisions of the thousands of faces that would cross my path and drivers that would accelerate while blowing the horn at passing pedestrians and talking on the telephone. I saw men in cars stopped in the middle of a roadway while an emergency vehicle sat behind them, trying to get a patient to the hospital.

It could have been me, I thought. *It could have been me and still this asshole won't move!*

Shut up, Number Thirty-nine, I calmed myself. *Go forward.*

At every turn I began to feel like I was avoiding death. At that, I was staying alive only to prolong a deeper kind of dying. Coming home was preparing for the next day, and the next day was an attempt to survive, and soon weeks passed without a moment of reflection. "Survival is the one break point between *not living* and *not dying,*" Darren, Number 6031, said during a strangely off-the-cuff moment chillin' at the foot of the Tower.

How true it was. I had put living aside and had reduced myself to the baser existence of evading death. I would take risks only if they seemed necessary to accomplish a day's work. But even this, I quickly learned, would require doing shit that I never thought I was capable of.

A cab started pinching me into a curb, not knowing that I was at his back window. The passenger was blithely enjoying his ride. I was only a few inches from the Crown Victoria and a few inches from the curb and still I felt invisible, so I punched the rear window with the butt of my fist. In a single action the cab swerved and the passenger jumped up in the backseat, nearly hitting his head on the roof of the car.

I barreled down Ontario, extending my arm across the cabbie's windshield and pointing to the empty lane beside us. *"Move!"* I shouted, and he pulled away timidly, giving me the space I needed.

On Franklin, a suit ran out behind a bus near the end of the day, blind to the oncoming traffic. I was unraveling the chain between the crank arms, galloping at him like a linebacker, drawing up light rain with the spin of my bald tires. I expected him to turn but he didn't, and I kept closing in. Then he stepped right into my path just as I was approaching. Had I hit the brakes or turned quickly, I would have hydroplaned, causing me to fall and slide. I would have clipped him at the knee and spun into the curb like a stray bowling ball. I had to find a way to control him, inhabit him, possess him like a magician, move his body as if it were my toy.

Inside of a second, I caught a glimpse of his silver watch and his weak chin under the umbrella. *"Yo, FUCK!"* I blasted. The man froze like a house cat, standing straight up in the air with his mouth agape, just as I passed inches from his bent elbows. "Look before you cross the fucking street!" I followed up, releasing him from my spell. He probably still thinks I am an ass, but I saved us both a lawsuit and a few weeks in recovery.

An SUV ran a four-way stop sign in the Gold Coast at the same moment I did, and we met in the intersection like rival lions in a forest. He jammed on his brakes, skidding at me from the right. He was a sports-bar local, a guy's guy with sideburns and a gut. Two attractive women were in the cab with him. I continued forward, making no adjustments, shaking my head as if to say that he was way out of line.

He spun the wheel and peeled out toward me. I let him follow me for a few seconds. Then I spun to a stop, ditched the bike in the middle of the street, and began walking toward him, wielding my U-lock in my clenched fist. He stopped and tried to say out of his window that he *could have killed me.* But then he was still poised to kill me, and that deserved a response in kind.

As I got closer, filled with rage, I could see more details. I was dissecting him, piecing out his weaknesses. I raised my arms: "Here it is. This is my life. Come and take it, you piece of shit!" Soon he was trying to find reverse. The women in the windshield had silent screams on their faces, their hands flitting about in the cab. The SUV started pulling back. I shook my head in disgust, pocketed the Kryptonite, and continued up to North Avenue while the driver got bitched at by a dyad of womankind.

This was the real work: managing the crowd, learning how to protect myself from the deadly negligence and rage of motorists. On Damen Avenue, while I was working the West Side, a silver-haired playboy in a white convertible Porsche started revving up behind me.

I rode into the center of the street and he came up on my left side, sitting halfway in a lane of oncoming traffic. Then he started pushing me into the curb. "What the fuck is your problem?" I asked.

"You're riding in the middle of the goddamn road and I'm trying to get through."

"But I'm going the speed limit, you fucking idiot."

"Get in front of me again. I dare you."

"You want me to exercise my right to the road? No problem!"

"I'll run you right the fuck down."

124   "And why don't you kiss my ass while you're at it, pretty boy."

I accelerated and cut him off, coasting into the middle of the lane again. What was incredible to me was that, rights and rules aside, I was keeping up with traffic. If I were to have gotten out of his way, he would have been tailing a blue van instead.

He stood on his horn and issued threats but nothing more. I doubted he would bludgeon the hood of his car for my measly ass. When the blue van fell into line behind a red light, I got bored of the bluff and started rocketing up the yellow line. I passed the blue van and a Volvo and eight other cars that waited at the light. I toasted Division and continued routing off a set of West Side.

Dude, that was stupid, I thought, walking out of the swinging doors of a neighborhood hospital. *You could have gotten hurt, man. You gotta think.*

I went for my pen, to mark the time of the drop on my paperwork, and accidentally it flipped out of the side of my radio holster and twirled through the air. I kept walking in the direction of the Grinch. I checked my watch and planned to take Milwaukee Avenue back into the city. When the time was right—I was in no hurry—I reached out and plucked the falling pen from the sky. It seemed to hang there in space like a coquettish invitation until I snapped it up sharply.

Nah, fuck thinking, I said to myself: *Act before thought can catch you. If you question. you hesitate; and that is dangerous. If thought can catch you, so can language. If language can catch you, so can death. Move, and trust your movement.*

Thomas, Damen, Augusta, Milwaukee, Kinzie, then Wells—not streets but actions. Connecting them, action to action, I'd suddenly made it back to the city, and yet, strangely, I felt that I didn't have anything to do with it. I was following something else the whole way.

I FIRST HEARD the term "exposure time" from Iris, a friend in Critical Mass who was commenting on how disrespectful the drivers of Chicago were to cyclists. She was going on about how careful I would have to be if I were going to take this messengering thing seriously. "As your exposure time increases, so does your risk," Iris said seriously. "Are you sure you're ready to do this?"

Honestly, I didn't know. I wanted to quit, but how could I? I would lose everything—the apartment, the steady cash, the tiny chance I had at redeeming my faith in the world. I recalled the image of the five bikers standing above their bicycles, arms in the air, wheels still and balanced against gravity. They were proof that I could survive this, and they showed me that I might actually be able to make a life out of it too.

Quitting was always an option, but I knew that the longer I could delay doing it, the more likely I would be to succeed. In this way, being defeated would be an honorable thing. I would have to give myself over completely to be, in the end, defeated. Think about it: those who try sometimes win; those who quit never do.

Nonetheless, her phrase "exposure time" stuck in my head. It posed a serious problem because it seemed undeniable that the more time I spent on the bike, the more likely I would be to get seriously injured. A casual biker, riding to work and back, would have a very small chance of having an accident, while a messenger who spent over fifty hours a week on some of the most active streets and intersections in the country would face substantial risk. A quote Iris read somewhere said that an average biker should expect to have a serious accident every two thousand miles—about a month's work for me.

I had to wonder, Was this a job or a suicide mission? I wasn't so sure anymore. Had I chosen this job to call for help? Perhaps by becoming a bike messenger I intended to end up in some horrible accident. Maybe I wanted to be maimed again, punished for the failure I had made of my life. Was I not crying out that I needed, in some way, an ambulance?

If so, it never came. Instead, a guy running to lunch stepped out in front of me after I took a left turn onto Grand Avenue and began approaching the curb of 515 North State to lock up. I'd swung my leg over the saddle and was coasting onto the sidewalk, gliding in on a sharp angle. Then he appeared, a white man in a suit, pulling his momentum to a stop as I plowed into him. We both went down, but I fell faster. While my head was down on the cement sidewalk, I could see him falling backward as if in slow motion. First his butt hit the ground, then his back rolled along the sidewalk, and then his head reached back, the curls of his white hair pressing into the floor, until—*tap*—he stopped. He hit his head, but only lightly.

I leapt to my feet, asked him if he was okay, and offered him a hand up. He took my hand without hesitation and we both apologized profusely. The guy was fine, just a little dusted by the spillover of a nearby construction site. He looked up as if to ask me a question, but instead he took a step back and regarded my brow. I reached up to inspect a correlating itch and found my palm covered in blood. I leaned over, surprised to find a stream of blood falling from my eye like a little fountain.

"Thirty-nine to base."

"Thirty-nine, go," Chris responded.

"I think I should come into the office."

"Why, wha's up?"

"I hit a ped and now I'm bleeding down the side of my head."

"You're what? You said you're bleeding down the side of your head?"

"And I hit a ped, that's what I said!" They could hear my laughter while I tried to take the ridiculous rhyme seriously.

"And you're laughing?"

"10-4!"

"All right, get in here."

"Shouldn't I drop the 515 State? I'm here?"

"No! Get in here!"

The suit and I parted amiably. I climbed back up onto my bike and started rolling up State Street. The stream of blood was now coming down my chin and running along my neck in the wind. Something about this was, I don't know, appropriate.

Goldberg wanted to get me to the emergency room, but I refused. I had been able to stanch the flow with bandages and tape, so I felt I should keep working.

Messengering bloody was kind of cool. Secretaries would offer me napkins and things to tell me that I needed to freshen the bandages. I'd have to wipe off the lines of blood that would periodically roll down my cheek. At first I couldn't distinguish sweat from blood, so I kept wiping everything with a blood-drenched hanky.

That night around six, I called Haewon and told her about the accident. She told me to get to her apartment as soon as I could. By seven I arrived, still smelling of car exhaust, my face lined in soot, and my hair matted down in body salt. She held my head over the sink and rinsed a day's worth of sweat and dirt from the wound. Then I heard her pulling boxes out of her closet. I trusted her. She'd gone through years of medical training and was now working as a resident at University of Illinois Hospital. I knew I was in good hands, but then she showed me a little purple envelope that she'd torn open. From within she pulled out a small curved needle with a long black string. With the needle she started punching holes in my eyebrow. While she tugged at my face and tied little knots with the string, I watched lines of blood, diluted by .9 percent sodium chloride irrigation, fall into the sink and slope inward to the drain. I was so in love.

When I sat up and saw her handiwork, she looked at me, trying to read my reaction. "What do you think?"

"Brilliant work, Doctor," I said, knowing full well that if I had gone to the emergency room, even though it would have been covered by the company, I would have been called "dangerous" and canned.

The next day, with my head bruised and my eye stinging, I found that my legs and arms were not particularly sore. It was not that I was no longer *in pain*. It was only that I had lost track of what it was like to *not* be in pain. Everything was in pain. My cut stung in the wind. My legs were swollen and hot. From the pounding vibrations of the bike, my hands had lost all sensation. But with these injuries, a deeper wound had begun to heal. Now that I'd bled for the first time, the ice had been broken and the fears I'd once had of living this life had simply vanished. I had faced my fears, quite literally—I'd been baptized. Soon I felt like I was unstoppable, then invincible. The job actually became *fun*.

If a car coming toward me at thirty miles an hour didn't offer me enough room to pass, I would lunge into his path, coming at him dead-on until he slid to a stop or avoided me outright.

I would ride into blind corners, recognizing up front that I might be only a second away from a person or a FedEx truck or a dumpster. I would pull off the blind corner on Haddock Place and LaSalle and enjoy the gamble I was making. I began to feel that any moment could be my last, and that fact began to seep into me like a steady stream of adrenaline, growing more intense with every hour. After all, I remembered, the city could just flip the switch and I'd be out. But it hadn't flipped the switch—so I just kept riding, fostering a powerful sense of fuck-all, hardening my spirit and learning to love the feel of collision.

There is an exhalation in a collision that is almost seductive.

Once, in pouring rain, I slipped on the newly painted lines of South Michigan Avenue. To my left was a long hatchback, to my right a white, compact rental with a timid-looking Asian man at the wheel. I had been keeping up with traffic, moving a good twenty-five miles per hour. When my front wheel slipped out from beneath me, I fell forward, smacked the asphalt with my back, and began sliding in a straight line between the two cars. I could feel the white lines in the road skipping beneath my messenger bag, *thump-thump, thump-thump, thump-thump,* and I could see that the front wheel of my bike had slid beneath the rental and was being tenderly pushed forward by the guy's slopping wet back tire.

The hatchback hit its brakes and got out of the way. I raised my hands in the air, getting eye contact with the rental's driver— *thump-thump, thump-thump, thump-thump*—and gestured for him to slow down easy. He looked me in the eye and nodded in agreement. *Thump-thump, thump-thump*—I was slowing down; he was slowing down. It was all very graceful. When Michigan Avenue finally came to a stop, I stood, pulled my bike from beneath the car, spun the front wheel to see if it had been bent, and then rode off feeling like I'd just come from the freakin' ballet.

One afternoon, swirling through traffic like I was some kind of break-dancer, I planned on cutting an illegal left off Clark so that I could lock up on Randolph. The only obstacle was an old Buick waiting at the light. Just as I rode by and prepared for the sharp turn, the driver reached for something in his backseat, unintentionally letting pressure off his brake. As I turned and the car rolled forward, his bumper tapped my back tire. The whole back end of the bike swung out from behind me. Now, completely out of control, I was hurtling eastbound against the westbound traffic on Randolph. A cabbie parked at the curb looked up at me, petrified. I yanked the handlebars to the right and leaned to the left, coasting out into the middle lane as a line of cars was coming right at me. I yanked to the left, saw the two bike racks that mark the service entrance of the Chicago Title Building, and pointed myself toward them. I swung my right leg over the seat to dismount and *crack,* the pedal hit the ground and bounced. The bike went up, I went forward, and somehow I landed between the two racks, looking right up at the sky. Two couriers looked down over me, amazed.

"Now, dat was *smooth!*"

I generated a small, embarrassing round of applause from a nearby crowd, but I felt like I had just had an orgasm. My heart was pounding. I was all cuddly, my vision was blurred. Guys tried to help me to my feet, but I was too busy laughing my guts out.

"*Move!*" the radio shouted, and my vision focused instantly.

Chris dispatched me on five different jobs that needed signatures in thirty minutes. He gave me the information once. Addresses, contacts, suite numbers, destinations—it all came at me in a storm. Was I expected to remember all of this? He sure didn't have time to repeat it.

As I got up, dropped the 171 N. Clark, and began again swinging my way through traffic lights, signaling when each car should move and where it should move to, my thoughts fell into an incredible rhythm.

It was like I'd begun to see the second hand ticking through time itself; all the mechanics were transparent. Every street sign and parking meter was part of the machinery that kept the world turning, synchronizing, in sync with every desktop computer and every pipeline, the flush of every toilet and the signals that tell garage ventilators when to spark up and suck the fumes. The rhythm was in sync with the political polls and the oil drillers, the interest rates and the new technotyrannies of the Internet. I could actually feel the earth's rotation.

But this clarity would come and go. With a bag full of rags and a head full of numbers and names in a spin-cycle blur, I started to get confused: *Pick 311 S Wack, drop 200 Jack, 175 Frank, and 333. Grab 190 State and shake it off on the Sun-Times building. Three out 500 Mich will take me north to Oak Street and my set of 980s. No! Pick 190 State and then drop the 35 Wack. Then hit the Times. WAIT! I still have the 10 Hubbard on! Fuck!* I rode along, cursing, shouting at the buildings and the lines in the road, chanting, *"Kiss my ass! Kiss my ass!"* until it all became clear again.

"I retire next week," the owner of a small company at 541 Fairbanks said to me. "I think I'm going to get a job as a courier. What do you think? Will that make me feel young again?"

"Doubt it."

"You're probably right. It's too dangerous."

"Hm."

"But the upside is I won't die of a heart attack then, would I?"

This got me laughing. "No. But there are a few thousand other things you'd have to watch out for."

"Yeah, but it wouldn't be a heart attack."

"You make a very good point."

Two cabs collided at the corner of Canal and Harrison, only six feet from my back tire. Little pieces of plastic and glass flew everywhere, and I had to wonder how much force it took to knock a vehicle sideways some ten feet. I jumped into a passing lane to find a flatbed holding a pile of rusted pipes moving in reverse. I stopped only a foot from the brake lights and had to hobble my bike backward before the truck's rear wheels devoured me.

On Jackson I had to dodge a pair of paramedics who were wheeling a corpse across three lanes of traffic. In a gust of wind I dodged a flying hamburger as napkins flew into the air around me like little birds. A bus full of Orthodox Jews, all hipped out with long sideburns and black hats, passed me on Monroe while I watched the Adams Street Bridge on the river get drawn up ten stories into the sky and stand there. At the same time, an old schooner crept through the river playing rap music.

I closed my eyes. Opened them. Closed them. Opened them. I tried to retain, even for just a second, blackness—but it would instantly turn into an onslaught of reflected glass and headlights. I would see, in the back of my mind, crowds pressed into the shadows of buildings like ghosts. Skid marks and potholes had scarred my pupils.

How can all this fit into my eyes! I wondered to myself, half amazed, half sick from the visual intoxication. By the rear entrance of 111 Wacker, I tore the goggles off of my face and planted the nappy palm of my glove over my eyes. It smelled like exhaust, chain oil, and sweat, but my burning eyes needed the moment's rest. My shoulders relaxed and my breath began to slow down. Then I saw lights flashing at me, moving quickly. My chest started to shift in place to avoid the illuminated meteors that shot from my glove and disappeared into the ether. Soon the feel of my thighs burning, pushing my wheels, returned through the blackness of my smelly glove. Even in rest, I could not get off my bicycle.

The blackness behind my eyes had been turned into an infrared war zone. The omnipresent danger of automobiles and city streets had printed itself on that delicate film that ran through my cervical spine and skull, looping together all of my childhood fears, renewing them in the form of eighteen-wheelers, paper trucks, and taxicabs. I felt like I was coming closer to god, but it was only the light, the whiteness of the city's low-hung clouds that was burning itself within me. The light was everywhere and overwhelming, like a divine vision that kept expanding until it became cruel.

The problem was that I needed to process information more quickly, but how could I do that when I could barely manage my own speed and temper?

My body started to jitter beyond my control. I would find myself tapping the wrong buttons in elevators, shouting at drivers who had done absolutely nothing wrong, getting into arguments with security guards about where the bike racks were or weren't. The more work Zero offered, the more I took and the more I became enmeshed in the phenomenon of extreme speed. The greater the distance, the sooner the deadline, the more fury I would need to handle it. The more fury, the more the complexity and detail would be shoved into the back of my head, to haunt my sleep and corrode the fringes of my life-world.

This was the cost involved: the mania, the schizophrenia that came from having your reality snapped under the weight of a ten-hour anxiety attack called Chicago.

The psychological weight of this exposure principle led to a strange sense of megalomania. The faster I moved, the more I realized that all movement was an extension of my movement. I became the source of all human interaction, the scramble of computer chips and modems. I became the dial tone, the sound of a generator. I glanced at the mirrored walls of a huge silver skyscraper. In this reflection I had become the substance mercury.

I was telling guards how to do their jobs and commanding crowds of pedestrians to clear a path. They would follow my directives because I was hurling myself at them, shouting with a command that was completely paranormal. I was skitching police vehicles, bunny-hopping medians, and charging into lobbies like I was some kind of fireman. The aim: cut a few seconds off the Business Life delivery, snatch a minute off the U.S. Bank route, spike home the Henderson & Lymann to 2 Pru and slap Ms. Fletcher with the Amoco shuttle, and do all four maneuvers inside of sixteen minutes, start to finish.

But the work, the speed, the mania wore on my temper. I was not alone in that. I saw a messenger drag a driver out of his car window. In another company someone lit a package on fire and threw it into the Chicago River. When the elevator arrived at the forty-first floor of a building I heard the words "FUCK YOU! ALL OF YOU MONKEY BUREAUCRATS!" Before the doors closed a courier stepped in, looking very satisfied. He cleared his throat and said: "I'm Timmy. How ya doing?"

I heard from a Cannonball guy that he'd hit his head so hard that he couldn't think. He described it to me after a day's work in a severe heat wave. He had some kind of lapse. For less than a second he closed his eyes. In that time, he said, he could feel himself fall asleep. In that sleep, he said, he hit a pillar of the elevated subway that snapped his clavicle and nearly broke his jaw.

I chased some guy four blocks to give him hell about his driving technique. He told me to get out of his way, that he was in a hurry. I stood in front of his car shouting, "This is my fucking road! I live here! I do whatever the hell I please here!"

He tried to drive, threatening me with his bumper.

"Bring it on, you piece of shit! I want every ounce of it, you bitch! Bring it on!" I pulled my U-lock out of my bag.

"What the hell you want?" he asked.

Holding the U-lock to my right, I began: "Left blinker!"

"What?"

"Give me a goddamn left blinker before I kick your ass!"

He turned on his blinker.

"Right blinker!"

"What the hell are you doing?"

"I swear I'll smash it in! Gimme the blinker!"

He gratified me. I repeated the process a few times and walked back to my bike thinking that I had done some good. I had made someone aware of the difference it can make to signal before making a turn.

I was clearly losing my mind. In an elevator of 10 South LaSalle, I put my fists up at my reflection in the doors. "Stick and run. Stick and run," I whispered, throwing punches at my image. My fist accidentally made contact with the door, and soon I was pounding it in, trying to beat the fury out of my head. It didn't work. The steel doors just looked back at me, a little scuffed from the oil on the gloves. My chest heaving, adrenaline rushing, I was at war with the world. Even in the stillness of an express car going to the sixty-fourth floor, I was trying to push the machinery—make it hurry the fuck up.

Only in movement did I find peace. Only at thirty miles an hour, inches from tractors, drafting emergency vehicles, dodging cars, ducking truck doors, and floating four-lane intersections like I was Casper the friggin' Ghost, would the world seem to have any balance, any peace at all.

Stillness would generate a violent convulsion somewhere in the center of my cognitive navel, the generating point of all my thoughts and feelings. I had found in stillness a nerve-twisting tremor that I could not bear. *Stillness equals death. Stillness equals death. Stillness equals death,* I ranted while stretching my legs and taking long breaths.

I thought back on that handful of messengers rising above the sidewalk on their bicycles with their hands in the air, their chins high, the feeling of blood rising upstream, filling their eyes with a masterful and intuitive sense of self-control.

"One foot," Superdave said cautiously, aware of the absurdity of his request. Jimbo and Bobcat each lifted a leg and fell away. James fell forward, catching himself on the handlebars. He pulled away from the line, disqualified. For a moment Pee Wee and Jerry looked like they could hold it. They lifted their left legs off their pedals, keeping the right ones as tense as possible. Pee Wee fell to the right only seconds before Jerry rolled backward, picking the bike up with him and falling in the grass like a circus clown.

Like them, I was attempting the impossible, and the full effect of this was only starting to become clear.

EVEN IN DEEP SLEEP, the world hurled forward at me. I would have dreams that amounted to nothing but snapshots over a feeling of general motion: the flash of an aluminum drainpipe, a bird on the grille of a building's ventilator duct, an upturned garbage can, a missing license plate, an ink stain, a pile of boxes on the other side of a dirty glass windowpane, then *crack*—I was being thrown over a mailbox. Black water spinning up from beneath my front tire, the cables of an elevator seen through an open hatch, the wrinkled palms of a receptionist unwrapping toffee—then my bike slips and I am sliding along Wacker Avenue on my side while a truck speeding toward me bounces over the asphalt moguls of the State Street intersection. My eyes could not allow these images to merely pass by in their natural blur. They couldn't sit back, enjoy the ride, and let the colors mix and the contours trail because at the end of each stream of images was another dramatic rendition of my death or dismemberment.

The same fear that had forced my eyes open was now flashing a catalog of details down my half-conscious synapses with a furious and yet strangely disembodied urgency. My pupils would be forcibly exhausted, caught in this gallop of leaping forward into the landscape, grabbing something, and then leaping forward again, only to be slaughtered by something new.

The injury of this exposure principle was not about collisions every two thousand miles or the stitches or the stretched muscles or the sore joints. The injury, the injury at hand, was deeper. It was the accumulated effect of stretching perception across a convoluted distance, perhaps two thousand miles long, and losing, somewhere in it, the solace of the unconscious mind. That surplus of untapped human experience had gone dry.

Forward my mind reeled. *I am pollution. I am a hundred car doors. I am an ambulance. I am a bent street sign. I am a salmon, lying at the foot of a bridge on Halsted. I am an inflamed sinus. I am out of batteries. I am falling from upper upper Randolph and don't know where I'll land.*

"10-9, I didn't copy that, Number Thirty-nine," I responded to myself in the voice of my dispatcher.

I sat up to see the clock turn from 5:59 to 6:00. The digital screen took a single breath with me and then the alarm came on. *"Move!"* it said in an electronic groan. *"Move! Move! Move!"*

I got geared up in bike shorts and a colorful jersey, then I hid the fruity sportswear with a pair of military shorts and a cut-up company T-shirt. I tied my radio, with its newly charged battery, onto my strap, hung the strap over a two-inch band of bruised skin that crossed my chest like a sash. My butt, still sore from the stiff seat, pushed me out of the alleyway to work the routine again.

The sky stood high overhead and the streets were splashing with warm rain. My face was filled with sticky hot air as my tired eyes tried to navigate the wet streets. The sun came out huge, like a desperate god, a predator. Everything I saw when facing east was in the form of shadows, thousands of them, some living, some moving, some shaping the sun-bleached world in front of me, just shadows hiding from the intense light. Riding into it I felt my soul being fried up and smeared out behind me. I looked toward the light even though it too caused me pain.

Soon I was laughing, pedaling harder, squeezing between cars and cops and trucks and crowds of people that I could hardly see. I knew that any minute this mighty god on its golden chariot could snap its fingers and take me away. So I pedaled harder, faster, reacting to things that I could not see but only sense, and I headed straight east as if to be in the act of leaping. I was tempting the danger, I was trusting the predator. *I will arrive,* I said to myself. *I must arrive. What other choices do I have?* As I broke that first sweat and heard those familiar voices on the radio, I stood up in my saddle and spun, full speed, at the world once again.

CHAPTER SIX

THE PHYSICS OF FLOATING

A bicycle can dodge, defend, disappear, and reappear. A bike can attack. It can talk, fly, and it can trail, like an Indian. It can hunt down a specific muffler or a brand of cigarettes and follow it anywhere—anywhere. A bike can think. Right or left? Inside lane or outside lane? But you gotta be "true," at one with the wheel, to hear it. You gotta be in tune 'cause if you're not (I've seen it happen) one second everything is cool and then you're hearing sirens or . . . you're dead: poof!

Gino, Number 214, Deadline

THOSE FIRST FEW MONTHS AT SERVICE FIRST COST ME A set of tires, a rear wheel, a set of brakes, and a cassette. But none of this really worried me until I heard my bottom bracket split. The bottom bracket is the swivel that connects the two cranks inside the frame. Since I'd biked through a few Chicago winters, salt had accumulated in its tiny gaps, dried out its oils, eroded its metals, and made it weak. Serious cyclists and messengers can go through two bottom brackets a year. I had gone through one in four years.

"Thirty-nine to base."

"Thirty-nine, go."

"I think my crank just snapped."

"*Snapped?* That doesn't sound good. Does it still work?"

"Well, it doesn't sound good. You had that right."

"10-4. You're on your way to Yojimbo's."

"*Yojimbo's?*"

"Yojimbo's Garage, 1310 North Clybourn. You'll see a heavy door. Knock on it. Call me when you're done."

I paused and repeated the directions to myself because I thought I'd missed something: knock-on-door and call-when-done. *Whose door? Where the hell am I going?* I wondered, though I was really too intrigued to ask. I just 10-4'd the man and started on my uncertain way.

I found the building sided up against an empty lot, along a sidewalk buckled and full of holes. A mousetrap nailed knee-high on the battered door carried an old folded piece of paper that said KNOCK LOUD.

The door was so heavy that it stung my knuckles. I pounded again with the butt of my fist, but it made no sound. As I wound up to rap the door with my U-lock, it opened. Marcus Moore, whom I'd once met at the Grant Park races, leaned out. I remembered him as the unwilling and yet serious partner in our three-part relay team. He looked down at me from a tall step, a man with filthy brown, curly hair that seemed drenched in black bike grease. He wore thick-rimmed glasses, and when he saw the company name on my shirt, his sharp smile opened wide. Then he motioned for me to follow him inside. At first I felt a little out of place. I thought I was going to be walking into his living room.

I lifted my bike to my shoulder and stepped up into a dark room. As my eyes adjusted I saw a full-service shop with all the fixings. There was a workbench, a bike stand held up by cinder blocks, a glass case filled with shining derailleurs and colorful racing pedals. There was a rack of beautiful KHS bikes. Brand-new Fuji frames hung from the ceiling, along with a row of used fork-and-frame sets. A torn-up sofa against a far wall was littered with high-end racing magazines and catalogs. Boxes of bike parts lay around everywhere, labeled with names I recognized: Superdave, Bobcat, U.V. In a little loft above a small bathroom was a bookshelf. I'd found the messenger Batcave.

"Sit down, man. Bracket snapped? Was that the problem?"

"I don't know. Whatever's in there is fucked."

"Bottom bracket," he said, as if it was perfectly ordinary.

"All right, whatever. I just need to get back to work."

"Yup." He exhaled and hoisted my exhausted bike onto the stand. I stood behind him to see what greasy mess he was going to pull from the belly of my gearing, but before he got to work he looked back and said, "You mind? I kind of like to do this alone."

"10-4!" I turned away and tried to occupy myself, but the moment I sat on the big green sofa a smell hit me, the smell of new bike tires and machine oil. Even though I knew many bike shops, this particular whiff of bike-shop sweat I hadn't caught since I'd last visited my grandfather's shop in New Smyrna Beach, Florida. He'd opened a Firestone franchise in the mid-fifties and eventually, year by year, he turned it into a small department store. Then bit by bit he began carrying Schwinn bicycles. By the time of the oil scare of 1972, Fox Firestone was a full-service bike store, the only one in the region. My mother did the books there every summer from the time she was twelve to the year she left for college. My uncle and my grandfather would build and repair bikes with an unusual grace and speed. Father and son, they could snap together a Schwinn cruiser from right out of the box in fifteen minutes.

I leaned over and saw Marcus spinning tools through his fingers like Bruce Lee with a set of nunchaku. Somehow I remembered seeing that intuitive kind of movement. Marcus had attached a thin wrench to the inside of my pedal, and he began spinning the crank arms while the chain spun in place. In seconds the pedal fell to the floor with a thud and Marcus peeled the chain off the chain ring, to get it out of his way. Watching him with childish wonder, I soon felt right at home.

Marcus is more than just a bike mechanic with a bike shop. He also holds accounts with a number of courier companies so that their bikers, no matter how poor, can come in with bent frames and rims. Marcus gets 'em up again, hands them a receipt, and sends them on their way. At the end of the week he'll roll out to the offices of these messenger companies, drop off his receipts, and get paid; the cost of the repair will be deducted from the paycheck of the biker who needed help. What this means to the average courier is almost beyond words. Instead of paying cash, these young, starving, and hardworking people get to work off their repairs. Because he accommodates poverty, Marcus the mechanic instantly becomes Marcus the savior, the legend, the almighty messenger godhead of Chicago. Because he is a good mechanic, he keeps this title with little dispute from others.

As I sat and flipped through some racing catalogs, I fully expected that I would be walking out of there in a few minutes with my bike and a smile, praising Marcus for looking out for the lowly messengers around him. He'd said that he just needed to get the old bracket out and put a new one in. It would cost twenty bucks, twenty-five with labor, and it would take about ten minutes. He handed me back my pedals and said, "I think your frame is shot."

I encouraged him to give it another try because I had nothing else to work on. Everything hung in the balance. If I don't have wheels, I don't have work.

A day and a half later, I came back to find Marcus with the frame on the floor, a collection of cinder blocks and wrenches all strapped together to maximize the torque on the bracket. Marcus was standing on the handle of the elongated wrench set, sweating and cursing. When he saw me he climbed down from his contraption, grabbed a huge wrench, and began walking toward me. He put the wrench in my hands and then righted it so that I could see the tool's twisted and gnarly teeth. Something had chewed it to pieces. Marcus said very calmly, "Your frame *is shot.*"

We began talking about building up one of his used frames. I looked at a yellow Cannondale frame-and-fork set that hung from the ceiling, and he quoted me a price for it that was three times the amount of my life's savings: six hundred dollars.

"Can I work it off?"

He agreed to schedule deductions over a few weeks' pay. A few days later I was riding a bright yellow road bike set atop mountain-bike rims. Everything that I could transplant from the old bike, I did: seat, pedals, bars with bar extensions turned inward for extra power. The thing was ugly, but it was fast.

I rode the yellow monster out of Yojimbo's, and what a brave new world it was. As hard as I had been riding, the drawbacks of my heavier frame had kept me from understanding something of the nature, or the special dynamics, of deep urban velocity.

The most impressive aspect of this new speed was its potential for making money. In a few weeks' time, I had the cash to pay rent, take Haewon to dinner, and replace the watch my mother had given me for Christmas. I nearly wept when I stepped up to the register, but I found myself laughing instead. I was doing it, surviving, working my way back into a world where my basic needs would be covered, where I could enjoy my life again, where I would never have to think about starving.

In three weeks, I had the income to purchase a new pair of cycling shoes with a metal cleat that would clip into a special kind of pedal. They took some getting used to, but they gave more power to my push. Their one really significant benefit was that the pedals and shoes together cost nearly two hundred dollars. That was more money than I had earned from September to January, and yet I could just toss the cash away. I could lean against the counter and smile lightly, as if the bike retailer were only bagging groceries. It was a big smile, concealing years of pointless, fruitless struggle.

At work, Alicia had taken Pat's post as "the early guy." (Bikers in the industry are often called "guys"—even the girls.) She was a balls-out serious messenger. Whenever she was on the air, she would move like a speeding train. But she'd been doing the job for years and was, quite understandably, a little burnt out. Eventually, I was called in to take her place.

Being the early guy is like being a center in the NBA. With the post came a certain respect. I could start to call shots, I could select the work I wanted to take for the day, I could tell Goldberg which rookies I thought should be kept and which ones we should let go. Service First liked me because I was fast and I was solid. I liked Service because the work was steady.

I would sometimes leave the office before dawn with twenty overnight packages on board. In the first hour, Sam, Number Thirty-three, and I would get all hooked up. Then the other bikers on the team would trickle in around eight, nine, or ten o'clock. By noon, when some guys would have ten or fifteen jobs dropped, Sam and I would have nearly thirty. By three in the afternoon I was doing more work than I had accomplished in a week at Joey's.

I was becoming indispensable, and I was *loving it.*

MAKING A DROP on the twenty-third floor of 190 North LaSalle, back toward the mailroom, where, down a green hallway, a few brothas were hanging out and talking shit while they waited on packages. I envied their sly street antics and language. Their prose was heightened and fresh, while my controlled speech seemed pale and restricted in comparison. Mr. Porter signed his last name on my ticket at 2:36:45, according to my new watch, and I moved on, organizing the next drop in my bag, taking no pleasure in the company or the diversity of others. I was preparing myself for the real stuff, concentrating, revving myself up to handle the workload that kept mounting on Chris's desk.

I pressed the DOWN button at 2:37:12 and waited. Six elevators served this floor but none of them were coming. My posture kept shifting: *At ease! Attention! At ease! Attention!* My heart was pounding in my chest and all I could do was stand there. *HELP ME! HELP ME! Maybe I should call the guard on the building phone? Maybe I should just jump out of the fucking window!* I looked, but there was no window.

Ding, ding. A red light lit up over my explosive temper. The massive doors opened up onto a golden carriage that reflected light like the elongated shapes of a polished steam train from the turn of the last century. At 2:38:33, I stepped in and my nerves calmed. At least I was moving.

Fizzzzzzzz. I heard my freewheel roll, passing the Federal Reserve, coasting down Jackson Avenue, slipping past the glowing facade of the Chicago Board of Trade—once the tallest building in the city. Atop this landmark, where the roof leans in, siphoning into a dramatic obelisk, a metal figure stands, basked in sunlight. The figure rises up as a combination of curved geometric lines and polished steel. While the highest building in Philadelphia was capped with a sculpture of William Penn wearing knickers and a ruffled coat, the highest building in Chicago was topped by this anonymous, featureless steel symbol of a humanity at large, a humanity trapped in space and yet bravely (and mechanically) penetrating time.

As a tourist, years ago, I'd once tucked into the observatory windows of the nearby Sears Tower. A crowd of thin shoulders looked down at this sculpture, commenting unknowingly that the features of this metal figure may have been *unnecessary.*

"Who would ever get close enough to tell that the figure did not have eyes or ears?" a tour guide asked rhetorically. And yet here we all were, leaning down over the figure, calmly amused by the romanticism of that early modern era.

As I compared those shapes with the current cubist patterns of the Sears Tower and the kaleidoscopic spectacle of the Thompson Center, I was amazed by the aesthetic shift that steel had given us. The Doric columns and the triangular pediments of the classical order could be reversed, erased, or made out of glass that rose and fell from floor to floor, carrying passengers.

These aesthetic shifts do not end at architecture. Portraits of the aristocracy once included the ruins of Greek temples as a backdrop. In these paintings the subjects stood with one foot forward, like old Greek statues. This *contrapposto* is lost in today's portraits of an ideal human type.

In its day, this gentle sway of the torso having carried one foot forward showed us the possibility of marble hinting at motion. Today, as we look back, this posture has shifted. We are no longer carved in marble but projected in electric currents through copper wires, radio waves, and telephone lines. As sculpture and painting once hinted at time, we now, using film, photography, and digital signals, only hint at space.

In the story of ancient sculpture, bringing that one foot forward and revealing the space between the legs was an enormous advancement—*once, a long time ago,* buried now in the ambulatory acceleration of modern man. In our age, most motion is done with the assistance of technology. The farther we go and the faster we go, the less our bodies have to move at all.

As technology, legs themselves are almost obsolete. As technology, they have buried themselves in cars, elevators, and the telescopic hallways at the gates of airports. They are the evolutionary experiments of a *Homo erectus* man. Though we keep the hardware, we have lost the application. The intensification of man-in-time has made our bodies merely units of transport, personal storage containers, carry-ons. And so our modern posture is one of accelerated time, giving only an accent, like one foot backward, to the realm of real shape.

I suppose that I, at the time a tourist in the windows of the world's tallest building, could have easily recognized that very few of us would have been looking out that window if we'd had to take the stairs. Elevators, like expressways, subways, and jumbo jets, help merge constant motion with constant stillness. In some ways, then, the steel figure on the Chicago Board of Trade keeps its symbolic primacy over the city: we are without features, without faces, cased in steel and floating, like Pegasus, on the hooves of technology itself.

The messenger signifies exactly this, the hooves, whatever human power labors toward this engineered ideal. The messenger commits himself to the development of a single day's work in the city, spinning through the machine while his legs transform into airplane cables and hydraulic cylinders moving around a series of titanium discs. His calves weld themselves to the die-cast pedals with small metal clips. His knees push the bike forward. This force vibrates through the fine metals of his bike until his bent arms absorb the stress again. He is not the passenger but the engine. His legs expand and contract like pistons, hardening with every cycle until his entire body, legs and all, are strong and thin like tough iron pipes, maintaining, physically and perpetually, a modernist, if not futurist, *contrapposto.*

With his seamless warp and woof of form and function, the messenger seems as timeless as human communication itself. The image of the messenger persists in the postindustrial mind as a flashback, the vision of Mercury. It is perhaps a testament to the power of the myth that messengers are still associated with theft: Mercury was occasionally invoked as the god of thieves. However, a more direct correlate is Mercury's role in commerce: he was often portrayed as a young beardless man, helmeted, carrying a purse in his role as the agent of merchants. Dressed like an angry court jester in GI gear and purple tights, on a bright yellow bike, I am reminded of another attribute of Mercury: he was a trickster.

But there's more at work here, something even deeper than mythological archetypes. The human mind seems to favor forms that represent an elegant and efficient solution to a problem. How else to explain the beauty in something as simple as a bicycle? Beyond the wholeness represented by the balanced and compact geometry of two circles and two triangles, our recognition of the form's function canonizes the image in our mind. There is a mathematical imperative that favors the bicycle in our view of the romance of motion. A few years back I heard about a study of the energy efficiency of all means of transportation. In the company of cars and airplanes, in the company of flies and frogs, in the company of eels, alligators, cheetahs, and eagles, the bicycle, as ridden by a professional, was deemed the most energy-efficient means of transportation.

Even while the bicycle itself develops along the lines of common technology, accumulating computer chips, hydraulic shocks, and fine metals, the messenger rig has done something remarkably different. It tends to progress in reverse, toward greater simplicity, losing brakes, gears, and cables. Messenger bikes are built to be light, quick, strong, and geometrically refined to the point that more engineering would only get in the way. Serious couriers think of their bikes as weapons, like swords; whatever is added to them takes away from their speed, their dependability, or their razor-sharp edge.

I found these traits in the yellow machine that Marcus built up for me. It was simple, effective, and built for speed and maneuverability. I named it the Grinch, and on it my body understood optimum efficiency. I saw clearly that, even at the height of our present technological savvy, the bicycle could never be buried; it could only be misunderstood and unappreciated.

RIDING A COURIER RIG in the city, looking out over its handlebars, I feel that the Grinch and I are one. I don't worry about the machinery. I avoid broken glass, vehicles, and people.

As I navigate head-on into oncoming traffic, twisting my shoulders through tiny gaps between side-view mirrors and oversized bumpers, I am exercising a specific kind of kinetic intelligence. I register only solids and fluids. I read the street itself and all the details of the urban world that could possibly obstruct my path, because speed alone is worthless. I need to have an out for every obstacle in a perfectly unpredictable blur of movement.

The effort is intuitive. When riding, I do not concentrate on what my hands and feet are doing. I focus on the space at hand, what is there, what is not there, and what is coming into being. I rarely dodge. It's more like I swim toward emptiness, analyzing what is in front of me by the speed with which it comes at me. I am not moving through space as much as I am expanding space where, in speed, it seems to fall away.

In a car this shift is evident. On a motorcycle it is almost ever present: space is transformed by speed, flattened. If the laws of nature depend on the perspective involved, then, from my perspective, mounted on an aluminum speed machine, riding through a constantly changing landscape (much of which is also in motion), physical laws are inverted; some are negated, others dramatically expanded. The laws of the universe change when you become part of the equation, when you figure into the dynamics of distance over time.

Extreme speed can feel like a long, narrow hallway. The direction, held in the mind, reduces the world to a series of positive and negative signals. For a professional cyclist like Greg LeMond or Lance Armstrong, speed necessitates a kind of tunnel vision, directed at the path he is on. If the path is interrupted, which it rarely is, the racer leans into a new vantage point. The racer does not have to focus on weaving through obstacles the way a courier does. He concentrates on his breath, his cadence, his posture, and his heart rate. "Keep your line" is a mantra for the roadie. As his perspective narrows, his vision crops down to an almost singular dimension; he knows the flatness of forwardness.

In the city, however, this "line" winds down a street, around buses, over curbs and medians, through the pocked asphalt of Little Italy after the snow has been cleared, through four lanes of cars and buses coming at you flank-side. Because I am an urban cyclist being hurled through traffic, I have to remember the stillness of things, *the flank reality*—I cannot let space flatten.

My mobility is not about the speed of going forward. Speed merely determines the rate by which I process an obstacle and set myself on a path to avoid it. In the right state of mind I can outmaneuver fate, I can outflank a head-on collision, I can manipulate my way through a mind-bending convergence of space. Slipping in and out of streams of traffic, this flank reality is an intelligence, a skill that must be cultivated and refined because a courier's ability to process is his only protection. There is no safety net.

My life and work depend upon unraveling all the dynamics of the city street and then speeding a path, like a signature, through it—always arriving at the end to dot the i's and cross the t's. The physics of floating is the basis of my agility. It is the magic that ultimately pays my rent.

MY SECOND YEAR in Chicago, still just an average bike commuter, I was not so aware of these distinctions between sight and foresight, between keeping my line and keeping my flank. One summer morning I caught a glimpse of those special laws of a courier's mobility, though I was too inexperienced to understand them.

I had this nice rhythm going, coasting through tight traffic, keeping my head low, zipping out into the median to crank past clumsy traffic on Ashland. When I turned onto Lincoln Avenue, a courier—a real hottie—appeared from behind me without making a sound. A little shocked, I gave him a sharp look, but he didn't catch it. A moment later I was glad he hadn't because, when I saw him more closely, he was a rabid dog of a man and I preferred not to stir his macho calm.

He wore a short-sleeved T-shirt and pair of weathered gloves with the Velcro straps open and flapping in the wind. I could see in his eyes the cocky comfort a Doberman pinscher has guarding an estate. He was at home, living in transit as he does every day, sitting behind his handlebars as if they were a desk, looking at the street as if it were his office—knowing the whole city, as it was, quite literally, *his business.* Instead of cruising along with his nose up like some messengers do, this guy gave a kind of a pirate smile. "Ahoy there!" he seemed to say, and I felt no intimidation.

I looked down at his bike and noticed that something was missing. His bike was simplified to the point of having no brakes and no gears. The lines of the chain streamed right back to the axle of the back wheel. There was only one cog! He had no derailleur, no cables, and no helmet. His bike was the simplest expression of a bicycle I had ever seen.

The messenger, a combination of muscle and hair and artwork tinted green beneath his skin, steadily pulled ahead of me on his clean piece of engineering. His head was hidden from view behind a big envelope stuck halfway out of his thick waterproof bag. I couldn't believe that with one gear—a fixed cog with no freewheel!—he was faster than me. I had twenty-one speeds, and yet it seemed he was going to be faster than every one of them. In high spirits, I stepped up to the challenge he offered. I shifted up and hammered my way into his wake, coasting until he heard my free-wheel rattling softly behind him. He suddenly shot forward, racing full-speed down the choppy diagonal street toward downtown. The game had begun.

I stood up and began muscling forward, and when I got closer I coasted, waiting for my chance to sprint ahead. As he turned back to check my distance, I made the move, passing him on the right, turning the pedals so quickly that my knees felt like they would spin right off. I shifted to an even higher gear and kept pushing, taking advantage of his single-speed handicap. As we leaned into a curb and swung around a gray van planning a left turn at the Southport light, I stayed in tight to the van, forcing the courier to squeeze into my wake. Then he threw me.

Only inches from me and from the van's door, he sprinted forward between us, ducking beneath the van's broad side-view mirror to pass me. He was moving like a barracuda, navigating across the ocean floor through sharp rocks and crags without a thought. I tried to imitate his moves, clumsily, apprehensively, desperate to regain my lead. He fought back, ducking around sport cars in adjacent lanes.

We muscled each other neck and neck until he quietly disappeared behind me, along with the blur of brownstones, storefronts, and construction sites. Even as I started to feel confident, my thighs were heating up like an overworked engine. I was sweating, panting, but I pushed forward, slashing the front tire right and left as I shifted my weight around for extra speed.

I glanced backward to check his position. He was tailing me, smiling. It was cool to be in the lead, but somehow he still had the upper hand. I had pushed myself so hard that my breath was narrowed, and my eyes darted with panic through the world of blurring colors and shapes (the truck backing up, the white car rolling out blindly from the right, the red Camaro coming up behind us).

Amid the chaos, timing my way through the independent rhythms of the street, I began to worry that I would push myself too far. Would I lose control and coast into the oncoming lanes? Would I miss details and become blind to textures of the pavement? The pedestrians? The brake lights of the cars in front of us? I began to brace myself for a high-speed collision or a scrape that could crack an arm or a rib or worse. But I was compelled to keep pushing. Losing didn't matter, but with this guy, contending did.

I felt that the harder we fought the more we would understand each other, as if speed and agility were a language—the tribal language of the city cyclist. I wanted to show him that I spoke his language, that I too was young and proud, daring, vital—that I was not afraid. I don't think I needed to impress him, but I wanted to be acknowledged for my respect of him.

As we approached the six-way intersection of Lincoln, Fullerton, and Halsted, my competition rapidly moved out from behind me and went for the lead, passing me on the right, gesturing that the intersection would be our finish line. The look in his eye was knowing and relaxed. This *would* be the end of the race, like it or not. I seemed to have little say in the matter.

He had refined his relationship to time and space to such a fine point that motion and direction were synonymous. I could still put some speed behind the wheel, but I would not be competitive. It wasn't strength I lacked, it was my lagging perception of this special speed-driven geometry. I was riding a bicycle. He was falling through crosstown traffic like a skydiver with his own horizontal brand of gravity. I was processing information. He was predicting it.

In time, I too would learn that an experienced messenger can see anywhere from five to thirty seconds into the future. The traffic can be read so closely that he is rarely caught off guard. Most people think that this comes with having good reflexes, but who needs reflexes when you can actually see the future? The truth is that reflexes are put to the test only when knowledge is inadequate. Reflexes, like helmets, are not the keys of a biker's survival. Riding in this manic plateau requires just the opposite: a sense of cool intelligence, a knowing before knowing is even necessary, a foretelling—and *that* was the look in his eye.

This messenger was like a magician drawing me closer, bringing me clumsily to the foot of his stage so that he could perform his magic right before my naked eyes and I could be amazed.

Traffic on Lincoln was hit with a yellow light. I thought I would have a chance to catch the courier at the intersection; then he stood up in his pedals and began to push forward as if he could catch the light that we were a full forty yards away from. In seconds this yellow light on Halsted would turn red and traffic would start pulling forward into our path, but my mysterious friend was still picking up speed. I tried to keep up with him, and when I saw the arenalike six-way intersection fill with cars rolling across our path, I thought I was being led to my death by a man who clearly had no fear of it. *Wait! He doesn't even have brakes!* I remembered in a panic. I stopped pedaling, trying to read the pattern of the cars crossing our path to see if he would be okay, but the situation was too compli-cated. I saw buses, a charity worker on the curb, a truck with tool-boxes and racks, eighty to a hundred cars and SUVs moving around wildly, a station wagon waiting on a left turn and three cars around him lurching for opportunities to jump in some direction. Still midmotion, I was ten feet from the competition and he was ten feet from the merciless blur of traffic, still going way too fast to stop. He even had his head down, like a charging ram. The pedestrians, an-other bicyclist in the intersection, six lanes of traffic trying to get to work before 9:00 A.M., a school bus, and this courier were rushing toward one another all at once, and only he knew how it would all play out.

Then I saw it: he leaned forward on his handlebars until his back tire was drawn up off the road. He stopped pedaling and planted the fixed back tire on the asphalt, dragging it through a carefully managed skid as a school bus passed like a long yellow wall only a few feet from him. He turned his head away and swung his back tire to one side, tearing it into the street with a scream. When the back bumper of the school bus finally cleared his path, the messenger stopped the skid and resumed his progress, clearing vehicle after vehicle as traffic flew toward him with no time to brake or react. Slipping through all six lanes in a straight line, he van-ished, consumed by a wall of cars and trucks that melded into a multicolored smear.

I held my brakes, skidded to a stop, and was in seconds sur-rounded by blaring car horns. I was standing with my bike in the middle of the three southbound lanes, consumed by a flock of angry drivers. I picked up my bike and walked it back to the curb, defeated and a little confused.

UNDER THE INFLUENCE of this unique physics, a courier's path can hardly be a legal one. Many of the maneuvers we make are illegal. We often get hell for it, but then, we get hell for anything we do.

More than thirty private buildings in Chicago will actually ban a messenger from a building if he's caught taking his own bag up to the suite with him. Most of the buildings managed by Miglin-Beitler work this way. In response to this, we pin I AM NOT A THIEF buttons to our courier bags and let that be our defense.

I had a suit on the twentieth floor of Hell (a.k.a. One North Franklin) actually tell me to use "the freight." I didn't think an envelope in my bag constituted freight, so I complained to a guard, who started yelling at me the moment I stepped toward him in the lobby. According to him, I was not allowed to stand on the ground floor of their building, much less use their passenger elevators. If he could have told me to use the garbage chute, he would have. He threw me out, threatening to have me banned from the building.

"What? Am I really that offensive?" I shouted from the revolving doors. It stinks when you get shafted not for who you are but for who you represent.

Darren Miller, while working with Advanced, was stopped in the lobby of 900 N. Michigan because he tried to walk past the guard without showing his I.D. He saw that other people were walking past the guard without showing their identification. What made him any different? Building policy. After arguing the ideas with the guard and getting nowhere, he decided to relent. "Fine, fuck the delivery. I'm not going in," he said, and went to leave. Again he was stopped. Now he had to show his I.D. to *leave* the building. As more guards came to manage the situation, Darren called into base and quit his job. Dispatch understood. He was no longer employed by Advanced Messenger Service. "I am not a courier anymore, so you cannot keep me here. I want to leave your building!" When he went for the door he was tackled, detained, and eventually dragged away by police.

Our clients give us hell for dropping a package a few minutes late, while at the same time the aldermen give us hell for the shortcuts we make through the city. In Illinois, a motorcyclist is not required by law to wear a helmet. In the Loop, a courier can be fined or arrested for exactly that. It is not a bad idea to wear a helmet, but it is a bad idea to enforce it only on messengers. The shit flies in this occupation no matter how you cut it, and so many messengers have stopped trying to please anyone. When the attacks come, they come, and the experienced couriers, like that hottie who toasted me on Halsted, just keep moving. Remember, I stopped at the intersection and I was the one who had to deal with the drivers.

There is a politics to the movement of a courier and it doesn't end at crazy building policies. When a motorist sees a biker run a red light, cutting through four lanes of traffic going twenty to thirty miles an hour, the driver is generally going to think that he is totally insane, that he has no regard for anyone, that he doesn't even care enough about his own life to look before rolling out into a stampede of steel. They think, *Someone should stop that person before he kills himself.* I understand the sentiment; it is a petrifying thought that someone could seem so careless with their own existence.

Don't be mistaken. Couriers want to make a living—that's all—but motorists will likely never understand this because they will never address the innate advantages a bike has over a car.

The kind of perception that a driver has behind a windshield, a set of small mirrors, a thousand-pound engine, and dashboard seriously limits his view of a cyclist's experience. The speedometer, the doors, the little sticker that says that the steering wheel is equipped with an explosive air bag, the seat belt, all of these aspects to driving a car condition the driver's mobility and perception.

A cyclist works with a much more open sense of immediate space than a driver does. He has at least 330 degrees of unobstructed vision (looking forward, tilting the head left and right) and about 720 degrees of hearing (two ears, tilted left and right). As I glance down a street and see a white truck with a red bumper, my eye sees the truck first. It doesn't need to register the parts of the truck, the windshield, the white grille, and the red bumper, to understand that a truck is coming. I see wholes, even at the highest speeds I can reach.

In a similar way, the element of hearing alone is extraordinary. A truck sounds different than a van, which sounds different than a car or a Harley-Davidson chopper or a squad car. Their presence is registered immediately in a way that makes the visual appearance of those things seem obvious.

Because of our high levels of observation, couriers have entrée to a whole world of character that most drivers have little access to. For instance, the most dangerous thing on the road is a taxi without a fare because that driver's intent is difficult to read. He can lunge in any direction at any moment: for a pedestrian, for an illegal U-turn, for a sharp left when you are passing on the left.

A cab with a fare is different. He won't make erratic turns or abruptly stand on his brakes. If the passenger is a man, the driver will likely be a bullet train, taking his turns at a high speed to earn his tip for effort. A woman in the cab typically transforms a taxi into your best friend. He will tend to offer you the right of way. He will use his signals. He will often become considerate. Again, this is probably because of the tip he's working for.

But cabdrivers are remarkably sensitive. I have never skitched a cab whose driver wasn't aware of it instantly. Hanging on to the back hub of a cab is tantamount to hanging on to the ear of the cabbie. They and their cars are all-seeing and all-knowing. That is pretty damn impressive.

Most drivers don't have this kind of metaphysical connection to their cars. The car for most people is an anesthetic, a wall between themselves and the world. The importance of this separation is hard to underestimate, but the most important consequence concerns a driver's safety. I find that most drivers' sense of confidence is artificial; they cannot see and they have little notion of what it means when the odometer reads sixty-five, seventy-five, or eighty-five miles per hour. They don't know what kind of danger they are in. Even though the annual rate of auto fatalities is perfectly predictable, collisions are still called accidents because they seem to take everyone by surprise.

This shutting off of the driver from his surroundings even endangers the world around him. His mission to reach a destination is clouded by a few confusing messages: one, that efficiency demands filling spaces that appear open; two, that obeying traffic signals and calming devices is actually in his best interest; and three, that other people on the road are *obstacles* rather than *drivers* who are as confused and selfish as he is. Facts are: most drivers are bad drivers, and bad drivers are dangerous.

John Dollard, a behaviorist, outlined long ago how aggressiveness can be clinically understood to be a buildup of frustration.

Though the larger implications of Dollard's frustration-aggression theory have been disputed, the central thesis holds: the regular interruption of a specific action or goal-directed activity leads to aggression. What remains to be understood, in the context of the car, is what kind of aggression it leads to.

Because of mixed messages and constant interruptions, driving is stressful. If this stress doesn't come out in the form of physical aggression (or at least in the form of exercise, which would be the best way), the driver will resort to symbolic action, for instance, an aggressive expression that says "I'm pissed!" Being that stressful situations so often happen inside the car, where physical aggression is either limited or impossible, this aggressiveness tends toward symbolic action. The driver shouts, hits the horn, or hits the gas.

Two things worry me here. Primarily, it is profoundly disturbing that a driver as young as sixteen or as old as time itself can assault with the same force what he is entirely cut off from understanding. Seeing only a pedal and glass, he can launch a couple of tons of steel into real people and still be participating in a *symbolic* attack. How is he to know what is a symbolic action when there is no one in his caged world to keep his perceptions in check?

Second, how can a government of car-numbed, suburban politicians intelligently manage a street or organize a city when they are unable to see beyond their dashboards and their own symbolic aggression? Can a governing body that is so remarkably ignorant of the dynamics of a cyclist's behavior represent a cyclist's needs? And furthermore, should a governing body that only knows how to drive through a city be chosen to manage it?

Oh, these thoughts get me down sometimes.

ON A BICYCLE, confidence and capacity are bound by a single chain. The more confidence a biker has, the more capacity he has—it is just that simple. The less capacity a cyclist has, the more he will tend to conform to the rules of the road. I believe that 90 percent of a city's cycling public fits this model. Most cyclists are aware, law-abiding, and respectful. But we can't expect bike messengers to follow their lead. A messenger following a commuter's level of caution and defensiveness would destroy his livelihood, insult his character, and impede his right to the road.

At a messenger party I happened to sit in on a great conversation about the politics of floating. A cycling advocate, very bright but unaware of the messengers' depth of experience, asked Pork Chop, a painter who rides on and off to cover his need for supplies, why he thought he had a right to run red lights. Pork Chop smiled brightly and said, "I don't live in a box, man. I don't have tunnel vision. I don't need to be told what to do."

The guy then asked if Pork Chop didn't think that a bike was a vehicle, and subject to the same laws as a car.

"No. I am a vehicle; I am aware of that," Pork Chop said smugly. "But I didn't sign any contracts about how I will act as a vehicle. I didn't take any tests, and I didn't get any mug shots for it either. Biking is a right I have. It does not have to be licensed because, you know, my bike is *not a deadly weapon*. I'd love to see a court try to suspend my right to bicycle." He started laughing. "The jury has reached a verdict. This man is too deadly to bicycle!"

Every once in a while, messengers do get stopped for breaking petty ordinances and traffic laws. You'd think they would just get a ticket, but they are often hauled downtown, held overnight—and *then* given a ticket. It happens all the time. I heard of one guy who lost his job because he couldn't deliver a package from his holding cell. He'd been arrested for violating a helmet ordinance. On another occasion, John Greenfield was arrested while talking to a cop during a small Critical Mass ride. He was charged with impersonating a police officer. They based their charge on the fact that one of the many patches on his messenger bag was a police patch that he had purchased over the counter from an army surplus store on Belmont. Twelve-Guy Rod (a highly respected messenger who seems to always be getting stopped for more and more absurd offenses) was once brought downtown during his lunch break. I think the story was that he had taken off his helmet while walking into a restaurant to use the bathroom.

The first time I heard that Rod had gotten arrested, he was running a set of thirty-minute specials to the North Side in rush-hour traffic. The Twelve-Guy whipped through a light on Michigan on his blue Cannondale. His orange sunglasses were clipped into the holes of his slick orange helmet, his trademark. He is a mature cyclist and very smooth.

Midstride, rounding Ohio at Michigan, a six-lane, highly commerical megastreet, he was spotted by a traffic cop. This is nothing unusual; cops are stationed at every Michigan light for the most part of a Chicago day, certainly during rush hour. We swirl around them all day with an implicit kind of camaraderie. Winks, nods, salutes—we are glad to know that someone is looking out for us. Street cops are generally cool people because they generally leave us alone. The cop who called in Rod was responding to one of

Sergeant Clark's ritual anticycling crackdowns, which he organized to fight Critical Mass.

Rod didn't know that he'd been radioed in. He didn't know anything about Sergeant Clark or why the Eighteenth District would suddenly be antibike. Rod was just cranking away like he does every day, loving that set of North Side specials, looking forward to ending the hour with another forty dollars to show for it. The intersections were all backed up, making things easier for him. Light after light he was in a beeline, burning straight through Erie, Huron, Superior, and Chicago with increasing speed. To him, there was no traffic. He saw space, holes, entire avenues open for his use. Pearson, Chestnut, Delaware, Walton—and then he heard the sirens. Cop cars were beginning to nose out of the intersections. Beat cops were starting to step out into the street. Two squad cars had pulled out into Michigan. By the time he got to Oak Street, there was a line of cops blocking the intersection like soldiers. One cop held his hand out, fingers spread wide. Rod hit the brakes and coasted right into his arms.

When he relayed the story to me, he was not upset—he was flattered. "I figure, I run at least, I don't know, what? Two hundred lights a day? I work five days a week, twelve months a year. That means I run something like ten thousand lights a year? Maybe? Give or take? That's a lot of lights—and I've been doing this for, what?, *nine years! Whatever, man!* It's cool, just give me a ticket—a behemoth ticket if you want to. One ticket out of some hundred thousand red lights? No problem! You won't get any dispute out of me."

By the time he got back to base from the police department, he was still blushing. He was proud, looking like a boy who knew he'd done well. He was chugging a long-neck Coors, gloating with a flat grin stretched across his face, "Yep, they got me this time." He kept up the sarcasm while the bike room was filling up with couriers, ending their day, matching their tickets. We were all laughing till our guts hurt while Rod continued: "What am I supposed to say? *I am so sorry, Officer? What was I thinking, Officer? I didn't see it. It was YELLOW, I swear!*"

What the driving public needs to understand is that speed is what we are paid for and floating is the skill that makes our work competitive. We can twist Madison Avenue into a runway and penetrate a crowd like it was a puff of smoke. There is no fear. These kinds of stunts come directly from our experience, and that experience should be trusted. An intersection burnt by a courier should herald cheers from cops, motorists, and pedestrians alike. It is the clearest expression of a messenger's technique.

CHAPTER SEVEN

IS / CHICAGO

Burnham Consultants
111 West Washington
Chicago, IL 60602

*T*HE ADDRESS WAS STUCK DIAGONALLY TO A CARDBOARD tube dangling out of my waterproof bag. Hunched over and forceful, I pulled out onto Washington from LaSalle, taking the sharpest left turn I could handle. Coasting toward the curb, I popped out of my clipless pedals and dismounted running. I spun the Grinch in one hand and planted it for the lockup. The key tied to my wrist spun the U-lock open. I locked it through a welded metal garbage can and ran for the revolving doors. Coming out of the elevator on twelve, I used the door that said ENTER and almost had my head shot off.

"Deliveries are *down* the *hall!*" shouted the receptionist. I excused myself and shuffled down the hall. There is not enough time in this business to combat every discourteous and ignorant remark that comes my way, so I followed her directions into the mailroom. It was strewn with paper tubes, blueprints, and people bustling about. There were two messengers. One was pacing rapidly and another was shouting on the telephone. Three people in white-collared shirts and uniform black ties did one person's work behind a countertop. I said the name on the label of my package and asked for a POD.

"Brown!" was shouted back at me. I smacked the tube down across a pile of papers and made it to the door.

This was the office of a permit-consulting firm named after the late Daniel Burnham, the architect most recognized for the 1909 plan for the city of Chicago. This plan, which carefully combined key aspects of major European cities, was a milestone in the urban-planning renaissance of America. To his credit, Chicagoans have one of the most widely used and loved shorelines in the country. The elevated and subway train lines exist now just as they were drawn up nearly a hundred years ago, and some of Chicago's parks, bridges, and railways are still identical to his model.

The broadly acclaimed plan was accepted immediately, as it accomplished the aims of many independent business interests of that time, and then, piece by piece, etched into the landscape. But as with any translation, some ideas were underplayed and some were changed significantly.

Burnham's Congress Parkway, the central roadway dividing the north from the south side of Chicago, was initially lined up with a number of city parks and fountains. The stately balance given to the roadway made it an axis of civic pride and cultural sophistication. Today, Congress Avenue in Grant Park is accented with a number of wonderful public monuments; however, it is no longer the primary east-west axis. Now the center of the city is a one-way street five blocks north of Congress that signifies only the center of commerce. The eastern end of this centerline butts up rudely with the lakeshore park and does not continue to the waterfront.

Surrounding the major metropolitan area on three sides was to be a broad semicircular boulevard connecting neighborhoods on the south, west, and north sides of the city. Between this boulevard and the lakeshore, a grid design was overlaid with a series of diagonal streets linking major public squares, in the style of classical European avenues. Only a few of these diagonals were ever built.

Burnham's vision of the major north-south streets, such as Michigan, State, Wells, and Halsted, had wide sidewalks with parks, and elaborately designed six-way intersections where the streets met the diagonals. Michigan Avenue is now the only north-south artery that is meant to accommodate heavy pedestrian activity. This boulevard-style throughway, lined on one side with skyscrapers and on the other with parks, is known today as "the cliff." Not only is this strip of Michigan pedestrian, but its line of masterfully designed and high-reaching buildings, which have grown and adjusted with the ages, is visually exhilarating. Side to side and block to block, this majestic avenue, which turns golden with the rising sun and purple with its setting shadows, is a testament to the human sprit, to the free market, and to architecture; but most of all, it is a testament to Burnham.

When the city gave his plan the chance to succeed, it did succeed, making Chicago an impressive prototype for the City Beautiful movement. Unfortunately, this chance did not come often.

The west side of the Loop was to have royal gateways where the residential zones met downtown's city life. Bikes were the transportation of choice in Burnham's day, and his plan called for paved streets so that cyclists could comfortably traverse the entire city without mud or cobblestones impeding their way. (Most of America still used horse-drawn carts and dirt roads at the time.) The city plan had a strong and dynamic transportation system of freight, elevated, and subway trains and downtown trolleys that led all the way from the suburbs to the boatyards. Burnham said he was designing the city for a hundred years' use.

Now, nearly a hundred years later, most of these amenities have collapsed. Neighborhoods are marked by their bad reputations, not by their architectural landmarks. Streets are paved only for the sake of drivers. The shoulders of streets and the seldom-used bike lanes regularly collect potholes, parked cars, and unswept glass. The train system was bought out by the city, and the trolleys have vanished. The hundred years that we have had to live out his design have seen a long political process of defacing it.

But these hundred years were more than Burnham could have ever imagined. Too many advances occurred even in the years before his plan was published. The first zeppelin flew in 1900. The Wright brothers made their first flight in 1903. Finally, only months before the Burnham plan was released, the Model T was introduced to the public. How could the future of the automobile have been figured into Burnham's great design? In 1909, when the city plan was completed, there were a little over seven thousand vehicles registered in the city. They were at the time astronomical luxuries. As the Model T became cheaper due to advances in assembly-line production, the plan of the city had to give.

This eventual transition away from the Burnham model is of special relevance to Chicago messengers. We look at the existing shape of the city as a kind of second skin. From our time working and living amid its every detail, the city map becomes the shape of free passage—the blueprint of liberty. Much like the limbs of our bodies, the geography of the streets becomes a human tool, an innate capacity like motion, a partial object that we use to reach, to move, and to attain other objects. The city, to us, is a form, like the image of our faces, which we identify with. It is a muscle that provides leverage and stamina to many young, struggling, and resourceful people. It would be difficult to feel the messenger's motion and understand our special perspective without seeing how the body and the city are, in this, united.

ONLY A FEW YEARS after the approval of Burnham's plan, traffic became unmanageable in the Loop. Every week over a thousand new vehicles were added to the Chicago streets, and new engineering techniques appeared necessary to control the problem. Burnham's partner, Edward Bennett, began exploring new ideas for wider streets and elevated roadways. In 1923, construction had begun to create bilevel and trilevel streets to divide into groups the kinds of traffic that would use them. One level was designated for walking and light local traffic. Another level was designated for through traffic and underground parking structures. The lowest levels would accommodate freight trucks and subway systems.

Once the experimental Wacker Drive was finally completed, congestion in the Loop actually increased. There was no design error. It was just that the city planners could not build the roads fast enough or streamline the city well enough to manage the growth of the automobile industry.

After the Second World War the automobile had become an essential part of the American experience. By 1950 more than 75 percent (roughly 8 million) of all the vehicles in the world were on our country's roads, and the numbers kept growing. The automobile allowed millions of people to buy land and settle on the perimeter of urban centers. In these suburbs, residents could have the best of both worlds, living in the country (though that changed rapidly) and working in the city. This postwar influx of vehicular transportation further shocked the existing infrastructure and created whole new problems for America to complain—and campaign—about.

General Eisenhower was elected president in 1952 and, against sharp criticism, decided to keep Roosevelt's New Deal programs active by instituting the largest construction plan in history: the Interstate Highway System. The project, grander than even the Great Wall of China, was adapted from a military model that was developed to support and supply troops invading foreign countries. By the end of the decade, the IHS would be moving millions of drivers from city to city or from the suburbs of America to their major business districts.

The once majestic gateways on the West Side are now industrial zones that rim a ledge along the deeply inset highway system. A series of bridges breach the humming and smoking canyon. The cars on the expressway change their lanes and sound their horns as often as they wish, speeding beneath these bridges.

As I scramble through the West Side, I remember Burnham's yellowed draft of this area. In it, fountains stood where two interstates now swirl together. Parks and wide sidewalks lay where black buildings now tower over hopeless people. The surrounding area is plagued by its wanderers and homeless. Lonely old men sitting motionless with their coffee fill twenty-four-hour breakfast places nearby. Their backs slump from heavy lifting and old age. Like me, they are not protected from the cold, the sun, or the wind. The

179

world is passing right by them only one block away, over a nearby cement cliff alongside the Eisenhower Expressway.

By learning these early maps and the chronology of how these streets have changed, I know the intent of every road that I travel on and the reason why some of the initial intentions were not met. Knowing these specifics helps me navigate any point on the map. It helps me understand why this street is cracked and that one smooth, why one part of the city is shrouded and dark while another is gilded in sunlight.

THE UNDERGROUND

IN MY FIRST few weeks living in Chicago, I got together with a friend, a dancer I had known from arts school. Around nine P.M. we decided to take a walk. As we began covering old and new ground within our friendship, we found ourselves also covering more of the city than we had ever known. By three A.M. we were many miles from where we'd started, and we couldn't conceive of turning around. The walk became a kind of spiritual journey through the empty streets and the dark shadows of our friendship.

"The earth is where the soul is located," Layla told me. "I should know—I have learned my body well enough, and it's not in there. If it exists at all, it must be beneath me. That's why the soul is collective: it's the earth that is holding it together. We can't lose our soul. We can only become disconnected from it."

As we considered this idea, we tried to walk only on grass, sand, or parklands, avoiding sidewalks and cement whenever we could. The story of Antaeus came to mind and I did my best to relay it to her. He was born of Mother Earth and was invincible as long as his feet were touching the ground. Hercules battled with Antaeus and defeated him by lifting his foe into the air and squeezing his chest. Antaeus, disconnected from the Earth, suffocated.

The conversation continued through the Gold Coast and we wound up on Michigan Avenue, walking barefoot right into the heart of the Loop at sunrise. The two of us were swinging our shoes from our fingertips, our bare feet stained from the mud and dirt of Lincoln Park. I could still feel the soul of the city between my toes.

When I looked across the bridge at the skyscrapers on the riverbank, the lower layers of the city were exposed. This first encounter with Wacker Avenue, which connects the city to Lake Shore Drive and the Eisenhower, put our theory of the soul under immediate attack. I counted the levels and discovered what I now know to be Wacker, Lower Wacker, and Lower *Lower* Wacker. If the earth beneath our feet is our collective soul, how do I explain this buried highway?

As a messenger, I have found places down there that have never seen the light of day. Alleys shoot out from Lower and Lower Lower Wacker and plunge into crevices between solid skyscraper foundations. In this city, the soul we were talking about is a high-speed strip of asphalt that seems to spiral and snake into pure cement beneath the water level. It is a hidden zone for taxis, freight trucks, suburbanites, and wild-eyed messengers on scratched-up racing bikes.

On a slow Tuesday morning, I descended a steep ramp into the dark corridor of South Water. It led to an underground alley lit twenty-four hours a day by dim yellow lights. A block away, the highway roared under a blackened cement ceiling. I turned around, avoiding the traffic, to find another ramp going farther down, leading to the Lower *Lower* world. Descending this ramp, I found what seemed to be an eternal construction site. Here men were burning thick steel, tearing trenches through asphalt. I hustled into the dark of the unknown terrain to find a line of empty parking spaces and a sparse group of black men carrying their pillows or coats, or a pair of pants taken off to stay cool. Their faces were glistening, placid, looking drained to numbness. They stood in their underwear with no shame about their distended stomachs or where they might choose to relieve themselves. They could piss on the open ground staring you straight in the eye. Blood, urine, and bile stained the air.

Looking farther I saw, on the Lower Michigan Avenue Bridge, a woman sitting on a road bike. She was smoking, watching the water pass beneath her, and letting the time slip away. She seemed at home here too, wearing black shorts with huge pockets down to her knees, black tights that strapped her legs into boots, fingerless gloves that had seen as much work as a lumberjack's or a coal miner's. Tattoos along her arms were her only armor. She looked emotionlessly upon this underworld. She was searching, counting, *ghosting*—sneaking in a short break when she would otherwise be in transit.

On her bike she crawled through the shadowed block of half-naked creatures. I rolled up next to her with a generic "Wha's up?" She was Laura, Number Eleven, one of the few female messengers at Velocity Courier.

"Winter is coming," she said. "I gotta remember these ins and outs. It's sometimes the only way to stay dry." Then she spun off onto Lower Wacker Place, an underground alleyway, and disappeared.

The underground architecture of the city is so vast and complicated that beyond the Lower and Lower Lower Wacker territories, there is a virtual honeycomb of tunnels, five stories deep. On April 12, 1992, the depth and design of this many-layered terrain was, for the first time, fully understood. On a dreary, drizzling day, a small leak near the Merchandise Mart cracked open because of nearby construction. The tunnel's wall caved in, the bank caved in, and the river followed, creating a huge blast of water that found its way through the empty network. The water went underground along the north bank of the river and into tunnels underneath the river itself. The Chicago Flood never came aboveground; instead, it filled the basements of nearly half of the city's downtown buildings. Whole electrical grids were shut down. People were evacuated. Tow trucks fished out hundreds of cars that blocked access to buildings. Streets were blasted open and water pumps were installed. The Marshall Fields basement showroom was filled chest-high with century-old filth and sewer water. Army engineers arrived to help manage the water flow. Emergency vehicles responded to calls from hundreds of related flood sites, making a diagram of fire trucks and street barricades that traced every detail of the tunnel architecture.

Legend has it that these paths which connect all of downtown were once ruled by Al Capone. The tunnels were supposedly used for transporting contraband, robbing banks, and disappearing conveniently. One of the tunnels in the basement of 215 West Superior hides behind a crudely patched and suspiciously convex wall. Around the corner, in the hallway of this building, stands a massive green bank vault. It has six-inch-thick cast-iron doors and sits on wheels, though it can hardly be moved. The vault is empty, but the combination lock still turns. It would require the hands of twenty to twenty-five gangsters to even get it up the stairs and onto the street. It would require at least ten people to move it down the hall. I think Al Capone was one of the first to navigate this underground, making the soul, the earth beneath our feet, actually function.

The messengers inherit this subterranean intelligence. It is to us a free zone away from the traffic and congestion and the law and order of the world. It is a sacred territory protecting us from the conditions up above. This city is imprinted in my mind like the palm print in my hand, and with the help of these underground alleyways, tunnels, bridges, lower bridges, and highways, the city can seem to work like a hand, opening and closing, touching end to end.

My two-way radio caught my ear. "Base to Thirty-nine, Thirty-nine this is *base*!" and my Capone daydream was left swirling in a nearby drainpipe while I was dispatched to 150 North Michigan for a Hinshaw special— "Yesterday!" Zero barked.

I followed Laura's lead. I shot south on a side street from Lower Wacker Place to Lake Street. I downshifted and spun out of the sloped alley, through clouds of steaming vapor billowing out of an adjacent basement, and flew toward a crowd of pedestrians. I found a hole between a yellow dress, a gray sport coat, and Grandma in a navy blue jumpsuit—fake pearls. The oncoming truck, which I had seen all the way back on Michigan, stood on his horn as I skimmed past his passenger door. The eastbound traffic had just begun to speed through the Wabash intersection at me.

I balanced the bike in place, straddling the yellow line in the middle of the street, waiting for a hole in traffic. Taking a sharp left into the oncoming barrage of cars, I timed the cross off the back bumper of a speeding cab and got out of the road. On the far side of Lake a young woman was pushing a baby carriage, blocking my entrance to the alley. I always pass babies on the mother's side. Mothers should never feel that their babies are unsafe.

As I passed, giving the mother a gentle smile, I jumped a pothole, shot to the right, and began sizing up the slip maneuver between a dumpster and a cherry picker just pulling through the alley. I stood tall in the pedals and squeezed around the oversized side-view mirror. Finding the dock entrance of the Stone Container Building at ground level, I biked right inside the building, muttering, "What are all these people doing out here?" Someone heard me.

"They are just moving around, *man:* A to B, A to B. One is a banker and one is a lawyer. Like you and me, A to B—all day long."

"Thank you, Bones. You're always so helpful."

"Anytime."

Bones smiled, scratching his new bright red Mohawk in a twisted-up posture, his arms crossed, his radio feeding dead air quietly. I signed for a large white envelope at the delivery window and turned around to stuff the package into my bag. Bones had gone.

I followed suit.

THE ARCHITECTURE OF MOVEMENT

FROM THE BLUR of salesmen rushing from place to place, to the crowds of yellow-jacketed stock traders summoning elevators to their floors, from the buses and trains filled to capacity, to even the gentle rise and fall of the buildings themselves, it becomes clear to the messenger that *movement* is the city's collective priority. Millions of people bustle into downtown Chicago every day, contributing their own velocity to the bustle. No matter the cost, on the trains and expressways, in the cabs and on the curbs, everyone is in the same kind of rush.

We say that time is money; the measure of time is movement. Courier services, for instance, depend on three factors: weight, distance, and speed. If I were to deliver one airplane ticket one mile away in the span of three hours, I would be earning about as much as an average parking meter. But if I had to get a subpoena or a contract or a tax filing one mile away in thirty minutes, I would be earning about as much as a public defender for that half hour. I can easily do three similar jobs in the same half hour and earn the salary of a commercial pilot. In a single day, some of us will move fifty-five to sixty-five packages, earning more than many of the professionals we share elevators with. The work put out equates to money coming in, and so messengers like to stay in constant motion.

Yet the same principle seems more or less true for the rest of the city. Competing businesses, predators and prey, those who say "More" and those who say "Less," the archbishop's retinue and the ad salesmen of *Playboy* magazine all look beyond their personal and professional differences as they work toward this larger mission: getting there. I have seen companies switch locations. An accountant in 120 North LaSalle moved to 120 South Michigan, while a corporate foundation moved from the same building on Michigan to the one on LaSalle. Hundreds of thousands of people walk in specific yet contradictory patterns as they head to and from lunch. Though these daily sprints from place to place may seem self-interested, they are marked by a kind of guarded behavior that facilitates the broader picture of public flow and accessibility.

This spirit of cooperation is deep and powerful, active in every facet of our lives, helping to make movement possible. When cooperation breaks down, the flow of our motion does too. Tickets are issued, arguments escalate, and people are sued. Cooperation is actually policed, publicly enforced.

The American metropolis, with its ever-climbing towers and endless highways, is built to facilitate this worship of speed on both horizontal and vertical planes. By spreading roads out to the farthest reaches, city planners give more people access to a city's business district. But this great downtown (an American idea if ever there was one) limits distance to make commerce move more effectively. For example, ten people, each driving a package ten miles, yield less productivity than one hundred people, each biking a package one mile—even though the net distance for either scenario is the same. Downtown is built to *accelerate.*

Skyscrapers, too, limit space between offices and other companies, fueling the common goal. The Sears Tower, on an average business day, will have more than 150,000 people in it working for hundreds of different businesses. Imagine the entire population of Normal, Illinois, floating into a single building by the morning and then leaving it a ghost town by 7:00 P.M. A building like this must provide a complex internal infrastructure to accommodate this tidal population, moving them from place to place in huge quantities. The primacy of movement is made clear in these buildings by how they capitalize on efficiency and proximity. A building is not real estate; it is a machine, a factory *of* real estate.

But however dedicated we are to increasing net motion, the automobile, with its obvious dangers, has to compromise its speed for safety. To this end, traffic and congestion are actually helpful to a city. Braess's paradox (discovered in 1968 by the German mathematician Dr. Dietrich Braess) describes this fundamental conflict between cars and space. His theory suggests that adding extra travel lanes for regular traffic increases congestion problems because, given extra room, drivers will pass more often and try to move more quickly. This results in numbers of cars trying to get ahead of one another, fighting to take the same traffic opportunities. When every driver speeds until they find traffic, wolf packs grow like viruses, and soon whatever caused the delay—a pothole, a police car, a fancy billboard—becomes a thirty-minute backup.

The positive side of congestion is that it lessens the potential for fatal accidents. People just don't die as often going seven miles per hour as they do going seventy. The city's architecture, initially built to expedite commerce, takes advantage of tight road conditions for safety and crowd control. The constant break-flows of traffic lights and stop signs work to slow down (but not stop) the car, since stopping the car for long periods of time creates serious frustration. The New York architect Harvey W. Corbett once said, "The movement of traffic is just as essential to the life of the city as the movement of blood is to the life of the body."

The city, too, like the body and the building, is a machine, and its health can be seriously threatened by only a few accidents. Therefore the intention of a city street is to limit speed (preventing collisions and clogged intersections) and to maintain motion (quelling what we now call "road rage"). Today, a car downtown is about as slow as the horse and buggy of a hundred years ago, averaging about ten miles per hour.

On a bicycle, I pose little danger to the flow of traffic. I see the slowly choreographed processions, but I float right through their rules every chance I get. The streetlights and moving parking lots do not hold me up. Red means red and green means green: I keep tempo regardless. I am free to move as I wish, piercing gridlocked intersections, snaking between cars, and running the wrong way up one-way streets. I get juiced by this. I feel like I'm flying—I can be anywhere all at once, like I can fucking evaporate!

Coasting down the hill on Randolph, a ramp that sinks down over Edward Bennett's three-layer freight contraption, I can look out upon a traffic nightmare, raise my fists in the air, and stick 'n' run, punching jabs into the sky, psyching myself up, sometimes shouting, "I am the greatest fighter of *all time*!" as I warm up for another round of headlights and horns and crowds of people walking in line. I use every inch of the city to my advantage. Each detail spurs me on until I become a blur to the world of people caught in the clumsy A to B of taxicabs and SUVs. It is a huge thrill to cut through parades of crawling cars. I can go full speed in my heaviest gear, flying past hundreds of hurried people all unable to shift into second. I flaunt my freedom to the motorists, who thought their cars would save them time.

NOISE

LAKE, FRANKLIN, WELLS, WABASH, and Van Buren are all partially covered by a massive steel construction known as the El (an abbreviation for "elevated train"), built near the turn of the twentieth century. To this day, the trains are more or less on time, but their efficiency is sacrificed. They are crude and overbearing. Their tracks, lifted at some points only thirteen feet above the street, are made of nothing but steel joists and lumber, and the architecture of movement sacrifices one important commodity: quietude.

One summer I put away the bike and the messenger bag and took a trip out to the small town of Dixon, Illinois, to visit some distant relatives. Their huge house was one of hundreds in the area. Each house I saw had big lots with front, back, and side yards. Where I live, you are lucky to have a planter on a fire escape, much less a *yard*. Their guest room was larger than many Chicago apartments. Their sprawling neighborhood seemed to me a huge, yet polite, waste of space.

The first morning there, I took a short walk. I heard the grass bending and snapping beneath my feet; on the street I heard my footsteps. I was about thirty yards from the house when I heard a door slide open behind me. Looking back, I saw Kate, my second cousin and my host for the weekend. She told me not to walk too far; breakfast would be ready soon. I listened to her soft and easy voice carry crisply through the air. Communicating to someone thirty yards away in downtown Chicago would require shouting. For a moment I saw the appeal.

I walked along the green country road to the Rock River. When I arrived, I sat on a small dock over the motionless water and was struck by how long it had been since I had seen nature. Farms across the river were plush and colorful; the sky was open and blue; the horizon was all the way down by the earth's surface! I'm used to a rectangular horizon marked by the rooftops of buildings. It was a jarring scene. The sky was too bright, the air was too clean. I closed my eyes, as I often do, and began to just listen. I heard cows from at least two hundred yards away. I heard the water, smooth as velvet, climbing slowly up and down the dock's wooden posts. I could hear birds. I could hear my breath. Then I heard a small engine.

I listened closely to judge how far off the little boat was. I figured it would come into view any second, but somehow it did not show. I waited for ten minutes while the sound of that single engine increased. As the boat, and its sole driver with a fishing pole and canvas hat, finally passed my field of vision, the colors faded, details vanished, the singing birds flew away, and the cattle were sold, maimed, and ravaged for their parts. The grass turned to asphalt and the trees became street signs. The environmental impact of internal combustion became clear to me as my mind was sent right back to the city's trenches. I was listening to the second industrial revolution. In another minute, the boat was out of sight, leaving behind it a punished landscape and a ringing in my ears.

In Chicago, oppressed by millions of cars, city buses, sirens, people, police whistles, construction cranes, drills, trucks, and horns, you would think that the city has reached its limit of noise pollution. We messengers carry our radios attached to the strap of our bags, with the volume turned all the way up so that we can hear our dispatcher's transmissions. The receivers are only inches from our heads, and yet we often have to shout to be heard over the air. I don't see how the city's noise problem can go much further without completely deafening its inhabitants. If a million people were to drive their little boats through that river in Dixon, it would sound like the apocalypse. But somehow, in Chicago, the problem goes largely unrecognized.

A day after my trip to Dixon, I was on a delivery westbound on Lake Street; riding on a beaten-up road sheltered by the train tracks above, I began to hear a train coming. I was alone on the part of the industrial corridor where trains pick up speed. The sound of the westbound train was then joined by the sound of a second one, an eastbound train, that would cross simultaneously overhead. The road began to tremble. The trains began to scream. I felt assaulted, as if there were two monstrous freight trucks the size of battleships bearing down on my little head. I had gone deaf. The sound had smashed out everything but its own metallic thunder. My heart was literally responding to the intense vibration, rattling like a tribal war drum. *It's an El train, Trav, no big deal. No big deal! NO BIG DEAL!* I pulled my bike to the side of the road and covered my head as it passed. When the monsters had gone, I looked up. The shadow of the trains passed on beyond me. Still trembling, I crept back up onto my bike and moved cautiously along my path, westbound on Lake.

THE SPIRIT OF THE PLACE

ABOUT AN HOUR or so after work, I'd crash. I would have just enough time to shower and eat before it would happen. Sometimes it would be gradual. Sometimes it would be abrupt and would topple me into unconsciousness as if I were a capsizing ship. My last words would spill out unconnected and absurd, to float away until dawn.

Once my body learned to adjust to the exhaustion and the workload, I'd find myself waking up, ready to start the day—at midnight. After surfacing, I would have a panicked surge of energy that would go uninterrupted for two hours—whereupon I would capsize again, only to be rescued by an alarm clock. This little window of frantic activity between sinking ships became the only chance I had to write. I would sit down at my computer and put out five to seven pages solidly in one steady stream of excited ideas. By two A.M. the text would look at me and I would look at the text; we'd have reached an understanding.

When it was time for work, I'd find that having taken these hours to write was actually helping to regenerate my physical strength. I would feel lighter, my breath would come more quickly into my diaphragm, my eyes would seem clearer—much clearer. By writing, I could actually see more.

"Life is revolution," couriers often say, and for me a new revolution was coming into view: without writing, I would feel heavy and sluggish at work; without work, my writing would become clipped and incoherent. But this new work cycle, once in place, would go around and around, giving me productivity and creativity—more than I could hope for.

One night I booted up my PC and waited for that wave of inspiration to come through my veins again. My head was lowered; my fingers were hovering lightly over the keys. Haewon had rolled over and buried her head beneath a pillow so that my typing wouldn't disturb her. But then an image came to me: I saw roads and signs and words painted broad enough to be read from a helicopter. New asphalt was laid building to building, wall to wall. Arrows and electronic signals gave directives to passing cars. Even when the streets were empty, they kept their careful barriers with signs and markings: NO STOPPING ANY TIME, BLIND INTERSECTION, DO NOT ENTER, RIGHT TURN ONLY. Behind all of this was a spirit. I could feel it in the street itself, in the width of lanes and the height of curbs and in the random aggregation of right angles that burgeoned out of the modern metropolis.

But how do I write a spirit? I wondered.

Suddenly I turned off the monitor, threw on a pair of sandals, and ran through the hall of the Gold Coast apartment complex where I had recently moved in with Haewon. It was a shoddy building with nearly two hundred residences stacked atop one big fancy address. I called up the freight elevator, which I had come to know from doing a move with the guys at the warehouse, and took a ride up to the top floor. *The page, the page,* I meditated, eager to reach the one good vantage point that this building had to offer: the rooftop. When the doors opened, I darted up the emergency stairwell and shoved open the two doors that led me out to the—*Boosh!* The feeling of enormity, lightly cloaked with the shadow of night, surrounded me on all sides. A strong breeze was coming in off the lake, inflating me with an awestruck fear even before I stepped from the doorway. But as I leaned over the ledge of the building, this welcome vertigo energized the atmosphere as if it were a black light filling the darkness with thick invisible electric currents. Lit up by my own exhilaration, I felt that I was a single glowing piece of paper that could be swept up and carried through the sky for the next hour, zigzagging a path to the ground, where I would scuff the asphalt and pick up a light coat of black ink.

Through the collage of architectural lines and the epic effect of thousands of yellow and white beams swordfighting in negative space, I could feel the spirit I wanted to write about. The amber glow of streetlamps made the tall buildings around me seem to float off the roadway like the features of a face set above a row of lightbulbs. Even from the roof of this midrise apartment, that face seemed to look down upon me. The collection of stone facades took on a fleshy tone, and the cavernous gaps between towers created shadows like hollow cheeks.

It was some kind of essence imbued with a discerning mind; it was a ghost gazing possessively over the territory it had claimed a long time ago. Ultimately, it was the ghost who drew these streets and the shapes of these blocks. It was the ghost who arranged these solids and hollows and painted the lines and arrows in the road. Its plan had none of the careful craftsmanship of Daniel Burnham or Edward Bennett, though it did have a specific intent. There was a reason the ghost's cheeks were hollowed, and there was a reason I could not see its eyes.

IN THE SUMMER OF 1993, I'd followed a small trail through the Roosevelt National Forest in Colorado. Along it I found old homesteads, wells, campsites, and streams. I could leave the trail to explore the massive boulders and caves. I could climb a hillside and set up camp, and when the sun rose again I could always return to the path, *the trace,* that human experience had left along the foot of these mountains. The path was my landmark, and with it I could always make my way home again. This was the earliest form of roadway. From it, all of our streets began.

As I turned back toward town after seven days in the wilderness, I reached an intersection. At my feet I saw the white earth separate from a single meter-wide square. Before me, the land was divided into four pieces, exactly like the quadripartite roots of the city of Rome, the city that marked the center of the earth for nearly a thousand years. Around that intersection, surrounded by seven hills, the Eternal City was built—but not with highways and shopping centers as we build today. Rome was made of towers and gates encircling a radial street pattern that was used to feed the city walls with weapons in the case of an invasion. The most primary function of a city was self-defense. It had to protect its prosperity.

But this prosperity could not have been achieved without a degree of assistance from neighboring developments. The founders of Rome knew that their young city, having few resources, would have to be cunning to earn this assistance. They would need something to offer as collateral.

At night, a small group of Romans would sneak over the walls of a neighboring city, gag the women, and drag them quickly off along the roadway. The husbands, forced to retaliate, would gear up, leave their city all prepared for battle, and walk right into a carefully planned ambush. The road was the weapon, and with it Rome was able to acquire another city's arms, tools, and rations without actually having to carry any of it. They now had slaves and, therefore, the assistance of neighboring developments.

As these surrounding cities weakened and were eventually overthrown, the Romans' need for defense shifted. Walls around their city were no longer needed. The surrounding cities could keep their strong defense. Soon, small residential developments, built of brick from the now unused walls, began to safely spread beyond the city limits. With the rise of these suburbs, the shape of the open city was established and a civilian economy was built to support it.

But the falling of the walls did not mean that the military was any less central to the further development of the city. To protect the wealth and the rights of Roman citizens, the machines of war were simply turned inward and brought down upon the Romans' own civic spaces. After all, the enemies of the empire were no longer foreign; they were now slaves. To keep the social lines carefully drawn, the industry of war was internalized as the industry of governance.

Holding on to the ledge of the rooftop and looking back at the city, I was bothered by this line of inquiry. What's the connection? Yes, there are governments. And yes, they make decisions about how we manage and organize our civilian lives, but that doesn't make governments evil. America has resources, and we try to share them. We have a market-based economy and a government that wants to sponsor our business interests. Where was the warfare? I didn't see it. But then I leaned a little farther over the edge of the rooftop.

The street, that glowing and gray matrix with its markings and arrows that cuts its way through the high-rise apartments and office buildings, did not happen overnight. Those streets were planned, designed, and built into the American landscape, almost as an extension of the cloud-filled factories that once produced the automobile itself. It's interesting: as the smokestack has receded from public view, the tailpipe has become ever-present. But why did this make sense? I wasn't sure.

I have heard about these bustling and contentious times back in the days of the Depression and before the war. The factory, a political stage at the time, was also the only way for many working-class families to stay alive. In the manufacturing of the cars, die-cast tools, and steel that made this economy strong, the American Dream of that time had something to do with *working*.

From my perspective, I don't see anyone working—at least not in the way we used to work, producing boots, sewing machines, and light fixtures. I see only the productivity of an *information era* in which we produce envelopes and architectural drawings. I see computer disks and fancy letterheads. I never see the brick. I can go in and out of the Amoco building twenty times a day and never see anyone drilling oil. But the oil is being drilled because we are using it; the brick is being dried because we are building; the work boots are being made because I see them in stores, merchandised like jewelry, carrying hefty price tags.

Where is the factory? Where is the labor? Where is the work? I wondered, because that is where the war is being fought. That is where the machines of control are nailed down upon the working class. Isn't it simple? Our businesses feed on the labor of the poor. Fortunately for the businessmen, there is a poverty class in America, an enormous one. Like Dzevade, they work to feed their families, they work to stay alive. Why else would anyone man a factory, or maintain a warehouse, or stitch boots? Why else would anyone deliver packages for a living?

On domestic and foreign ground the working poor are used, but the moment the businessman can choose *between* domestic and foreign labor, the skewed governance that becomes warfare is suddenly crystal clear. To be competitive, business interests must move toward cheap foreign labor (which, in turn, increases the problems of poverty in America). But on a deeper level, when we are putting factories in the fields of our enemies, America can usurp the entire economy of other countries. Foreigners become slaves, without ever leaving their own cities. In America, minority populations, slaves in a past age, remain slaves to poverty.

198   This is no accident. The development and protection of a working poor actually makes a good deal of economic sense—for some. With a healthy population of poor people, there will be a steady demand for work, any kind of work, no matter the conditions. This group is willing to work themselves to death for the protection of their families and the possibility of forging some kind of quality of life. While one group is pushed into hard labor, another group becomes dedicated to consumption. One group produces supply, the other group demand. It is an uncomplicated, even fixed, economy where the working poor are farmed, ghettoized, and eaten by what politicians call "jobs." For the producer, poverty is a commodity.

Today, as trade relations expand, the same kind of economic engineering can be seen. The wealthy countries consume, while developing countries produce. A forced supplier serves a force-fed demand. In the end, both sides are being used.

But what is a "forced demand" and how does it work? An object is introduced to the market to increase the competitiveness of the worker. When one person gets an advantage, it becomes necessary for others to develop the same advantage. The cell phone and the personal computer are fine examples of this, but the archetype is the private automobile.

Beyond simply mobilizing the affluent, the automobile has actually shaped the city around its use in order to make the car a competitive necessity in the American workforce. How can you compete in a free market without a car if you can't get to work without a car? This is a forced demand. And yet even in the engineering of the car is another forced demand. Like people, cars die if they do not consume oil products. Once it is necessary to drive, then it is necessary that someone, somewhere, the hardworking poor, the sweatshop laborer, even the government of so-called developing nations, produce to the level that we are forced to consume.

This is why our highways strangle neighborhoods and our lanes of traffic are crammed so close together that there is little room for anyone who is not driving. This is why the city is violent and fully enclosed. It is *supposed* to be violent. It is supposed to be so violent that we demand cars to serve even our need for protection.

Streets in Chicago are not open for public use and they do not allow people to freely find the resources they need to survive. To fund larger battles elsewhere, these streets must be open only to those who are driving. By driving, the civilian is supporting the oil and automobile market that gives the United States the economic green light to weaken and even invade foreign countries. With the design of our cities, America has learned to create enough demand to feel justified in taking the resources of other nations.

It is a fancy kind of strategy that creates these amazing towers, and it is a fancy kind of soldier who is meant not to fight but to desire and consume. With this military-green, structurally reinforced consumer addiction, America, like Rome, has found a cunning way to engage the assistance of neighboring developments, and it has created a tricky kind of collateral. With roads built only for automobiles, the city itself has been taken from us. To retrieve it, we give in to a forced demand. We are ambushed on the highway.

For a moment I was amazed that I could hold up against the layer of violence that has been built into our landscape. But then my pride receded and I just felt angry. That ghost, being a function of the state, has not helped me. That ghost, being a function of the state, thinks I am an enemy. It has opened up the streets for motorists to speed through and it has drawn the lines in the road right up to the curb so that I would feel endangered, so that I would feel that I did not belong, and it is the ghost that is responsible, the ghost that won't show me its eyes.

I saw its face glowing through the skyscrapers and lying out upon the flatlands of sprawling suburbs. Staring deep into its empty sockets, I told the ghost in simple words: *I hope we can reach an understanding. I am from this place. I belong here. I will not serve in your war.*

CHAPTER EIGHT

BETWEEN THE CLIFF AND THE BANK

He who cannot obey himself is commanded.
That is the nature of the living.

Friedrich Nietzsche,
Thus Spoke Zarathustra

CHRIS UNDERSTOOD.

He'd seen bikers retire due to knee problems like mine. He told me flat out that there was not a lot I could do about a blown knee because "once the window of recovery is gone, you remain, and such is life."

I was working as hard as I could because I had become one of the company's *anchors*. It was a station I respected and wanted to live up to.

"You do what you can do," Zero said compassionately. "Besides, how long did you expect you could keep up this kind of work?"

I had been booking for the company more than three hundred dollars a day for the past six weeks. That's not called doing a job, that's called being a *rock star*. While Sammy Sosa and Mark McGwire were out slugging each other over Roger Maris's home-run record, the Punk, Number Thirty-three, and I were leap-frogging each other for the company record. I had taken down sixty-eight packages on a Wednesday only to see Sam hit seventy-one that Friday. This competition didn't come from some need to show off—though neither of us was above doing just that.

The company had been working on a skeleton crew, and the jobs were piling up from 7:00 A.M. to 7:00 P.M. Matt, the German from the office, was taking cabs from place to place and walking off packages that the bikers couldn't handle. And so, injury or no injury, someone needed to put in the miles.

Chris and I developed a system. When the knee was in good shape I would tell him I had a green light. When it felt weak or iffy or if I was having only sudden bursts of sharp pain (usually at around 2:00 P.M.) I would give him a yellow. A red light meant that I could hardly walk, that my day was *over*. Red meant *red,* and I would crawl home in agony.

Sometimes the biggest challenge of the day was the knee and sometimes it was the overall physical exhaustion. I did my best to avoid them both, but the problem of exhaustion was by far the easier to solve. I would take a host of vitamins and drink nearly a gallon of water a day. But mostly I would eat. Dinners were early and they were huge. Getting off work became a hunt for food. Steaks, potatoes, thick pastas, and fat—I judged all of my meals on how many calories were in them.

Before dawn, at the HoJo on Huron, I would sit among a host of old fat police sergeants who grumbled and belched over their food, smoking pipes and cigars at the break of day. These guys were in it for life, and by the size of their guts and the color of their skin I could see that their forced retirement was not far off.

As disgusting as the smell of their fumes was, my appetite remained unaffected. Ordering a large helping of eggs, a side of pancakes, and a bowl of grits, I would begin the process: eat while drinking only enough watery coffee to realign my head from that night's sleep.

I would treat the process like a ceremony because this food was responsible for firing my ovens for all of five hours—half a day's work. No matter how bland the pile of wet yolks and cholesterol mixed in my stomach, or on my plate, I took it all down like I was shoveling coal into the engine of a steam train.

To supplement for the remainder of the day, I would carry with me sixteen ounces of granola mixed with M&M's and dried fruit that I would start munching on at the first sign of hunger or 11:00, whichever came first. If I didn't eat at least three ounces by noon, I would be brain-dead by 1:30, slurring my words and overshooting my streets, stoned from depletion.

This is what they call "the bonk" in cycling. The blood runs out of sugar and then it draws on the muscles' stores. Once this is drained, sugar is taken directly from the brain. First the body loses strength—they call it "hitting the wall"—and then you bonk.

To avoid this I needed to eat before I got hungry. In elevators I would pull out a Tupperware container, twist off the top, and drink the dry mix. The granola gave me the complex carbohydrates and the chocolate gave me the quick, high-burning sugar. The two of them together are necessary, like the oil product in gasoline—one part ignites, the other part burns. Between 11:00 and 4:30, I would munch. The idea was to eat lightly and constantly, so that there was always something keeping my blood sweet.

I would stop eating only if I had to stop riding, and that was now happening about once a week. Generally it would be cool with dispatch. As long as I toasted the morning rush, Chris would not be concerned.

I was concerned. I was deeply concerned. I would hobble home around 2:40 or so in serious pain, and though I could sit down and rest, my mind wouldn't shut off until 5:00. I needed to know that the day had gone okay at base.

I tried to exercise the knee. I iced it. I thought back to how the old injury had happened to see if it could be fixed by surgery.

I remembered seeing the gold four-door coast through a stop sign as I flew north on Clark Street. Had he stopped at the line or just blown the intersection wholesale, I would have been fine. But when he saw me coming at him only a few yards from his window, he hit the brakes and sat smack in front of me. I was leaning right to clear his back bumper when the bottom of the bike slid out from beneath me. With my left leg outstretched and my right ankle pinned all the way up under my armpit, the bike and I lodged ourselves beneath the car's back tire. I was looking up at a smoking muffler and a back wheel that then slowly crawled forward and drove away.

Immediately I jumped up to shout something, but my knee would not open and I fell back to the ground, screaming. The pain was so deep that I began to shout and cry instantly. I found myself lying in the road screaming my head off.

When I told Haewon about the accident she said exactly what Chris said, that nothing was going to fix it.

In a world where everything seems to want to stop you, all you can do is fight. You continue because you must, you continue because you are living. And so I pushed forward, horns bowed in advance. I would force myself onward, lunging ahead with the last bit of strength I had left. As with the bull, the attack remained my only defense.

I did what I could. I adjusted my seat. I stretched every morning. After breakfast, I would spin on a high gear for the first hour of every day. I had a stash of horse pills, generics, made of 800 mg of ibuprofen, and I would pop one every few hours if I had to. But no matter how hard I tried to defeat it, in the end I was exploring whole new dimensions in pain. No matter how many people told me to sit out for a few weeks, and no matter how many times I agreed, the next morning, I'd be back at work like some kind of addict.

BY 9:30 THREE BIKERS had called in sick. The bolt fell out of a new guy's spindle, so I was ordered to run off his packages. I found him on Madison and Canal furiously trying to forge a method that would temporarily hold his pedals together. He'd fallen, tearing a chunk of flesh off his elbow; the wound deranged a large tattoo that spindled down from his triceps to his forearm.

I called in: "Thirty-nine to base."

"Number Thirty-nine, go."

"I found Number Thirty-six on Mad. His elbow is cut up and bleeding but he doesn't seem to care. He wants to work and he's making that real clear."

"10-4. Grab his Modem Media, his Quarrow, and let the crankless wonder walk off the West Side. Number Thirty-six, wack off that Wacker stuff and then get over to Yojimbo's. If you want to work, I've got work for you, so don't go disappearing."

"10-4. I'll be back on-line as soon as I can."

Number Thirty-six was still off the clock when, four hours later, my 1:30 shuttle was finished. I had six new Rosie's combined with the Quaker roundhouse from Foote, a set of MCIs, and I hadn't had time to stop for liquids since I'd left Number Thirty-six on Canal. Stepping out of a Jenny Jones drop in the Peacock, standing right out in front of a big cafeteria, I heard my radio crackle. "*Punk!* I got fires lighting up all over this desk, man! Have you dropped Marina City yet?" Chris asked in a demanding voice.

No response.

Shit, I thought to myself, looking at a refrigerator with bottles of juice behind a line of suits toting lunch trays. *Three minutes. That's all I need.* I was dizzy and my mouth felt like I had eaten glue. Every chance I'd had to stop and hydrate I would hear something outrageous like this from the dispatch room, dragging me back out onto the street again.

"Sanchez dropped a bomb!"

I could hear Goldberg in the background: "Dammit! How many?"

"Nine specials all at once. They can kiss my— Shit, man. Number Thirty-two, Matt, Number Thirty-two, Matt, Number Thirty-two, Matt. Where is my cowboy?"

In broken static he replied: "Wait . . . time . . . on . . . Three First National."

"Man, Number Thirty-two! I've got crap dying all over this board and you've got wait time? I don't have time to wait! Stop filing your goddamn fingernails, get the package on, and get the hell out of there. Where is my Two-oh, Two-oh, Two-oh."

Fred responded: "I am right now having a long talk with a police officer, dispatch. We are having a bit of a con-fron-ta-tion! It is a losing battle, Chris. I think it's a losing battle. I am looking at a set of handcuffs, talking to you with the ass-istance of this new municipal friend of mine."

"Ah, shit. I'll deal with that later. Three-nine-three-nine-three-nine! Where is my Energizer bunny? Thump, thump, thump,

Thirty-nine. Are you out of the Peacock, holding Rosie, a pair of MCIs, and a Quaker round-trip?"

"10-4. Exactly."

"I'm a *hound dog*! I can find you *anywhere*!" he gloated passionately.

"Well, I'm a step ahead still, Chris—on Columbus looking at the Litter Box. Is it my lucky day or what?"

"I would hardly say that. Nine! Pull nine out of Triple Three and we'll talk."

"10-4."

I took a hard right off the metal bridge and started weaving along the speedway of Lower Wacker Drive. I was still dying of thirst, but I pushed forward, burning through the line of highway traffic, squeezing myself through the two-foot crevice between a tow truck and a twelve-foot-tall UPS monster truck that was gaining speed.

Together the three of us streamed through the underground cavern like Blue Angels in a tight formation. Inches from my wristwatch the brown freighter started pulling past me. Behind its huge loading doors, a machine-made wall of air enveloped me. My sleeves were being sucked into an undertow.

Suction! Shit, I've heard about this! I grabbed the cast-iron hardware of the tow truck to my right and launched myself forward into the windy wake of the brown freighter. I hammered, hoping to keep up with it, and was surprised to find myself actually gaining on the back bumper of the truck. I was going forty-two miles an hour when I tapped the brakes to keep my distance.

Now, drifting back slightly, I could feel a wall of air pushing me forward again. I lifted my right arm out to the sky and straightened my back as if I were giving praise to Muhammad. Worship aside, I was giving the wind more surface area to push me with. I was a human kite, a wing and a prayer.

As lanes merged, the tow truck filed in behind us and started flashing his headlights to warn the trucker. Because of the speed the UPS carrier was going, I really doubted he would take the time to read his mirrors. The flashing lights worked instead like a disco ball, adding to the miracle of the moment. My right hand, once in praise of Allah, started swinging like I was some kind of nutty rapper in a music video.

I knew my exit ramp was coming on my right side and so, when I saw the beams of sunlight flash across the cement supports of the underground tunnel, I swung out of the truck's wake and flew straight out toward the light's source, up a long curving Lake Street ramp. As my eyes adjusted, I stole three lanes of southbound Wack, two lanes of eastbound Lake, and three lanes of northbound Wack in a single move and skidded to a stop outside the Nuveen building.

When I emerged through the rotary door with a stack of Sanchez for distribution, that Punk, Number Thirty-three, was there to help share the burden. I still had a bag full of shitty, slow jobs, a small set of Loopy routes, and I had just taken most of the Sanchez specials. I had to keep moving. Running the hot stuff, virtually throwing packages at mailroom clerks and tossing them onto the desks of corner offices, I was still dying of thirst. In elevators I would stretch, trying to keep the circulation going to my weakening right knee. But then, what was there to circulate? I could feel frothy spittle building up at the corners of my mouth. My teeth felt like they were covered in hair. I stopped eating my granola mix because swallowing the hard pieces was too difficult. The veins in my arms looked thick and pronounced, as if my heart were pumping blue putty through them.

When I stepped into the air-conditioned lobby of the Quaker Oats Building for the Foote Cohn round-trip, my whole panorama went flat. The environment looked like it was drawn in pastel on rice paper, like I could reach out with my finger and tear a hole in the world. I gave my I.D. to the guard at his desk and stumbled to the elevator. I rested my head on the metal walls adorned with thousands of little Quaker Oats emblems and dropped down to LL2. The mail clerk took the front half of the round-trip and turned to find the pieces that would be going back. I ran to the washroom. Inside of thirty seconds I splashed my face and soaked my head in the sink, guzzled the water from the fountain, and ran back to the clerk in time to snatch up the batch of back-half from the clerk's hands.

Pulling into 101 East Erie, the FCB tower, I stumbled past the guard to the convenience store in the far corner of the lobby. I stood in front of the fridge, tore open a sixteen-ounce Gatorade, and guzzled it down without a single breath, dropping the bottle on the floor. I grabbed a second bottle and slugged away half its contents as the owner watched in disbelief. Then I spun around, slapped a five-dollar bill on the counter, and walked out, squinting my face to keep the liquids down.

There was a pile of work up at FCB, but I was only taking the northbound half of it. On a landline at the mailroom desk of the fourteenth floor, Zero had to tell me three times which packages I was taking and which I was leaving behind.

"Are you okay?"

In a strained voice I replied, "Yeah, I'm just letting the hydration kick in."

"10-4. I need you in top shape today. How's the knee?"

"Um . . . so far so good."

"Just be in touch with me. If it gets bad, we'll figure something out."

"10-4." I hung up, spun around (this time, too far), snapped up the three pieces he had for me, and stomped through the tiled hallway, tipping plastic cups stacked precariously on a rack by the cafeteria that shared the fourteenth floor. While the doors of an elevator were closing, now only two inches apart, I shoved my meaty glove into their way, opening the doors against their electronic will. The thirtysomething ad execs in the lift looked at me like I was a human corpse that had just dug itself out of their cafeteria's salad bar.

The liquids lasted about forty minutes. I was moving way too fast. I was out spinning my gears and swinging the heavy bag around my shoulders as if I were doing a geeked-out dance move.

I saw a Cannonball named Tommy get into a scuffle with a cabdriver on LaSalle. The driver of the cab had tried to pin him into a line of parked cars. I arrived in about twelve seconds, and by the time I got there, I was one of four bikers at the scene. A Velocity courier and an Arrow messenger had arrived and were telling the driver, fists in the air, to get back in his cab. The cabbie peeled open his clenched fists in an act of surrender and got back into his car. We looked at one another like, *Now what?*

The entire conflict came to a head and disappeared before we ever knew what had happened. One of the guys called it an asshole pit stop: "Got to fix the asshole!" We laughed for a second, brushed off the built-up tension, and cranked back into work mode again.

Nancy Coffin, the mail clerk in the Sears Tower, gave me an apple wrapped in a paper towel. I looked up at her through the Plexiglas windows, amazed. "Is this for me?"

"If you want it," she said coyly.

"Yes, *I want it,* Nancy!"

While she blushed, I shoved the apple in my mouth and turned it into a sloppy core in a matter of seconds. With my cheeks full of juice, I thanked Nancy for her kindness and burned off a line of Loopy airline tickets. The apple lasted about thirty minutes in my system, working its way straight through my pores like I was a screen door. To avoid the hundred-degree heat, I tried to stay underground. I took a Wacker ramp down into the Gothic estuary and zipped through to Grand Avenue, forcing my way east on three lanes of westbound traffic.

On a landline at 676 St. Clair I called base: "Chris, I am Topless for Men and I need to sit my ass down. The caution light is on and blinking. Do you copy this deep yellow hue?

"Okay, okay. The Chicago Title?"

"Dead."

"Miserable Financially?"

"Miserov? Dead."

"The Oat Box?"

"Dead."

"Hartmarx?"

"Dead."

"Topel Forman?"

"Dead."

"Okay. The Oil Can is yours and the 980 Mich is yours. I will get you in here as soon as I can. Out of Amoco, meet up with Number Thirty-seven."

"10-4." On the Fairbanks incline, my eyes began to tear and I noticed that I was starting to hyperventilate. I thought about keying in and telling Chris to fuck himself. I thought about lying down on the sidewalk and watching the clouds. I thought about riding east and throwing my white ass into Lake Michigan. *Boom! Splash!* I would have done anything to be subsumed by its cool waves.

The chaos mounted in the dispatch room to even more unbelievable proportions. I kept riding while Chris sat at the desk with his hand on the transmit button, rattling out orders like a cracked-out sports announcer. I could hear him running his palm against the shaved sides of his head beneath his dreadlocked patch as if he were an inmate. It was just his way of managing the stress. He was responsible for every deadline, and he was still short a handful of bikers.

"Number Thirty-two, out of Leo B. grab a Harrisse to 2 Pru. Run the Talent, drop the Peacock, and call me out of DDB. There is a North Side set building up there. Number Thirty-three, Punk! You should be out of Barney about now. Sit on the route, you are going to the Opera for the hill. Number Thirty-seven, if you have not met up with Thirty-nine—what's your twenty, Number Thirty-seven? Give me a reading?"

"Thirty-seven on the hill with the Triple Threes. Thirty-nine has my 900 Michs."

"10-4. 10-4. Thirty-nine, run the Cutters, the Jolly Wally, and pick up a Suzie Q for base. Thirty-seven, Rod, meet up with the Twelve-Guy, Rod. He's got a dying 500 Mad. He should be going into Amex right now."

"Negative. Twelve here, looking at Lake. I have an extra Amex to CMI special for Thirty-nine."

I could see his red jersey just rounding the corner onto the steep black slope of the hill. Dwarfed by a sky full of buildings, blackened trim, and tinted windows, his blue Cannondale tilted back and forth as he hammered up to hand off that CMI to me.

"10-4. Then, Thirty-nine, grab the Amex, run the Cutters and the CMI. Pinky and the Brain has—"

"I am not Pinky!" we all heard Matt cry from the back of the office.

"Shut up, Pinky, who asked you? *Anyhow*, Pinky just found another headache building up on the DDB phone and, Twelve, you're on it."

"Thirty-nine to base, 10-4 on—all that."

"Twelve, go."

"Rock over London," Thirty-seven affirmed.

"Thirty-two, 10-4. I got it."

"Thirty-three, um. Out of the Opera, holding the Ellis. I've got a rag for the Mayor. Should I drop it on the way to the Can?"

"Punk, drop it. Take the South Side out of DDB that Thirty-one is going to leave behind—is that a 10-4, Lu?"

A broken radio responded: "@#%#evator#**@EL$$&(tor!##* elevator." She could not transmit.

"10-4. Punk! Number Thirty-three, hit the Picasso. Get your rocks off. Run the hill and grab the DDB last. Do not call. Use your radio. I will be on the street. Is that a 10-4? All bikers will be dispatched off of the radio until Thirty-nine gets his ass in here. I am on the street. Zero, out."

The radio went dead, and I must admit I was glad of it. The silence helped me pace myself. I grabbed the CMI from Twelve-Guy and was carving a path through the Mich-Wack intersection, relieved to hear the silence, relieved to hear that I would be sitting down before night fell. I picked up my bike and limped down the steel stairs to a three-lane artery running beneath upper Michigan and dumped the Cutters (515 North State on twenty-five). As I

216

dumped the CMI (150 East Huron) I found two suburban runs that I knew would be coming into base, so I swiped 'em up. I dropped the J. Walker (900 Michigan on twenty-three) and hit Suzie Q (108 West Oak Street, first floor) for a Schaumburg set.

COMING BACK INTO BASE, hobbling in through the back door, I dumped my bike in the back room, gave Little Dave the West Side suburban set, and hurried into the dispatch room.

"Two more," Tom said, handing me a set of floaters with specs on two new jobs. My number was scribbled in the corner of each: a Mart to a nearby Kinko's and an L&R Realty to the courthouse.

I tried to say "Tom, I can't. I'm down. I can hardly walk." But I couldn't. That would mean failure. I just looked at the floaters and tried to think *Fuck off, fuck off, fuck off,* but they couldn't hear me.

Leaning on the photocopier and reaching out, I took one step in the direction of the board and stuck the floaters beneath my magnet, which already had more than fifty jobs pinned beneath it.

On the board, up in the corner, I saw the magazine cutout of a crying baby, which is a notorious attachment to the Service First board. It gets stuck under the magnet of whatever biker is being the biggest pussy for any given day. It's kind of like probation, I think. If a biker is a baby for three days in a row, he gets canned. I added the baby to my stack of floaters and limped to the door, sure that I could be stronger than this. I forced the metal fence open and mounted up clumsily in crippling pain.

Superior to Clark, Clark toward the Mart, I could hear my right knee grinding. I let my left leg take the weight until I caught a little speed. Then, rolling up Kinzie, I clipped out of my right pedal and started stretching out the knee. I pulled my thigh up to my chest, grabbed my ankle, and stretched it down again. I sat on my shoe and leaned back while coasting. I took the service drive up the north side of the Mart and free-locked under the kiss-'n'-ride, a covered curb near the lobby doors.

Walking into the huge lobby, I was sweating like Dzevade had that day when he'd fallen in between the dock and the truck. In the elevator, I shared six feet of space with four women wrapped in red velvet and mink. I leaned into the right wall, looking at the illuminated numbers with my head against the steel paneling, trying to bear the pain.

I wasn't weeping, but tears began rolling down my face all the same.

"Did you see the new chair line at Cassetti?"

"Oh, aren't they so nice?"

"Oh, but I hate the new Knoll stuff—going in there I feel like I'm in a cartoon or something! The stuff is made for aliens."

They laughed awkwardly about the furniture lines, their faces too tightly stretched out to make a real smile. I was busy dying in the corner thinking, *Jesus, man, do they even know what a day's work means?* Haewon's ring gave me something to press against when my gripped molars weren't providing the proper anesthetics. I turned to two of the ladies and swallowed a horse pill from the palm of my glove. They looked up at me, saw the tears brewing in my red eyes, and took a step back, as if I were a werewolf.

The doors opened and I hobbled out like a wounded deer.

I climbed out of the Mart, grabbed the Grinch, and coasted all the way down to L&R Realty. Out of there, I headed east until, finally, on Franklin, I couldn't move my leg.

I coasted half a block away from Franklin and pressed the button on my radio: "Man down! Man down!"

"Number Thirty-nine, what's your 20?"

"Illinois between Frank and Wells, copy? Between Franklin and Wells!"

"Thirty-nine, what happened?"

"My knee is stuck, totally frozen. I can't move it. No blood, 10-4? No blood."

"Is your bike okay?"

"It's beneath me. My head is on the bars. I cannot get off my bike. Copy? I *cannot* get off my goddamn bike!"

"Should I call an ambulance?"

"Negative. Negative."

"Base to drivers. I need someone on the North Side. Who's North?"

"Two-nine to Three-nine."

"Dave, go."

"Sit tight, Thirty-nine. I am North, shy of five from Illinois and rolling. 10-4?"

"10-4."

"Are you still on your bike?"

"I'll make another go at this but—"

"Hey guy, why don't you sit tight. Big Dave is on his way. He'll make everything A-OK. All right?

"Two-nine to Three-nine, do you copy?

"Shit! Come back, Thirty-nine!"

I'd fallen. My body was stiff and as sensitive as an eardrum. That fall would echo in my bones for weeks. I dragged myself and the bike between two parked cars: a bad idea. I should have waited in the street, but I was like a wounded animal, hiding beneath anything I could find. When I saw Number Twenty-nine's minivan drive slowly past, I didn't think to use the radio. In a stale whine, I tried to shout. All I could think was that this helplessness was perfect. It was just what I came for, just what I deserved.

"Dave! Two-nine, Two-nine, turn back. Stop!"

There was no response. I was hugging the radio with my head pinned against the curb, tears rolling down my face, my leg twisted and stiff. Big Dave, Number Twenty-nine, had pulled over and leapt from his car; he'd seen my bike tire peeking out between a van and a gray Benz. Soon he appeared above me with the gentle words "Surf's up, killer. Let's roll."

As I laughed, he reached behind me, pulled me forward, and shoveled his right fist behind my back. With a glance I told him to continue. There was simply no other way. Screaming and clutching on to the bearlike man, I was drawn up into the sky and carried from the wilderness.

BACK AT BASE, as I limped in, hauling myself from car to car through the alleyway, Chris made a curious proposition over my radio: "Number Thirty-nine, dispatch."

I would have begged Chris to reconsider, but there was no time. It was the end of the day and we were looking at the five o'clock rush. I tried to tell him that I just needed a moment to get circulation going, and that I could still finish off the day if I could only sit down a while.

220   "Well, bikers use bikes; dispatchers use chairs. So you can sit your butt down because you are on the mike."

"10-4."

Tom, having heard all this, spun Chris's chair toward me as I came in. "Are you okay with this?" he asked.

"I'll figure it out. I'll have to."

Pinky and Mikael were on the phone taking orders from clients, slapping the service tickets onto the dispatch desk. Tom sat in the driver's chair. His head was buried away, talking to an upset client on a telephone. Everyone in the small room was talking to someone, and no one was talking to each other. Bikers were trying to get directions, trying to find Chris, who was out making deliveries. Every mouth and speaker in the room was shouting and everyone was in motion, compartmentalizing data like a hard drive. Papers were everywhere, scattered on the table. I looked at the mess and started to arrange a few biker sets, shuffling the little white pieces of paper into careful lines like it was a game of solitaire. Two Sanchezes were looking south. Taitei had a special round-trip for 546 Jack; and two out of the Tower were heading north. I was arranging the floaters in a line on the table when I realized that Tom, to my right, was sitting very still and watching me. A moment ago he'd been listening to a client shout his ear off on the telephone.

It didn't shake him at all. He held a gentle smile and seemed a little curious about the organization I was making on the table.

I looked at him as another floater was slapped on the windowsill near Mikael's desk. Tom took the floater from the sill and slapped it next to my pile.

The radio continued: "But no one wants to sign for the package because no one knows the sender!"

Zero keyed in to help: "Marlene. Ask for Marlene. She is the only person in that building who knows what the hell she's doing anyhow."

"Man, shut up! People can hear you."

Pinky slapped another special on the table next to me and Mikael at the customer-service desk picked up the phone: "Service First, this is Mikael. How can I help you?"

I was still looking at Tom. He sat back against the filthy orange office chair. His heavy face looked back at me carefully, trying to find the right words. I just kept arranging the floaters into groups.

"Good instincts, Trav. But give the Towers to Number Thirty-one, Lu, because she is on her way in from McNutty and I think she can use the work. And look at the Taitei. That's a round-trip. Have Number Thirty-one pick up the back half first and have Number Thirty-seven run the front half. That way Taitei might get their business done within ten minutes, as opposed to an hour. What harm can that do? And if something pops out west, Number Thirty-seven will be there to catch it. He won't have any back-half to deal with."

I rearranged the tickets agreeably—a little surprised at how well he'd read my hand—and reached for the microphone. But Tom stopped me before I could speak.

He leaned forward, silently telling me to hang on, and gently took the microphone. "Number Thirty-three Punk, Number Twenty-nine Dave is hanging out on Stetson, waiting for the Needham special to Rolling Ghettos. Are you out of the Can yet, Punk?"

I looked over at his arrangement of suburban floaters. They were in nice orderly piles for each driver that he would be dispatching. My floaters were in a total mess but I knew that, to him, they all made sense.

"Yeah, Tom. I just stepped out and I have the Ghettos. I see Dave waving."

"Wavy Gravy, Number Thirty-three, thanks for your help. Big Dave, get out of Dodge."

"Yeah, I copy that. I'm outta Dodge."

"10-4."

Tom was so cool at the helm, so impressive. Even his sweat was not like mine. It was not the perspiration of labor or stress or pain. He was always relaxed. The beads of sweat that rimmed his forehead were just a matter of his being a big man.

The pressure, the deadlines, and the holdups that would get Chris screaming like a little girl would not even make Tom twitch. He was above worrying about packages and people and angry clients. It was as if he wore a special ring that had one magic power: the power to know illusion as illusion, to see through fantasy and fear, to perceive only what is actually there—and nothing more. Clarity is magic.

His relaxed demeanor glowed with this strange wisdom. And yet he was a simple working man, doing his thing. If he wasn't dispatching drivers he'd be managing a small restaurant, or maybe he would be driving a truck, but he would never change. No matter what he would be doing, he would always be glowing with that stillness and ease, having worked out all the glitches of the world and its many mysteries.

"Number Thirty-one, Lu, what's your progress on the McNutty's?" I asked the microphone.

"Number Thirty-one here, I am at Canal and Harrison, coming inbound."

"Are you clean?"

"10-2, 10-2, I'm clean like you," she rhymed self-consciously.

"Who said I was all that clean? What you need to know is: Nancy's got two for you out of the Tower, but they won't be ready for another few minutes, so why don't you hit Advanced Engineering on Jackson. They will have a set of blueprints for Taitei. Get that on and call me out of the Bates Motel with three on board."

"10-4, I'm on it."

"Number Thirty-seven, this is base, what's your progress on the Monroe?"

"I'm out of 225 with the 801 Moe, looking at Madison."

"Let's sit on the Mad for a moment, pull a set of AT&Ts out of the Litter Box on five, Sanchez and Daniels. They have a West Jackson getting dusty. I am hooking you up with a heavy West Side run. Are you into that? Do you find that *hip*?"

"That's groovy hip, Thirty-nine."

"10-4. And, Rod!"

"Twelve. Go."

"If you are the guy I think you are, you'd be on South Michigan *without* a set of photos on board. Are you *that* guy, Twelve-Guy?"

"Twelve."

"10-4. 310 South Mich just dumped a Britannica on the Tower, and there is an old 55 East Jack daily run around Amex for 200 West Adams. Can you reconcile this?"

"Twelve."

"10-4. Zeeeeerrro, what's your twenty, brother? Where you at?"

"Zeeeeeeerrrrrrrrro, I just picked up with Little Dave, Number Twenty-four."

Then Tom grabbed the mike. "Dave, Number Twenty-four, you've got a Marina City to pick up and then you'll be out of time on the Aurora. So grab the City and . . . *Rrrrrrun 'em.*"

"10-4, that's a 10-4, that's a big 10-4!" Dave replied while his two kids screamed in the backseat.

"Zero, there is a BRA special for the IBM and an FCB for Linda. Can you grab the BRA, run the Hub, and call me on the Foote?"

"10-4, *boss!*" Chris replied, imitating my voice sarcastically.

I couldn't laugh. I was still in shock from all the excitement and fatigue. The pain had vanished and my pulse had calmed; all of my energy was just rising up into my synapses. Dispatching is a skill of the mind, and I was beginning to see the whole picture of Chicago laid out in my imagination. Looking through the white metal board covered in floaters, some of them just scribbled scraps piled up under thick magnets, I could see the streets and the traffic, as if I were in a hypothetical helicopter circling above. I could see each of my bikers cutting lines through traffic, taking holes through red lights, locking up, and disappearing into buildings. As I stood behind that desk, I knew who was on the West Side and I knew who was running the Gold Coast and I knew how many pieces each of them had on board at any one time. I could see the packages in their hands as they ran up the steps of a building.

Soon the dispatch table started to clear up. The traffic began to loosen. I was very close to having cleared the pile of floaters, but every minute a new one would come in. I kept scribbling a biker number on the corner of the small ticket and sticking it under the magnets on the board as I assigned the work. Before I knew it, the table was clear and my head was spinning.

I tried to watch Tom and understand his calm. He was dispatching Number Twenty-one, Larry, north from the 'burbs.

"Have you got the Steakhouse on, Larry?"

"That's a 10-4, that's a big 10-4. Tom, big guy, can you do me a favor?"

"Sure, Larry, what's up?"

"Tell that rookie up there, Number Thirty-nine, he is doing a damn good job. Really, he's tops. I think he should know that."

"I'll pass the message on, Larry."

"Thank you, Tom."

"And Zero, what's your progress?" I called out.

"The Peat is dead. The two One-elevens are dead. The Braun is *on*, and Bates is in view. I'm looking into the sun as we speak, 10-4?"

"10-4, Zero. I'll set you aside a cold one. Is that a 10-4?"

"That's a 10-4, *boss*."

"Yeah, 10-4, 10-4," I replied.

"10-4 on that, Thirty-nine."

"Zeeeeerrrro!" I shouted.

"That does sort of say it all, don't it?"

"*Yeah, boss*, it does. When you're clean, just bring it in. Your day is done."

CHILLIN' WITH THE BIKERS, who were sitting around in filthy red jerseys getting a light buzz on weak beer, Tom leaned over and handed me a pile of checks. I started handing them out, like I was all in charge. Having paid off the entire room of bikers, whose faces and hands had gone black from exhaust and soot, I saw that my check was not in the pile. I asked Tom what the story was and he told me that I should go to Goldberg, ask him.

"But then I would have to walk there. Wouldn't I?"

"Yeah, but it's your *paycheck*."

"I suppose."

226   I limped into the cluttered office, which hadn't changed; nor had he. Goldberg, with his company shirt and trimmed gray mus-

tache, looked just like the day we'd met. He sat me down, clearing a place on a chair, moving accordion envelopes and piles of paper. For a moment he glared at me, trying to find the right words.

"How do I say this? Well"—he thought for a moment—"I don't have to say it! Here." He handed me an envelope. "In the past two weeks—I should say, steadily for the past eight to twelve weeks—you've had a higher average than any other biker in the history of this company. This check, these two weeks, you have made more money at this business than I have."

After local and federal taxes, Social Security, insurance, and the cost of radio time and pager service, I had a check that I could live on for months.

"Congratulations."

I didn't know what to say. I was too freaked out. "It's a pity," I finally said.

"Why, what do you mean?" he asked.

"I can hardly fucking walk."

Goldberg took a deep breath. He didn't know what to say. I lifted myself to my feet, limped out, and shut the door behind me.

CHAPTER NINE

ALLEY CAT: OF SICKNESS AND SUCCESS

There is no immortality and no reward for heroism, except in the glory of being remembered in some great poem.

Walter Kaufmann,
Tragedy and Philosophy

*T*O HAEWON, THE IDEA OF RACING MADE LITTLE SENSE.
She'd come from good schools and had spent most of her life in college and career-related studies, residencies, fellowships. Her life had gone from graduation to graduation, degree to degree. She'd spent most of her life building up credibility in her professional field. How could she see the sense behind what looked like the bloody foolings of a bunch of crazy messengers?

But I had found that the world down here was remarkably organized. Even if it was loud and bombastic, rebellious and unconventional, the people were often fixated on levels of personal status. With one another, messengers were highly cooperative, and yet competing against one another, they were fighters to the bone. It was a tight society where one could be promised lasting respect and recognition for what one could offer to the community.

For most of us, there was no religious incentive to strive for greatness, or even goodness. Most messengers were not divided into souls and bodies, goods and evils, or egos and ids—our psyches could not be cleft or viewed separately. Why live? Why fight?

Because history could just roll right over our heads and forget us all. Young men and women with years of hard living inked or etched into our skin, with the jeans and sweaters that we'd worn since we'd run away from home, with limited resources and limited opportunities, we, some of us, were still striving for glory with the will to be remembered for what we do well.

Seemed we had little else. Outside of our artistic pursuits and our useless degrees, what else might have marked a messenger's status? Some of the messengers I had gotten to know had no solid education; some of them had no aspirations beyond covering a few outstanding bills and then *taking it easy.* Some of us looked like militia and spoke of ourselves as anarchists, but this self-governing ideology was not entirely adopted by choice.

No one was watching out for us. We did whatever we wanted to do because no one seemed to care. The free market, the family, the IRS, and the Social Security system had done little for us. Our anarchy was not idealized; it was actual.

Most of the messengers I met seemed to surf a tide. They ran from poverty while committing most of what they earned to their own work and creativity. After paying for school or musical instruments or art supplies, after covering the rent and putting a little food on the table, they spent their earnings on bike parts and pints of brew at a bar named Phyllis's, on Division Street.

They were black, Asian, Latino, Latina; they were parents and the runaway children of wealthy lawyers. They were thirteenth-generation Americans whose lineage has suffered the sagas of our war-torn farmlands. They had come from Poland, Japan, Hawaii, and Peru, from the suburbs, the homesteads, the war fields of Iraq, the public housing projects down Taylor Street and elsewhere, bearing the stretch marks of a deeply polarized political system. They got to this country by plane, by boat, and by land, and together, riding in groups or talking in groups, they looked like a rainbow coalition surviving on the outskirts of the Thunderdome.

They had stopped playing the games of the capitalist system. Instead, they had burrowed themselves beneath it and dug out the culture and the creativity that they were seeking. They weren't looking at the free market to find their reflection. They were looking at its buildings, its ventilation systems, its ducts and docks and shafts, its sleeping subways and its cracked asphalt.

To the world, these messengers were like rats, too low to concern the average man; thus they ducked his conventional rules, traditions, and the means by which he found his credibility. They were free but somehow, sadly, indistinguishable. No one seemed to ever shine a light on the differences between us. I had taken elevators with guys who stunk of liquor, wearing the last pair of clothes they owned. I had a conversation with a man whose Afro was mangled and tainted with his own vomit. I could see a line of the dried residue crawling back behind his ear. He was a messenger. I was a messenger. Yet we were so many worlds apart.

Then there are messengers on another level entirely. Kim Morris holds her master's degree in English and works as a bike messenger. Otis Gunn, Number Thirty-eight, was a stockbroker and a bike messenger. Chris Powell was a sponsored racer for True Value. To the mainstream, we were rats, all of us, and we felt like rats. That is why we'd scrape each other up when we fell. That is why we would stand together. That is why we raced. It was our way of establishing what Haewon called "credibility." It was our way of feeling important.

Cap'n Jack had first been known to me as the guy who won the "world's most dangerous messenger" award at the Cycle Messenger World Championships in San Francisco. He ran the course against the grain of traffic. Timmy the Drunk had gained his notoriety by messengering in Chicago for twenty-two years. Superdave won his credibility for being one of the most dedicated couriers in the city. He would come to every major race and every competition in full red, white, and blue livery, bringing up the rear. He may not have been fast, but he was Superdave—and he had a tattoo on his leg of himself *as Superdave* to show for it. John Greenfield had gained his respect for organizing charity-driven courier concerts in local clubs. He raised money for a few cycling organizations, a local community center, a domestic-violence support group, and a health clinic that offers free HIV testing.

Jason Neri, a young man, still a kid, earned his credibility the hard way. The word was that Neri began messengering when he was only fourteen. Now, hardly twenty, he had been through more shit than most people get in a lifetime. His hair was cut short and dyed lime green. He was pierced in his lip, tongue, and nose. Whatever he had tattooed on his back and shoulders traveled all the way up his neck to his jawbone and out his sleeves.

Beyond the harsh appearance, there was something magical about this kid. He was more secure and more damaged than most of the others couriers I'd met and talked to. Year after year, growing through adolescence, he had to face down drivers, cabs, and fellow couriers who were unsure how to incorporate him into their tightly knit and well-hidden society. Since he was too young and too intense, people had their opinions, but I think most people feared him. Had Icarus himself survived his fall from the heavens, he would have looked something like Jason Neri.

This was our kind of credibility. It was a story, a heritage recorded in the tombs of the local courier 'zine and remembered by whoever cares and for whatever it's worth.

IT WAS 4:30 that Sunday morning when I pushed open the back door of my building and mounted up in darkness. I was rolling through the silent and suspended atmosphere of downtown Chicago, spinning to warm up my tender right knee.

I had heard about these alley cat races. They are different from a professional bike race because they are designed to simulate the specific problems that messengers regularly encounter. I had heard of races that involved elevators, jelly doughnuts, stairs, oversized boxes, shots of vodka—anything these untamed minds could come up with. Alley cat races are both demanding and dangerous, as most of them involve intense speed and are directed through busy streets, where unsuspecting traffic is, to us, just another obstacle.

By the ungodly hour of the morning and the stillness of the streets around me, I knew this race would lack humor. It would be "a fifteen-mile breakneck sprint," as Crazy Todd, old Number Thirty-five, had described it to me a few days earlier. When Todd says anything that is not a joke, you know to take it very seriously. I remember when he did laugh it was after saying, "Marcus is probably going to race us into the cement train supports along Hubbard and give a prize to the guy who gets up first."

I didn't find his idea very comforting, but rolling past the abandoned tents in Grant Park, left there from the last of the summer events, I realized that there was every chance we would be run through very unpredictable terrain. *Let it in, Travis. It's just like the cold, you have to let the cement wall in,* I philosophized to myself morbidly.

I pulled into the gravel parkway surrounding Buckingham Fountain. The scene did seem a little bizarre so, for the fifth or sixth time, I checked the handbill. No question: there was supposed to be a race going on here. I waited. The sky was cool and clear, tense with an eerie stillness. My stomach trembled. I could smell the first signs of winter, like an airborne plague, coming in from the lake. Standing in front of the empty lot, I felt like I was staring at a paradigm shift—as if I were standing on a cliff that would, at any moment, fall into an abyss. And I think that is exactly the kind of ride I was up for.

Looking down, I saw tire tracks, ten or twelve thin rivulets snaking through the gravel past the fountain. I followed them to the east side of Grant Park slowly, cautiously, not knowing what to expect.

There, scattered along the steps, huddling and slouched in darkness, were the shadows of some of the top athletes in our hidden biker society. U.V.; Andy Gregg; Jimbo; Ken, Number Seventy-six; and Skull were deep in concentration, surrounded by their road bikes, which were upturned or lying on the loose rocks. Bobbo, Number 285, was there, passing out centimeter-thick joints for us to share while we waited for the rest of the group. His face, typically a bright Fu Manchu smile, was now round and clear. As he smoked and passed the bud, he looked outward at Lake Michigan—a black sheet of endless space. He seemed to be listening to it, as if it would come alive and speak.

I was sitting next to Zero. I felt comfortable around his un-barred cynicism. While the other bikers (including myself) were layered up in polyester and spandex, Zero was true to form in a leather jacket, a pair of torn-up corduroy jeans, and a baseball cap turned backward.

Talk between us was sparse and tense, occasionally bottoming out into silence.

"Did you sleep?"

"A little."

"Are you carrying anything?"

"No way. Not a patch kit, nothing."

"What if you flat out?"

"Then I'm screwed."

Then we both shut up and focused on our breath. I was drawing in long, clean breaths of air. He was dragging on a Camel.

Registration meant putting seven dollars in the cash award pot and having your name scratched onto the back of a crumpled piece of paper. Marcus, the messenger mechanic hosting the race, col-lected the cash and pocketed the final check-in sheet by 5:15.

The intersection of Congress and Columbus, which would serve as the start (and finish) of the race, began to buzz with speed-crazed athletes. Some of the bikers, like Skull, were spinning in wide circles, pedaling in a high gear to loosen up their knees. Others, like Eric Sprattling, were straddling their bikes and stretch-ing. Eric has, for many years, competed professionally on a cycling team, and he told me that if it weren't for "death games like these" he would lose his edge on the circuits. His shaved black thighs in a blue skin suit looked like tree trunks.

Ken leaned over to tell me that this was the most stacked race he'd ever seen.

It was clear that I didn't have much of a chance, but I pulled up to the starting line all the same. There would be no starting gun, no flag to drop. The stoplight on Congress and Michigan would do. We lined our front tires up along a crosswalk and prepared for the next green. Rehearsing the course in my head, I could see that this was going to be a unique way to spend a Sunday morning.

For the first mile, we would navigate ourselves, taking any route we chose through the Loop until we reached a checkpoint on the second Randolph Street Bridge. From there, we would follow a specific thirteen-mile course that made a triangular shape through the city. For the last mile, from the Des Plaines Street Bridge to the finish line, we were again set free to route ourselves until we crossed this finish line.

Our eyes watched the green light turn red. Someone called out, "This is it." My arms tingled; my heart began pounding. To my right were three cyclists, including Crazy Todd. His playful energy was gone. He was watching the light, consciously breathing in through his nose and out through his mouth. To my left was Jimbo. His gentle and handsome face was staring at the light as if he wanted to break it. On the other side of Jimbo were twelve more cyclists, forming an erratic line of helmets.

Marcus then ignited: "Everyone, listen up! The route can change suddenly. A couple of us have noticed street barricades down in the parks. If you can't get through them, detour around the entire park. If you can get in, best of luck."

Silence followed as we continued to watch the red light, knowing that any second now, in the middle of a blink . . . a thought . . . a breath . . . *Barricades?* . . . "*Go!*"

OFF THE LINE, I somehow took the lead and shot down the hill on Congress, following the course I'd plotted the night before. Leaning into a sharp corner I noticed Bobcat, one of the most notorious and dangerous ex-messengers, sharing my lead. He was tucked in behind me so that he wouldn't have to face the wind. I had never done anything like this before. I didn't know professional drafting techniques, and I certainly didn't know I would depend on them for the rest of the race.

A newspaper truck passed us on Dearborn, a major downtown artery. If Bobcat could trail me, it seemed logical that I could trail the truck. I ducked in behind it and tried to keep up. As a rule—which I had temporarily forgotten—one should never follow too closely behind a vehicle. A huge metal plate covering street construction suddenly appeared from under the truck. I jumped the bike, hoping to clear the plate and keep my speed. But I flew too high and landed too hard. As I hit the ground the chain popped off the chain ring, and Bobcat flew past me, dragging a pack of those big-league bikers along with him. Losing valuable time, I hurried to a stop, got the chain back on, and hammered off again.

My spirit was shattered. Looking up, I saw the whole group swarming through the streets, fanning out and converging into near collisions under the flashing yellow streetlights. *Throw in the towel, Trav. You won't catch them,* I thought to myself. Then: *But quitting is hard to live down, hard to forget.*

I shot forward into a sprint that burned my thighs and calves. Even my hands began to sting with heat on the handlebars. In this frenzy to make up lost time, I nearly killed my dispatcher. I didn't even see him until his back tire dodged my path. Had I, for a moment, gone blind? I didn't know.

I knew that we would all regroup on Randolph, through the first checkpoint. When I climbed over the first of the two bridges on Randolph, I saw everyone out ahead of me merging into the plotted course. Pedaling hard on the downhill side of the bridge, I managed to regain some lost time and pull in tight with the nearest group I could catch.

We soon formed a razor-thin line of seven bikes, each drafting the other like a toy train. *This can't possibly be the lead pack,* I thought. *I'll have to lose these punks in a minute or so. I've got to ride with those who are winning.* Once I caught my breath, I pulled out of the back and crept forward. Slowly I passed Skull, who was easy to identify by his short orange hair and black shades. He slipped in behind me as I came alongside U.V., a half-Japanese mechanic and courier. Next in line was Jeff Benjamin, a little guy, built like a hockey puck. Then came Andy Gregg, winner of the last alley cat. In front of Andy was Eric Sprattling. Eric has been known to bike from Chicago to Madison, Wisconsin, win second place on a six-hour time trial, and then bike home again. Leading the group (though not for much longer) was Bobcat, once the winner of every messenger race in the city for a stretch of two years. He still takes home trophies from larger races in the States and Canada.

By the time I got to the front, we were leaning into Ogden Avenue, a long, wide, quiet roadway that cuts through a few blue-collar slums tucked in behind hospitals and auto shops. Though I knew I'd caught most of the group, I was squinting to catch a glimpse of a lead pack that I imagined was up ahead of me. But I saw no one.

The wind soon became a problem, as I was pulling this entire group behind me. I tried to keep the pace but my legs began to tire. I was a human windshield growing weaker and weaker against the breeze. I realized that I had only one chance of surviving this race: I had to *follow the people who were following me.* I needed teamwork.

Skull soon pulled up ahead of me, whispering, "I'll take it, Trav." Thirty seconds later, Andy passed him, and then, like threads in a delicate fabric, we began to weave in and out, smoothly and efficiently, rotating the lead, sharing the workload against the wind. Soon we were attuned to one another's breath, rhythm, speed, and riding style. Our tires were, at times, less than an inch apart—so close that I could have reached out and touched Skull's spike-studded belt.

To the city, we were nothing but shadows darting through red lights on a silent Sunday morning. But from the inside of the pack, we were a single machine in seven parts, switching gears as the winds shifted, changing the lead before we tired out, calling out in line "Brake!" "Clear!" "Bump!" "Car!" and so on, as the hazards came up. The consideration and refinement of these maniacal speed junkies was incredible.

When I began to feel that we were getting close to Douglas Park, I didn't know where to make the turn. "Here?" someone called out. No one seemed to know. Confusion grew, and the whole pack began to spread out with uncertainty. I crept up behind Bobcat and set all my doubts aside. If anyone knew the route, he would.

240

Wearing a bulletproof poker face, hoping to trick and possibly shake the group, Bobcat whipped out of third place and took a hard right into a curved roadway going straight through the park. While the group panicked and scrambled back in line, I was tucked neatly behind Bobcat's colorful Klein road bike.

The street was smooth and black, newly paved like a road out of a racer's dreams, with bright yellow lines that drew out into a wide right turn. I stood up in my pedals and pushed forward to feel the wind, and I found myself exhilarated, laughing out loud, passing Bobcat to get a better view of this perfect roadway. Good roads in Chicago are rare.

Soon, these gorgeous conditions would degenerate into the cracked and broken asphalt of Sacramento Boulevard, the next leg of the course, which would bring us into Humboldt Park. The pack tried to keep its line, but now we were swerving around potholes, over railroad tracks, through periods of total blackness under bridges, and into intersections waking up with light traffic. Our teamwork had begun to fall apart.

ON SACRAMENTO, THE CHALLENGE was to maximize rest. This meant staying away from the front as much as possible, sometimes exhausting the leader by refusing to pass. Occasionally, the leader would have to swerve out of the front position so that he could find shelter from the wind, behind someone else. Not Bobcat. When he was out front he was tireless. But you had to watch him closely. He would swerve to shake the next rider from behind him or to swing the group into potholes.

We began to slow our pace to preserve energy. Then, suddenly coming out from the back, Eric Sprattling rocketed ahead. As he flew past me, going at least twenty-eight miles per hour, he glanced over and said, "Thought I'd change the pace." He had hardly broken a sweat! Panic set in, and we all stood up in our pedals to catch him. I was out of breath, my legs felt like they were ripping, but I managed to keep pace with the group.

By the time we caught Eric, we were rolling into the entrance of Humboldt Park. The course through this shadowed space was a wide street that led beneath a path of tall trees turning 270 degrees around a lake. But unlike the last park, streetlamps were rare here, causing long periods of near blackness. Once inside, I took the lead again and routed the group through a labyrinth of hazards. I could see only a few feet in front of me, and the terrain was covered with potholes.

Out of the blackness came two long yellow poles, bound together with a thick chain blocking the entire road. I didn't know what to say. *"Yellow bar!"* would make no sense. I stumbled over a few syllables and came up with "BRAKE!" I squeezed the levers in my hand and skidded down to a slow roll. There were two alternatives: right or left. The curbs on either side had deteriorated into loose gravel. I shot left over the street rubble, hearing the pack behind me calling, "Brake!" and scrambling to some decision about it.

The sky was just starting to lighten, and shadows hung over us like ghosts. The road opened up again and the group converged into the drafting system we had established. But the rough conditions kept breaking up our teamwork. "Gate!"—another huge barricade blocked our way. Scanning the curbs, I decided to stay right, hugging the inside of the wide turn. U.V. pulled up behind me as we slid over a curb mashed into dust and rocks the size of fists. The tires slid out from beneath me as I tried to push forward across Division, a major artery intersecting the park.

There was no traffic, but I had to jump down onto Division from an eight-inch curb I did not anticipate. I was halfway across the street by the time I registered the curb I'd descended. But having only seconds to save my health, my wheel, and the race, I could not figure out the *oncoming* obstacle. I shouted, *"Think!"* but had only enough time for a few groggy words to pass through my head: *Curb? I went down a curb. Up? Curb? Up? Curb?* Glancing up, I saw an eight-inch cement block looking me dead in the eye. *FUUUCK!* I jumped the bike, flew through the air screaming, and landed it onto a pile of rocks, wheels first.

U.V. was not so fortunate; he was right on my tail, so he couldn't see the curb coming. But I kept pedaling, trying not to think about how serious his accident might have been. Soon, I could hear trees, birds, and distant traffic. There was no one within earshot. The road was all mine.

I kept the lead heading toward the last barricade and California Avenue, where I stumbled out of the park onto the empty street again.

Turning eastbound on Augusta, I caught a glimpse of the rest of the pack behind me. A tight machine now in five parts, they were eating up all the distance I had gained, coming at me like a torpedo. All my agility and luck were turned swiftly into extra weight, as I had no one to hide behind, no one to draft. Soon all five of them were butted up behind me, hiding from the wind and refusing to pass. I couldn't hold it much longer. "Brake!" I shouted and gripped the levers. On both sides bikes flew past me, and I was left in the rear.

APPROACHING MILWAUKEE AVENUE, I noticed that something was wrong. My half-numb face felt as though it were being pulled off my head. My cheeks felt like they were back by my ears. My nose was sliding down my chin. "*Is this normal?*" I mumbled, losing control of my lips. I had been, for about thirty-five minutes, pushing my physical limits. Now it was their turn to push me.

I had only enough energy to keep my eyes open and my head up. Then my toes went numb and my hands began to feel like mittens. When the bike began to wobble, a different kind of panic set in: *Can I finish this race?* My head felt like a bucket of wet sand, and my vision blurred. The blindness I'd felt in the first leg of the race had returned.

I began to feel my consciousness slipping away. It was as if my ghost was trying to leave my body and I was telling it to stay. *What the hell is going on?* I began to shout internally. Then it hit me: I was suffocating. Difficulty breathing is a common problem in racing because, with one's knees rising into the armpits and one's head tucked over the drop bars, there is little space to put the breath. The highest point on a cyclist's body is the small of the back, and it is usually working like hell.

Losing the race seemed inevitable, but I could not give in. I kept pushing, hoping the breath problem would just go away. I was somehow keeping second or third place steadily—well, less than steadily. Uneasily, or weakly. Yes, very weakly.

As we neared the city, over the Milwaukee Avenue Bridge, I began to taste my stomach acids. Another bad sign. I tried to keep the bike straight and going forward, but if I didn't do something quickly I would wind up in a ditch or dumpster, or vomiting over the upcoming Des Plaines Street Bridge. I started taking deep breaths into my lower back. It was like sucking water out of ice cubes with a straw. I was gasping like a drowning man.

Then, flying through the air, I heard the spinning fizz of a tire going flat. Skull had disappeared. Now I was with four others, climbing up the thirty-foot incline of the second checkpoint. Across the bridge, it would be a mad sprint for the finish line, any way you could get there—if you could get there.

For a split second, I glimpsed the Chicago skyline. Some of the most impressive buildings in the world stood close together, like the flags of a finish line. I was trailing Bobcat, prepared to follow him down the bridge and left, onto Fulton Street. Fulton was clearly the best choice. It would link up with the last diagonal block of Milwaukee. I figured everyone would take Milwaukee to Lake Street and Lake over the river because *that bridge* had the smallest incline. As we neared Fulton, Bobcat, leading the group, stayed right. He wasn't going to turn.

Suddenly it occurred to me that the rest of the group would probably follow Bobcat. Why would they follow me? They didn't know me well enough to trust me, and that was my advantage.

When the turn came, I shot out of the group from second place and flew down the dark and chopped-up shortcut. There was only one rider I didn't shake. Andy Gregg, the manager of the Blackstone Bicycle Works, had taken the turn with me. At first sight you wouldn't expect much from him. But even in his thirties, and with a little gut and a regular-guy look to him, he could make younger bikers shake in their clipless pedals, myself included. He is deadly serious about everything he does, and now he was in my wake, timing out the final sprint. Over the bridge he tore out in front of me. I kept my shoulders within his wake.

How do I lose this bastard? my groggy mind cried. *Ditch him!* I plotted. *Leave him out on Lake Street with no one to gauge his speed against. He'll panic!* I stole a wide right turn onto Clark Street, leaving Andy ahead on Lake.

Now I was alone. That *wasn't* part of the strategy. "You idiot!" I shouted. "Is that all your thick head could come up with?" Now I had no one to gauge *my* speed. Where was Andy when I needed him? Amid all this adrenaline, exhaustion, and fear, I shouted as loud as I could, my voice echoing off of the empty office-building walls, "You idiot!"

In the heat of the final sprint, I tore into Michigan Avenue, now seeing Andy gaining swiftly behind me. Morning had come, and we were enveloped in a magical blue light. The streets were filling up with freight trucks and buses behind a blue veil of wet air. Andy trailed me as far as Adams and then made his move.

As we crossed Jackson, fighting for the lead, I saw Sprattling, Bobcat, and Benjamin, the three-pack that Andy and I dusted on Fulton. Seeing us zip past two blocks ahead, the group, all in unison, let rip: "*Fuck!*"

I slipped in behind Andy, catching the last few breaths I could. We leaned left into the Van Buren ramp to Congress and started to climb it. I had to pass Andy on the incline if I had any chance of beating him. Then, at the last turn, he went wide. I took the turn sharp, pulled only a few feet ahead of him, and carried the lead over the Congress Parkway Bridge. Arms shaking, I coasted past the line, toward an empty gravel parkway, lit by a gorgeous sunrise. Again, I was alone.

"WHERE IS EVERYBODY? Don't tell me they left us here!" I collapsed on the loose gravel dumbfounded and gasping for breath. Andy came slowly to a stop and seated his head on his arms, panting. Seconds later, the others in the pack rolled in, some of them collapsing like I did and coughing. Finally I sat up, my head feeling like a cinder block. The next pack rolled over the line, and I began to figure it out. Marcus appeared and pulled up to Andy. He was sweating and breathing heavy. He pulled out the crumpled paper and asked who won. But Andy could hardly talk. Instead he just looked in my direction, and Marcus's eyes lit up.

I looked back. "Me?"

"Hell, yeah!" Laurence said, emerging from a car near the finish. He'd seen those last turns better than I had. I couldn't see anything at that point—anything, that is, outside of the little buggish idea that was bothering me. Yes, I could see it now, an idea was fighting its way through my oxygen-depleted head.

"These hotshots need some humiliation! It's good for 'em, good for their game!" Sprattling congratulated me, humbly accepting third place.

"Okay, then!" Zero stood to face Bobcat. "You've got *competition*." As my dispatcher, he had a right to be especially proud of this victory.

247

I was clouded, confused. I was somehow less than everyone

here, less capable, less ready, less anything. During the entire race, I'd thought there was a group ahead of us. It was an illusion I had built because I could not accept the idea of winning. It was a miracle to me that I could stand at all, much less that I could stand among these very serious and talented couriers.

The weed was already being passed around, but I could not partake. I was standing up, walking off the fatigue. I leaned over, still dizzy, still confused, looking at those loose rocks again. Right there, from where I was, under the blue sunrise, on this red gravel, it was clear to me: I would never see myself in quite the same way. They would certainly not see me the same either. To them, I was revealed as an insider, one of the few. Somewhere between us, a new respect was being bestowed on me, in the way of a forty-dollar first prize.

I stood, walked away from this awkward shift in my sense of self, and joined the group in laughter. I celebrated the fact that these people who were my competitors were also my teammates. As red-faced as some of them might have been at my success, I knew that they would help me if I needed them. The bond was real, warm, and respectful.

This unruly bunch, these colorful dropouts and rebels, might be the only people I will ever be able to turn to and trust when my life is on the line. We all independently muscle through the same ignorance, the same abuse, and the same forms of disregard, but among us a kinship runs deep. As we sat in a circle and enjoyed the sunrise, we were of a single mind, a single spirit, not for the pains that we had all endured but for the love we shared, the strength we felt, and the spirit we celebrated in the underground domain of urban cycling.

Riding away that morning, the sun now high overhead, I felt a little sadness knowing that this victory would fall quietly on the world. For an hour or two I'd felt like the king of the city, but then, riding below its enormous skyscrapers again, I could see that my throne was fragile. Victory here meant nothing to the world. Outside of that tight circle, my newfound awards and accolades, my feats and heroic deeds simply vanished.

I was a new man, a graduate, but no one seemed to notice, no one really cared. This time we were sharing was the dark ages for the cyclist. Without one another our greatest struggles would disappear like a lost language, like an endangered species, like a dream disturbed too quickly. Without one another our history would vanish, our justice would vanish, and the culture that unites us would admit a sad defeat.

CHAPTER TEN

AMBUSH

In present society all usefulness is displaced, bewitched. Society deceives us when it says that it allows things to appear as if they are there by mankind's will. In fact, they are produced for profit's sake; they satisfy human needs only incidentally. They call forth new needs and maintain them according to the profit motive.

Theodor Adorno, *Oppositions*

The Vehicle Code defines "[v]ehicle" as "[e]very device in, upon or by which any person or property is or may be transported or drawn upon a highway, except devices moved by human power."

Illinois Supreme Court,
Docket No. 84246–Agenda 34–May 1998

IT LOOKED A BEAUTIFUL RIDE. THE LATE-SUMMER SKY WAS clear. The traffic on these back roads was uncluttered and calm. The Coors Light biathlon was only five weeks away and, from this rural Du Page County road, Jon Boub was heading right toward it on his customized Fuji roadster.

To win, he would have to train hard. A two-mile swim in the morning, a five-mile run for lunch, and a forty- to sixty-mile bike ride through rural Illinois after work were the ingredients of his past successes, so he stuck to them religiously.

A rear wind was strong enough that the leaves along the rural Old St. Charles Road were swaying forward like waving arms pushing him into a higher gear. As his derailleur pulled his spinning chain closer to the axle, he started speeding down the half-mile descent into a soft valley.

The bridge marking the bottom of his descent came into view, so he stood up to max out his nineteenth gear. With his back in the air and his lean thighs pushing through the weight of the aluminum machine, Boub watched the asphalt pass between the cork-wrapped handlebars and his rising knees.

Glance: the small covered bridge was closer. His head dropped and his legs rose up in the air to rocket him forward.

Under his arms he could see the few quiet residences passing, hidden beneath the shadows of tall trees. Concentrating, his eyes registered only pieces of the environment as it flew past: his speedometer reading thirty-three miles per hour, the lines of the road zipping beneath his bike frame, a woman mowing a front lawn, his speedometer reading thirty-four miles per hour. The conditions were ideal.

Glance: the bridge was closer. The one-lane road disappeared into the shadow of its twenty-foot A-frame spanning a small creek. Beyond the shadow, he could see the street continuing out the other side of a line of wooden pillars. That shadow would give him a moment's rest from the low-hung sun. The bridge was a gateway. He'd pick up speed on the downhill, hit the bridge, and then make his first big push uphill. Because the next seven miles of the route comprised a clean straightaway, this push would mark his tempo for the whole circuit.

Glance: his direction was on the mark. He was centered, the posts and railings lined up on the outside of his shoulders. His thighs were burning, his breath changing its rhythm to meet his cadence.

When Jon touched the shadow at the foot of the A-frame, he was curled up over his profile bars, eyes tearing behind a set of Oakleys, expecting the small incline. Every day he would cross this bridge, and each time through, he would coast on the pedals, watch the sunlight flicker past the vertical posts, feel the pillars breathe across his forearms. Coming out on the other side, he would hammer the hill. Preparing for this ascent, he vanished into the shadow at thirty-five miles per hour.

That day a construction crew had arrived and started a renovation project that would remove and replace the asphalt between the bridge's wooden floorboards. They'd finished the first part of the job that afternoon, meticulously blasting the old asphalt out of the wooden crevices, leaving gaps between all the lumber. When they left for the day, they took their caution signs with them. When Boub entered the bridge he had no idea of the danger he was in.

Beneath the covered roof, darting through the beams of broken light, he could see that the A-frame's shadow had changed. The black strips beneath the floorboards had the wrong density. Where there had once been pavement, there was, suddenly, nothing at all. His wheels, whirling through the wind, were only inches from a sharp descent into a void. As he breathed in, even before there was time to panic, his front tire swerved and fell six inches through the bridge's floorboards and hit a cross member of the superstructure.

His whole world flew into a vertical spin as the bike, hitting the crossbeam, knocked Boub out of the crevice. The bike, still connected to his right shoe, went completely over his head in a somersault. He landed on his back and bounced again, still carrying the bike between his legs. Outside the bridge the momentum continued. He landed on the pavement and was thrown into a metal guardrail that came at him like a bolt of steel lightning. He put his left arm out to absorb the blow but, since he was spinning, his arm went over the top of the railing. The metal gate plowed into his chest and bounced him into blackness.

"JON, YOU'RE HURT. I know you're hurt but you've got to get up. Get up, Jon. No one is going to find you here. You've got to get up."

Awoken by the sound of his own voice, he found that the sky had turned a deeper blue. His helmet was split in two. As he touched his face, he could see that he was bleeding from his right temple. His shoulder was dislocated and his entire right side was shredded and torn by asphalt.

"*You've got to get up, Jon.*"

In blinding pain, he leaned to his left to disconnect the pedal from his racing shoe. Using only one arm, he lifted himself to a sitting position. He held the bike up and, keeping his hand on the top tube, he pulled himself to his knees. Then, wrapping his arm over the bike, he stood.

The road was empty. The light over the western horizon had fallen away, and he could hear the sound of a small lawn mower about a hundred yards east. Using the bike as a crutch, he began to walk toward the sound. Stepping into the bridge again, he got a closer view of the naked lumber that had trapped his front wheel, but because of spinal injuries, looking down was impossibly painful. He had to keep his head up, his weight on the bike. He talked to himself to keep from losing consciousness.

When he finally reached the source of the sound, he saw the woman he'd glanced at while flying past this same strip of roadway. He shouted to get her attention. "Can you help me?" The woman turned and saw him—a tall man bleeding down his entire right side, leaning on a twisted bicycle, standing in front of a beautiful sunset. Her eyes and her mouth opened in an expression of complete horror.

Seeing the fear in the woman's eyes, he got a flash, a mirrorlike reflection of his own injuries. Instantly, Jon passed out and fell to the ground to be awoken sometime later by the touch of a paramedic.

He'd suffered a concussion, three herniated discs, a fractured hip, a crushed hip joint, a torn ligament in his left foot, a dislocated shoulder, and numerous muscle injuries. After insurance, his out-of-pocket medical expenses were nearly *fifty thousand dollars.* He decided to take Wayne Township to court for damages because the bridge, being an unmarked construction site, was clearly unfit for regular travel.

The township fought the suit, arguing in defense that the bridge was in perfectly operable condition for its *intended and permitted* users. This was the language of the Tort Immunity Act of 1965, which explains that claims cannot be made against the state for injuries in public areas that involved usage that was not *intended and permitted* for such areas. Beneath this language was a profound and important question: is a bicycle a legitimate means of transportation, as legitimate as the automobile? If so, the city would have an obligation to maintain the road for a cyclist's use. If not, Wayne would have every right to leave the bridge as Boub found it and let every cyclist suffer similar injuries.

The courts ruled against Boub, reasoning that a bicycle was *permitted* but not *intended* to use Old St. Charles Road. Because there was no bike lane, Wayne Township persuaded the court that they hadn't *intended* this roadway for bicycle use and were therefore exempt from any liability. Something as simple as a Caution sign or a No Bicycling sign would have prevented the accident, but because of the awkward position the bicycle has in our day, being (according to this court) permitted though not intended, neither sign applied.

Jon Boub appealed the Du Page County ruling and brought the dispute before the Illinois Supreme Court. Behind him were the

Chicago Bicycle Federation, the League of Illinois Bicyclists, and hundreds of Critical Mass activists and messengers. To dispute the charge of being an unintended user of an Illinois roadway, Boub cited the case of *Molway v. City of Chicago* (1909), in which a cyclist sustained injuries after falling into a pothole. The court ruled that Illinois was responsible for keeping the roads good enough for "ordinary travel," which to the jury at the time meant cycling, walking, driving, riding on horseback or in a carriage, and traveling by trolley. But the Illinois Supreme Court found this case unpersuasive because it was decided at a time "when automobiles were just beginning to appear."

In truth, the court of 1909 may have even been biased toward bicycles because cities first began paving roads in the early 1890s under the lobbying pressure of an organization called the League of American Wheelmen (LAW). These "good roads" were initially made expressly for cyclists because the cobblestone and mud, which were suitable for the trolleys, carriages, and motorcars of the time, were not easy to navigate with bikes. Paved roads meant bike roads. It wasn't until the early 1900s that the auto industry joined the good-roads movement and began to show their own muscle in the political process.

The *Molway* case is a reminder of a pre-Fordist age in the American city when the street reflected the principles of its constitution. The street itself was democratic, providing for many kinds of competing transportation systems. Not only did it give Americans access to the city, but it celebrated the diversity of its people by integrating the use of the most primary of public spaces.

The *Boub* case shows us the state of our current road system, which protects only the rights of motorists. Under the influence of the automobile, the court of our day has reversed its stance on the importance of an integrated roadway, tearing it from its democratic roots. As Nelson Algren said, "Nobody but an outlaw [can] maintain a semblance of order on the common highway." This outlaw was called National City Lines, a corporate conglomerate made up of many interested partners, including Standard Oil, Firestone, and General Motors.

In the 1930s, National City Lines bought and closed down forty-eight independent electric-rail systems that were serving major cities across the country. Later, the company was taken to court and proven guilty of antitrust violations. Though it may not have been conspiring to shut down the rail system to the benefit of more car traffic, it was conspiring to replace the trolley with, exclusively, GM-brand city buses. The conglomerate was fined a mere $5,000, though the ultimate cost of the transaction is beyond measure. This purchase, however much its consequences may have been unforeseen and unintentional, marked the end of the integrated roadway by making the public street the absolute territory of the auto manufacturer.

I don't think it is fair to say that the street was intended particularly for cars, bicycles, trolleys, or roller skates; what the street is *intended* for is travel. But I think it is fair to say that once the automobile had coaxed the roads out of the hands of light rail, the automobile could itself begin to transform the size, shape, scope, velocity, and thereby the *intent* of every road on every city block. Americans *had* to drive, or find a way to be driven, simply to get from home to work.

This decision, between driving and using the new city buses, was not entirely made by a fair and free market, either. The government played, and still plays, an enormous role in making the car affordable to the average American. To this day, buying a car does not mean having to pay for the expanded streets, or the extra police that are needed to manage traffic. Buying a car means buying a car. The costs that cars create for metropolitan areas in terms of damage of public property, waste, water and air pollution, the loss of wildlife, et cetera, are assumed wholesale by municipalities and state governments. These costs, many of which are hard to calculate, are inflated by a number of economic and building decisions that have amounted to federal grants for the expansion of the private car.

During the Depression, and with substantial federal funding, the New Deal public works programs ran the first set of state roads through America. This gave our unemployed workers something to do with their hands, but it also substantiated the growing priority of the automobile in America. The passenger-train industry was forced to make severe cutbacks in service because of the new "motor traffic."

But was this motor traffic competing fairly with the train industry? By no means. Huge subsidies on oil, used to keep production and transportation going through hard times, benefited the automobile more than any other industry because of the car's speed in consuming certain oil products. After the Depression, those subsidies were not released, and still today they are not released, forcing the taxpayer to pick up the brunt of the cost of every gallon of gasoline pumped. To this day, the cost of oil has been artificially suppressed by burdens on the taxpayer to the advantage of the oil and automobile industry. Could trains possibly have kept up? Not when drivers were kept from paying for their own roads, services, and fuel.

This heavily influenced demand for the private automobile soon translated into an equally strained demand for space. Today it is commonly understood that 400 square feet are needed to park a car, while the office of an average company requires only 250 square feet. Having to house these new (and artificially cheap) automobiles became a serious architectural problem. A wave of skyscrapers were developed that would house the car and the worker in a single building. In Chicago, much of the underground architecture developed in the early 1900s was opened and developed for parking. Today, these buried spaces are still operating and regularly used.

In neighborhoods, the problem of parking could not be handled with such ingenuity. Residential streets became so tightly packed that the neighborhoods themselves looked like parking lots. For those who had the money, this overcrowding was one element that made suburban neighborhoods with less density more attractive. On the outskirts of town, there was more curb space per lot. Houses were beginning to be built with garages. The wealthy suburbanite could drive his car right up into his new (and artificially affordable) home and shut the door.

These influences led to the great migration of the baby boom, spreading our cities outward entirely beyond the scale of human-powered transportation and creating the automotive dependency that we see today all across the country, in America's urban, suburban, and exurban areas.

PUBLIC SPACE, ONCE *INTENDED* for public use, is now managed by the profit interests of the machine age. And though the bicycle is what gave us the paved road, and though the bicycle is even today competitive with the automobile in dense areas, it has become the immigrant of the roadway, losing its rights to the road and its status as an equal in the public arena.

The Illinois Supreme Court phrased it this way: *"We do not believe that bicycle riders are, like drivers of vehicles, intended and permitted users of Illinois streets and highways."*

The repercussions of this kind of exclusivity are devastating not only to cycling but to the future of the city. How can we prepare for the city's development in this new millennium if aggressive, irresponsible, and intolerant business interests rule our streets? Does one have to subscribe to the auto industry in order to belong on America's roads? I don't think that's democratic. But more, I don't think it's competitive. Instead of giving alternative transportation a chance to compete with the car, it only gives car manufacturers the opportunity to compete among themselves. This kind of practice does not make America a free country or a free marketplace.

Should it stand that a roadway can be *operable* for drivers alone but at the same time *permitted* for cyclists' use? Does this not amount to, in the case of *Boub v. Wayne Township,* a kind of rattrap for the cyclist? The message is that the moment you get on a bike (or off a bike lane), you give up your civil rights.

Today in the heartland of America, if a cyclist, a motorist, and a runner fall into the same five-foot ditch in any average intersection, the bicyclist alone will not have the right to sue.

The Chicago Critical Mass was furious with the verdict of *Boub v. Wayne Township.* The case led us to question how liabilities will be handled when and if an *intended user* of a roadway strikes an *un-*

intended user. Could a defendant plead that the bicyclist was impeding an *intended user's* progress? If so, could this roadway be called *public in any sense at all?*

SEPTEMBER 25, 1998

AS THE COLLECTION of a few hundred cyclists accumulated around the Picasso sculpture, I was just winding down from work. I changed my shirt, slapped the sweat-drenched bag against my back again, and started handing out flyers. Around us on all sides were the relentless battles of metal machines that lurched forward foot by foot, jumping lane to lane so that some driver could advance himself one link in the citywide chain that was surrounding us for miles.

In my one year with the Chicago Critical Mass, I had seen a colorful and committed local movement grow. All the old faces were there, coming out for the last ride before daylight saving would swipe our six o'clock sunshine away. Smiles were bright and the cheer was high. Though we'd had some problems, on the whole we had enjoyed a summer of important victories. The group had managed to stay together for its first full season, remaining relatively steady even in difficult weather. We had garnered the support of other cycling organizations and made serious inroads with the city. We had first-time riders on every mass, and they were all welcomed heartily.

In fact, there were a few new riders here today: a doctor, a husband-and-wife team who had done masses in other cities, and a

few bike messengers who were giving the ride a try for the first time. One of them was Gregg, Number Thirty-four, a rookie at Service First. He was delighted to be there; he thought the idea was fantastic and it made his work seem more worthwhile. I wasn't elated. I was, in fact, quite on edge.

I gave a little interview to Digital Dan, who was shooting a documentary of the ride, and then mounted up and started circling the downtown square to keep my adrenaline high and my thoughts clear. My knee had gone out twice that week. I'd had to have Marcus build me up a new set of wheels because I had beaten the old ones to hell.

To make matters worse, while others in the group stood around quite casually, doing their usual jabbering and socializing, I saw that there was a bike cop in our midst, a *copsicle.*

Dan started interviewing Jim Redd at the foot of the sculpture. Redd was bright and optimistic. The officer from the downtown district didn't faze him. I overheard him saying at one point, "Everyone is invited—cops, kids, grandparents. They don't have to like us, but they're welcome to ride with us."

I saw a few people engaging the curious authority figure in careful discussions. Smiles were passed between the cop and some of the bikers. He asked for one of our route maps so that he could *help,* implying that he would hold the intersections for us as we passed through the downtown area. I inferred that on the other side of the river, as we came into the Eighteenth District, we'd be in the hands of God.

A guy named John, a computer animator, gave the copsicle a copy of our route. It was something we gave to everyone so that we could all stay together. It was a matter of hospitality. If the entire board of directors of the Ford Motor Company came to ride with us, we'd at least give them a route. But I was not alone in feeling uneasy about the police presence so near the start of the ride.

The cop called in the directions on his radio, turning his back on the bikers who were straining to hear his transmission. Our path was marked—we all knew it.

I kept circling, so that I would see Haewon when she arrived, via bicycle, from the hospital. When I saw her, clad in scrubs and a light jacket, my eyes lit up and my sense of safety returned. To the mass, I had come to represent the aggressive activist, the guy who would take the street by force if he had to. Haewon had come to symbolize the common rider, the middle-class constituent who could give our anti-car ideology a calm and rational voice. Together, we made a powerful team.

When the ride began, Dearborn filled up with three tightly packed lanes of cyclists, greeting pedestrians and handing out flyers. Bells rang, whistles called, and small crowds chanted. People rode with signs taped to their bikes or strapped to their backs. Bikers we saw riding independently were invited to come along. Once again, we were urban missionaries sharing with the world, in our loving way, a few simple solutions to the larger problems of our age.

While the mass tried to clear a major intersection, a fringe group stood in the road to hold traffic. As the lights changed and the bikers kept riding through, I looked for the copsicle to see if he was helping us at all.

He was on the other side of the crowd, hiding behind his radio. As we rode forward into the Gold Coast, he disappeared. Most of us were still smiling and thanking those waiting patiently at bus stops for not driving to work. Haewon was in a conversation with Gin

Kilgore, a sprightly and devoted activist. It was comforting to see, as we rode along Wabash Avenue near Loyola University and the up-scale shops of the Gold Coast, that our simple proposal had inspired such a strong community to come together.

But the positive feelings changed, as they always do, the moment we saw a set of police headlights tailing us. Alone, this wasn't unusual. It was, in fact, rather normal. Cops tail, especially in the Eighteenth District. They look for bait. They are like lions watching gazelles stampede through a field. To defend against harassment, bikers will try to switch out of the back position. The moment the optical illusion of running and interweaving gazelles fades, the lions set their sights on a victim. And when lions set their sights, there is always a victim.

Donny and Tim were arrested during our June ride when four squad cars converged on Clark and Schiller. They snagged the bikers, loaded their bikes in the trunk of a squad car, and drove away, letting the other 150 of us continue our ride uninterrupted.

T.C. at one point was arrested and hit with the charge of *inciting a riot*—but it was on an off-schedule ride that had only twenty-six bikers, most of them computer geeks. Can a handful of mildly peeved code crunchers constitute *a riot*?

During a winter ride, a squad car sped past us on Lincoln Avenue, parked, and then waited for the group to come toward it. As we rode past, a leather-clad cop lunged over my back tire and arbitrarily pulled a guy named Jon, one of our most peaceful riders, off his bike. We all looked around, dumbfounded, while Jon was cuffed and loaded into the vehicle. We happened to be only a few blocks from leaving that officer's district.

It seemed like a control thing. Some officers just had this need to piss on us so that we knew whose property we were. But not all cops were this way. Most of them, usually outside of the Gold Coast area, treated us like a quirky novelty. We were not challenging their authority—we were challenging the automobile's authority. It takes no time at all to see that Critical Mass is not a criminal organization. It is just a group of people on bikes.

In most cases when cops have met us in intersections and have approached warmly, they have gotten friendly, respectful treatment in return. I remember one cop flagging a mass through an intersection on Jackson and Michigan as we skirted the lakefront park. By the time I reached him to thank him for hurrying us through, the cop was smiling ear to ear, saying, "You're welcome, you're welcome, you're welcome, you're welcome" to virtually every biker that passed. He was blushing! We'd made his day.

Because of these positive interactions with police, riders have stopped getting upset or worried by their presence. We just try to stay out of their way when the cuffs come out, and usually we know when it will happen. When a squad car appears ahead of us, it usually clears the intersection and lets us pass. When a squad car appears behind us, a cop will wait a while and then strike—from the rear.

I was at the back of the mass as the squad car was coming up on us. "Clear the way," he called through a cracked window, and of course I obeyed him. I let him crawl at five miles an hour up to my right side.

"Thank you for your help, Officer," I said, trying to get him on our side. "We can really use some help up by the front. You know how crazy drivers can be when they have to wait."

"You need to disperse, now."

"What?" I honestly wasn't sure I'd heard him correctly.

"Realize that if all of you do not disperse in the next sixty seconds, every one of you, *every one* here will be arrested. Is that clear?"

I came in close to his window. "If you expect me to say anything to these hundreds of people in the next sixty seconds, you are asking too much. You know that would be impossible."

"I just have to make the order and then it is up to you to obey it. At this point all of these people are not obeying a police order."

Now I was seriously concerned. "Do you know who is in this group? These people are students, professionals, parents—there are children here!"

"It's not my fault."

"Well, what are they doing wrong?"

"They are not obeying my order to disperse and they are all going to get arrested for it."

I rode ahead and warned the handful of cyclists that I could reach by voice, but seven blocks ahead of us the front of the mass was merging onto State Street. Over my left shoulder I could see squad cars shooting up the parallels. I saw a paddy wagon sitting in the intersection of Dearborn and Elm. Its headlights turned on as I rode past at the end of the group. When the front of the mass came to Division, I saw the reflection of red and blue lights on the walls and through the glass windows of the restaurants and coffee shops that make up that intersection. There were no sirens. No warnings. The cop could have used his bullhorn. He chose not to.

Up ahead I heard shouts and loud gasps as cyclists veered through a pack of police, some of them jumping off their bikes and running them to the curb. I saw officers hurriedly walking against the grain of traffic grabbing cyclists, pulling them off their bikes, and throwing them to the ground. By the time I arrived, bikers were lying on the pavement, facedown, cuffed together. As I rode past, I saw a biker get thrown onto the hood of a squad car. His arms were up in a gesture of surrender; he was not fighting. Another officer then took him by his shirt collar and forced him to the pavement, where he cuffed one wrist. A porky, six-foot meathead of a cop wrestled another passing cyclist off his bicycle and conjoined the two with the same set of cuffs.

While mountain bikes and their riders lay scattered along the street, a formidable crowd formed on the sidewalks, chanting. The cops responded by pulling people out of the crowd and stacking them into the back of police cars whose trunks were overflowing with bikes that would be held as evidence. We asked what the charge was. None of the officers made a reply. I think they seriously didn't know. They were just following orders.

Fourteen bikers were arrested at the Division Street intersection and taken to the cop shop on Chicago Avenue. The remaining demonstrators, having followed the paddy wagons to the station, set up camp, strategizing, drawing on the sidewalk in colored chalk, and chanting loud enough that the inmates could hear us.

Haewon's eyes were huge and worried. She had never seen anything quite like this. I gave her my spare bike key and all my extra cash and told her that she should probably head home. She agreed.

"Are you going to be okay?" she asked in an uneasy voice.

"What's the worst they can do? Arrest another bike messenger? What would that accomplish? Nothing."

268   "If you get arrested, call me," she said in a whisper.

"10-4."

She nodded, aimed her road bike toward Clark Street, and rolled away, climbing on in one motion like a pro. I went to the Service First headquarters only a block away to make distress calls to local TV stations.

While I was thumbing through the Yellow Pages and tying up two phones at a time, Gregg, Number Thirty-four, was still in the crowd outside of the station. "Oh shit!" I heard on my radio. "About twenty cops just came out of the doors of the cop shop with batons and are pushing people away from the front of the building! Wait, wait, wait!" He cut off, suddenly.

"Are there more arrests?" I asked on the two-way.

"I don't know, Trav."

I told Gregg to keep his cool and not to get involved because I needed to know what was happening. One of the people at the Channel 7 assignment desk overheard the transmission and agreed to bring a news truck to the corner of LaSalle and Chicago.

I ran back to the protest surrounding the Eighteenth District police station on three sides. I saw for myself how the cops had forced the demonstrators off the sidewalk and out of the street. People stood in small crowds, tightly pressed together for protection. Cop cars pulled into the blocked-off roadway to fragment the crowd.

Why were we being separated like this and scraped off the street? Naturally, our angry mob could not in any way impede the flow of traffic along Chicago Avenue. Such is the state of our right to peaceful protest and public assembly; it is restricted to the sidewalk, the architectural equivalent of a Post-it. Somewhere down the line, our right to protest had been squelched by the need to facilitate car traffic! I found Gregg, Number Thirty-four. He was standing in front of the news truck, mouthing off to that meathead cop I'd seen earlier. "What happened to your billy club? Did the cameras scare it off? You can't get it up anymore? You going to play *Officer Friendly* now, you asshole?"

When the cop saw that the camera crew was still trying to get their instrument assembled, he came forward, grabbed Gregg, and started pulling him off his bike. In turn, I grabbed Gregg and started pulling him back onto his bike. "What is the offense? What did he do?" I shouted.

"He pissed me off!" the guy shouted back, looking up to make sure that the cameras weren't getting it.

"That's my First Amendment! I can mouth off, you son of a bitch!" Gregg hollered, trying to get the camera crew's attention.

As I hung on to Gregg's courier bag, the three of us were crossing the street and moving toward the station. I started yanking at the bike, but the cop wouldn't let me have it. "We need this for evidence."

"Evidence of what?"

In the end, I could get only Gregg's work radio, an expensive item that could easily disappear once in custody.

The cameras then clicked on and began quietly taking interviews that would never be aired. The night slowly and sadly dissolved into meaningless conversation and fits of useless anger.

The bikers were charged with *mob action,* an antigang ordinance that was written to give the police the power to arrest anyone in any crowd if it looked as though they had come together with the intent of breaking a law, any law. We weren't hit with *disobeying a police order* or *disorderly conduct.* We'd conspired to break an obscure city ordinance that supposedly made it against the law to ride

270

bikes two abreast. It was almost comical. No, it was more than comical; it was *wrong*.

The "mob" was released the next morning after spending twelve hours crammed into the city's cold, roach-infested holding cells. No one slept, not the prisoners or the demonstrators, because a harrowing realization had been made: cyclists in this town have no power, no rights, and no voice. Cycling itself is criminal.

RIDING THROUGH THE SHADOWS of a long, quiet neighborhood street, trying to find the location of our next meeting, I felt a peculiar strand of fear. It wasn't a fear of poverty, crime, or discourteous drivers, since this road was so quiet that nothing moved except for me, the Grinch, and a few leaves falling in the cold air—but I felt seriously endangered. I was told that in the meeting I was heading to, we would be planning an anti-police action.

The street signs were either missing or bent, so I could not be sure what street I was passing. Parked cars, whose colors had gone black, lined the road on both sides. I could make out their shapes only by the glistening light of the rounded edges and windshields. Their emergency lights still had an amber glow. They seemed alive, their consciousness measured by the tiny blinking of an alarm signal.

Small second-, third-, and fourth-story apartment-building windows peered out from behind and above their tenants' vehicles, which waited like guard dogs at the building entrances. I felt that I had to be very quiet so as not to unleash the fury of these gorgons too soon.

Since the ambush, the city had felt alien to me. The roads felt more dangerous; the police, once friends, now seemed untrust-worthy. That unsteady feeling of being passed by a car on a narrow roadway made me shudder. I was riding my bike carefully, like a grandmother. I felt weak, politically. I was no longer watched by some anonymous ghost; I was wanted by it.

The police had been doing the work of the lawman; but the law-man had been doing the work of the businessman, leaving us with what felt like the hit-and-run diplomacy of the GOP. It was confus-ing. Did they think we were against law and order, or did they un-derstand that we were merely *anti-car* and exercising our right to be that way? Or was there a connection between them that I needed to understand?

In the last few days, an officer had harassed Zero about where he was that Friday night; Rod had gotten arrested, *again;* and a rookie named Francisco had been drilled about who organizes Critical Mass.

"No one *I* know," he'd said adamantly. But then, no one orga-nizes the mass. It is an accidental reoccurrence, though many peo-ple in the mass do try to organize themselves. In fact, since the troubles began, every weekend there was another group of riders hosting a meeting to deal with different aspects of the twisted poli-tics we were confronting. Some of the meetings were about recon-structing the events as we all remembered them, some of the meetings dealt with finding the money to represent the mass in court, and, as mad as it sounds, some of these meetings dealt with techniques of self-defense.

Behind a shiny black van in the middle of the block, tangled through an iron fence, was the landmark I had been seeking. "Look for the bikes," Digital Dan had advised, and there they were, piled one atop the other and locked by a network of chains and U-locks, creating a giant Brillo pad of spokes, pipes, and Kevlar seats.

At closer inspection, I saw that the pile consisted of bikes that I had come to know. In the pile I could see Donny Quixote's light brown single-track, Jimbo's yellow thrift-grade fixie. Katherine's GT, Gareth's foldable mountain bike with the spring-loaded cable for a bottom tube, Iris's touring Trek, Dan's racing bike with his ubiquitous trailer, Greenfield's orange one-speed with the upright handlebars. These were not showpieces but rather work bikes built and designed for daily use. The paint was chipping, the tires and the gears were coated in mud and soot, and the chains were light brown, needing a teaspoon of oil.

I locked my bike to the last piece of exposed fence I could find and climbed my way to the third floor. Thirty-five people were piled into a sparse room. The question before us was whether, in the future, we should let the police snag us and continue the route or whether we should begin to stop and *retaliate.*

Jim Redd laughed about the idea initially. But then, once the crowd sat seriously, paying close attention, his laughter stopped. He stood in front of his mountain bike, which he'd dragged upstairs, and pulled his U-lock and key from his bag. He slipped the open U-lock through the bike frame and the spokes of his back wheel and locked the hard pipe around his ankle.

"Lock the ankle to the back forks; toss the key. Lie in the road facedown with your bike on your back. This will protect your vitals and make it harder for them to move you. Then reach out and hold hands with someone. Don't talk to the police and don't look them in the eye. Just lie there."

He explained, "The idea is to make it hard for them to move

you. You just want to be there until the cameras arrive. The cops might grab you, they might drag you, but if you are not a threat, they cannot harm you."

No one spoke. While we looked on, some thirty of us sitting or standing in the small Logan Square apartment, he went on to show us another technique. We watched him kneel by his bike, slip the curved pipe around the bike frame and the two sides of his throat. He attached the crossbar to the ends of the U-lock beneath his white beard—and turned the key.

Craig, a thirtysomething who had a stable job and a marriage to protect, asked, "What if no one is looking? What if the news cameras don't come? Are we ready to take it that far?"

T.C. piped in, "You say they can't harm you, but they can. It doesn't have to be right, but they can harm you."

Monetta interjected, "But is any of this *right*? We are being persecuted for using the very roads that we're taxed for. That can't be right. But cops aren't so concerned with right and wrong, are they?"

She reminded us that many of the sergeants on the force today had been rookies during the Democratic National Convention of 1968. They would not take these measures lightly.

But then, we were not the protesters of that time either. It was not fashionable to stand up for anything. Times had changed. Now, having a criminal record meant something. Most of these people had lives and careers to protect. They had families and reputations to uphold. The people here had as much to gain by fighting as they had to lose by fighting. Would the world be watching? Would anyone be watching? That question was wearing our confidence thin.

IN THE MEANTIME, the messengers had their own response to the arrests. Instead of confronting the lawman, they defended their right to the street by racing on it at high speeds, enjoying every turn and straightaway for what it was worth.

The Tour Da Chicago races that Marcus was hosting had been creating a lot of solidarity in the messenger scene. Messengers were taking their riding more seriously than ever before, sponsoring a racing team called Triple X that competed in races all over the country. These messengers were beginning to earn respect on a pro level.

They would schedule weekend training rides out to Wisconsin or the small towns that have, in the last few years, been turned into suburbs. Many of the rides went to Indiana and most of them were led by Eric Sprattling, the long-distance megastar whose first hundred miles were, to him, a warm-up.

Between these two groups, the community of messengers and the community of bike activists, I was somehow right in the middle. On certain issues, I found myself unsure of which side to take.

As the massers worked to influence the politics of the bicycle by becoming more extreme and more determined, the messengers backed away. They hung low and took care of themselves.

It was strange to see that the legit people, the middle-class massers with careers and families, were more willing to be arrested than the more extreme couriers were. The mass was going to the street without the help of the courier, and the courier was going to the indoor track at the expense of the street-level politics.

As a messenger in the mass, I would be reproached by riders for the freedom with which I ran red lights and sped into oncoming traffic. One guy, after a ride, told me I was holding back the movement because I was unpredictable and had no respect for authority. He asked me why a driving public would give cyclists any more respect if so many of them were willing to ignore street signs. To that person, I was damaging the respectability of the bike commuter with my messenger style.

I didn't know how to answer because on the other side of the issue, I would get attacked for staying mainstream. "Why do you care about *Commuter Joe*?" Skull asked me. "If there were more cyclists on the roads, there would be more people in my way," he said. Other couriers would justify their distance to the political issues by saying, as Ken did, that "masses ride too slow and then they get arrested. I don't want to do either."

To make matters worse, the Critical Mass group seemed to be pointing fingers in all directions to find someone to blame for the arrests. In the eyes of the mass, drivers were the problem, the media was the problem, the police were the problem, and couriers were the problem because they gave cycling a bad reputation. People from the mass would tell stories of being harassed in the lobbies of their own buildings because they looked like messengers.

"If messengers were to obey laws, we wouldn't have to deal with things like this. In fact, we commuters would probably find less antagonism from drivers if they didn't think they needed to defend themselves against messengers," one of the more conservative massers complained.

But the discord did not end there. It spread. When Digital Dan and I used a set of messenger radios to help self-police the ride, a firestorm of protest was generated. We had become authority figures because we were trying to defend against another police ambush.

If there was a route for an upcoming ride, some people would say that it was against the ideology of an "unplanned event." If there wasn't a route, other riders would get upset because it would mean poorly planned rides that would meander aimlessly. In either case, someone was unhappy. Our morale had grown inconsistent and undependable.

The November demonstration began, as usual, with cyclists accumulating at Daley Plaza. This ride had no route. The idea this time was that the cops couldn't ambush us if they didn't know our path. The mass ended with bikers getting yanked off their bikes on a dark corner of LaSalle Street. No one locked themselves to their bikes—there was no time.

The police chased us down a congested section of Michigan Avenue and its cross streets. With cops on our tail, we began to ride at full speed, taking turns against traffic on one-way streets to evade the squad cars and paddy wagons. We were no longer peaceful protesters. To them, we were *savages;* to us, we were *prey.* Objectively, we were a panicked mob, intent upon delaying another crackdown. Then Monetta, the host of the U-lock demonstration and one of our best strategists, was yanked off her bicycle by a cop who had gotten hold of her sweater. The cop pulled her into the air by her neck. She fell five feet to the ground, landing on her back. The cop then jumped on her, pinned her facedown on the asphalt, and cuffed her. Her bike rode another twenty feet before falling in the road, unmanned.

CHAPTER ELEVEN

REQUIEM FOR THE WORKING MAN

Good-by now to . . .
All the crazy wonderful slamming roar of the street—
O God, there's noises I'm going to be hungry for.

Carl Sandburg,
"A Teamster's Farewell:
Sobs En Route to a Penitentiary"

ROLLING INTO THE BACK ALLEYWAY AFTER BREAKFAST I saw someone sleeping in the gutter. At first sight, it didn't surprise me, but then I noticed that this half-drunk, unconscious soul was wearing a Service First jersey and had a beautiful blue-gray fixed-gear with upturned and sawed-off handlebars, bullhorns. I had never met the kid, but I saw in his slumber that beautiful rebellion that seeks not status nor shelter. Both lost and free, it seemed impossible to see him doing anything other than living a courier's life. No matter what the world was going to throw at him, he was going to *coast*, unafraid and mostly unresponsive, until he found his niche.

The back gate was still locked, which meant that Zero had slept through his alarm. I waited, resting on a guardrail, the kind you see on the side of highways. This one divided a city-owned alleyway from a private parking lot. Centered in the parking lot, a massive American flag flew above the alleyway. I thought that was curious. It was right at the back door, and I'd never noticed it.

When Chris pulled in, we stepped over the young man and started our normal morning routine. I brought the Grinch inside and began writing up tickets from a pile of overnight deliveries, selecting the ones that would work with my DDB and Rosenbluth routes. While we were sitting around in the dark dispatch room, using just the light that came in from the alley, I asked, "Who is that dude in the back?"

"New guy."

"What is he doing here so early?"

"He started yesterday and fucked up. Took a couple packages home."

"So."

"I told him to bring 'em in. He gave me a 10-4—which meant that he would bring the shit back into base, right?"

"He didn't do that," I said, understanding the problem.

"No," he said, pausing a moment. "It is too damn early to be firing people, right? Maybe I'll tell him to come back at noon, then I'll throw him out. I am just not up for it right now."

"That's why they call it *work,* Chris."

"10-4 on that."

When the sleeping rebel awoke, I overheard their conversation. "Can you give me one good reason why you didn't bring those packages in?" Chris said, frustrated. Finding no significant response, he let the kid have it. "Oh, get the fuck out of here. Hit the road, Jack. I shouldn't have to deal with this bullshit." The kid rolled his broken heart back out into the alleyway and disappeared.

Chris dragged his feet back into the dispatch room, once again neglecting to turn on the fluorescent lights. "Am I getting old? I used to love doing that."

"Dispatch?" I asked, changing the subject.

"Yo."

"I need to call it early today. Fourteen hundred hours."

"Why? What's going on?"

"I got an interview."

"*A what!*" he nearly shouted. He then sighed heavily and said, "10-4. Two o'clock, no sooner." He knew what was happening. I had found a way out. I left Chris deflated in the dark office, his elbows propping him up over a pile of floaters. I started my early route, spinning with a huge sense of relief.

That weekend, at Danny's, a bar on Dickens, I bumped into Cesario, the visual arts director of the Mexican Fine Arts Center Museum. The last time I'd seen him I was a broke preparator eager to get two weeks' work installing just about anything. But now, meeting again, it was clear—I'd changed.

"Where have you been, man?" He nearly shouted from a table not far from the bar. "I've been looking for you for months. I've been asking everyone if they'd seen you, if they knew where you were living, working, shopping, *anything*. What the hell happened?"

"I've been working, man—payin' the rent."

He looked at my clothes and gloves, the key hanging from my wrist. "Messengering? Are you a bike messenger?"

"Yeah."

"That's insane. Why are you doing it?"

"I've got to do something. Last I checked, the gallery district was dry. The Museum of Contemporary Art was giving me the runaround. Your Mondays weren't cutting it. I needed to get by."

"Then sit down, because there's something I want to talk to you about." He then gave me the scoop on a full-time job that would be opening up at the museum. It was not an office job. I would be managing the main building, a satellite building for a youth museum, and the storage sites for all the various departments of the museum. I would be supervising the maintenance on the galleries, doing installations, working with the theater festivals, and keeping the building up to code. The job seemed perfect for me. I had gallery and museum experience, warehouse experience, theater experience. The one drawback was that the job only paid $29,000 a year and, to me, as solid a job as it might have seemed, it would mean a pay cut.

At first I wasn't sure. After I heard about the long-term savings package, the three weeks of paid vacation, the time-compensation deal that would mean getting paid for hours worked overtime, and the top-notch insurance package that included life, disability, health, family, and dental coverage, I decided I had to take the interview.

That day at work, I was the drag-ass queen. I pulled off two jobs an hour, where I would normally do six or eight. The moment I thought about leaving, all of my strength disappeared. I was so fucking tired that I could hardly stand, much less ride. I just wanted to lie down and cry. *It was over. It was over. It was over,* I knew it. I kept moving, giving long, emotive stares at the city from the corners and the steps I had so come to know. Chicago had become a friend who'd shared with me all of her secrets. We'd developed a strong bond, a trust. I knew I would miss her. I knew that it would be hard to let her go.

I saw a few old heads that morning as I rode through the Loop. I saw Superdave, and we hung out for a few minutes outside of the Bank of America. His red beard and bright eyes were dim. He'd been out here for eight years, and even I could see that for him the glow was gone.

I saw Jason, once a water polo hotshot from California. He was heading north. I was heading south for the CNA. The two of us slapped hands in the middle of State Street and kept rolling. He'd been out here for at least four years, working his heart out, being unstoppable.

Through the polished metal doors of the Oil Can, I saw my own reflection, but it didn't look like me. The young man's face was covered in thick plastic materials, a warlike helmet and chain-saw protection glasses. His eyes seemed hollow and lifeless. He was an object of the external world, a tool used by clients and companies to facilitate business, capital. This young man was the act of commerce. You could see it in his face—my face. He was the material form of *intent,* a coil of densely packed electricity, a radio wave. He was a catalyst for meaning in the world, built to disappear the moment he filled his purpose.

I'd filled my purpose. I'd won the top prize, loving what I was doing and succeeding because of it. From the street to the museum, I was on the correct path, the path that would take me home again.

Chris called for me: "Number Thirty-nine, what's your 20?"

"Litter Box."

"Litter Box, what? I thought you'd be at the Cock."

"I found I like it better here."

"*Man,*" Zero groaned. "Do you want a—*never mind.* Dirty Thirty, Dirty Thirty, have you had your Pleasure yet?"

"Yeah, Pleasure Travel has died on us."

"Because the Energizer bunny's gone and died on us too, I'm giving you his Lockbox route. 10-4?"

"10-4. Thanks, Trav," Dirty Thirty added, knowing that he was getting a promotion.

"Yeah, dude" was my only reply, and I fell back on the steps of 333 Wack and looked up at the sky. The El passing by on Lake rattled a pigeon out of its iron superstructure. I didn't even think about the train; its clatter had become so familiar that I hardly seemed to notice it. The bird held my attention, though. Having flown from the tracks it now hovered overhead against the high rectangular sky, flapping its wings, uncertain of where to plant its feet.

IT WAS A CURIOUS feeling to leave the street as I did. It meant becoming, somehow, a part of society. For a while at the new job, I felt like I was living a secret life, like I would, at any moment, run out of the museum, mount up, and knock out a pair of specs at the Rush Hospital. I was worried that I'd be leaving behind all the kinship and the intensity that I was so proud to have achieved. I was no longer the maniac on the yellow Cannondale. But then, I was no longer going to be in crippling pain, in restless sleep, and up to my elbows every morning in egg yolk and cigar smoke, so it all paid off.

When a messenger moves on to another career, he does not *quit.* He *retires,* and his title goes from being a messenger to being an ex-messenger. The delineation only means that you have a good "hookup," and usually that's often accompanied by the purchase of a new rig. In a few weeks, that is exactly what I did. Marcus built up for me a 1998 Fuji Aloha with small, agile 26-inch wheels. It was a well-built speedster, and it spoke for my admission into a lighter, more credible world.

The first thing I did as the operations manager at the museum was have the city install bike racks at the sidewalk near the building.

I found that, with more time on my hands and better sleep, I could contribute to the bike community in ways I had never thought possible. Instead of seeking my own credibility in an automotive world, I found myself working for the credibility of cyclists at large.

I started heading the flyer-distribution wing of the Chicago Critical Mass. I wrote press releases for demonstrations, designed routes, and began, for the first time, to write about my experiences as a messenger. On an everyday level I encouraged the people at the museum to try riding to work once a week. Because I was not active as a messenger, I could be active in bringing cycling back to the working class not as exercise, or leisure, but as a legitimate means of transportation.

When I kicked the chunks of ice from my gloves and out of the rolled-up legs of my blue jeans, most of the people at the museum looked at me like I was nuts to be riding. Forget windchill; the *still-wind* temperature had been below zero for weeks. Over the New Year's weekend, thirty inches of snow fell over the city, and six more inches followed soon after. It was the worst blizzard Chicago had seen in three decades.

I had to explain to people at the museum that riding in winter was not so much a show of manhood as it was a skill. For long rides, a set of Gore-Tex socks and thick tights keep most of the ice, water, and wind from the lower half. Toes go numb in twenty minutes or so, but *you deal.* Ears should be carefully covered, and a thick layer of Vaseline can prevent some of the splitting on the cheeks and lips. Hands are a big problem. Serious riding should not be done without an investment in good gloves. For the torso, unless it's raining, go light. You need room to lose the body heat you generate.

Winter is brutal for all riders, but with the right gear, it becomes manageable. I would wear a jersey, a long-sleeved T-shirt, a thin but tight acrylic sweater, and a thick wool sweater on top. The cotton, acrylic, and wool combination was a low-tech way of keeping warm while still losing sweat. It also gave me enough padding to take a fall gracefully.

I could talk about it lightly and with enthusiasm only because I wasn't messengering anymore. I was a bike commuter now, and I was proud of it. I was still out there with the rest of the guys. I would see them every day on LaSalle, bundled up and exhausted. I would talk to guys on the street whose lips were purple and whose breath was short.

"How are you holding up?"

"I'm sweating too much," Zach replied. He was one of the more determined couriers in the city. He had enough gear to handle just about anything, though it took me a while to recognize him behind the extra layers.

I would cross paths with many other couriers while passing through downtown. Whereas we would usually slap hands and say hello, on very cold days many of them would just ride past, nod, and look away, defeated. It is hard to be sharp below twenty degrees on your sixth, seventh, eighth, and sometimes tenth hour. In the cold everything seems heavier, and so you burn more energy than usual. Your face can get windburned in minutes and your reaction times are slow. You taste salt for months, because it is kicked up from the tires. And then there are technical problems. Brakes become totally useless. Tires slip on manhole covers and icy bridges. Parts dissolve and fall apart. The bike slides at almost every turn.

Jeff, Number Forty-six, told me that a guy in a white SUV hit him intentionally. The driver got out of the car and started talking shit and getting in his face: "Whatcha gonna do about it, tough guy?" In an average situation Jeff would have been smashing windows in with his U-lock and dragging the guy down the street by his collar, but it was about 10 degrees and it was a Friday. Half the staff at Velocity had disappeared, ducked out, or been seriously injured in the last week. Jeff, usually in a team of twenty, was doing a quarter of the work on the board.

"Whatcha gonna do, messenger man?" The guy advanced.

Jeff realized that if he spared this guy a moment of his energy, he would not be able to complete the day's work. He dropped his head, pulled his bike from between the truck and a parked car, and walked away to a good section of road, where he could mount up again. He said nothing. He just continued his work. I saw him that afternoon outside of the Velocity headquarters. His beard was stiff with frozen spittle. His eyes looked like they'd been carved out of his head and then painted back in. He told me the story while leaning on his handlebars, trying to stretch the words through his purple lips and frosted face.

This was his fourth winter as a messenger, his second winter in Chicago, and, for him, it was the most unrewarding test of his life. "I wake up. I work. I go home and crash, man. On the weekends I buy gear and I replace parts. My girlfriend thinks I want to leave her, but I just don't have the energy to explain."

"Why don't you take some time off?" I asked.

"I've got a place here that I don't want to lose. Next year, I'll be calling the shots. I'll be getting that hookup, you know."

That's how it was for most of the guys and girls out there. In the offices of the different messenger companies, couriers would gather, waiting for work, sipping coffee, smoking pot, and sleeping.

Being awake meant being at work, and being at work meant suffering.

I remember seeing a messenger walk his bike the wrong way up Superior. A wind gust had picked up loose snow and spun it around him, creating a whirlwind of small ice chunks. I couldn't tell who it was and he couldn't see me riding carefully across Superior at Wells.

Piles of black and brown ice and snow were lined up along all of the major streets. Pedestrians had to walk in the road because the sidewalks were covered knee-deep. The parked vehicles along the curbs were buried: the massive snowplows had been charging through the city for weeks, and with each pass they would dig up ice, salt, litter, even chunks of asphalt, and toss it atop the block-length piles of the same. Locking up outside of a building to run errands, I had to climb a small hill of ice, turn my bike upside down, and lock it to the collar of a parking meter. These piles of ice would remain, like a Chicago head cold, unchanged until spring.

During these punishing winter months, like the leaves of the trees along the Old Town avenues, all the political passion and activity of the bike community fell away. The budding cliques at the fringes of the mass were being scraped away and muted, if not by futile legal disputes with the city, then with serious injuries that were becoming an everyday occurrence. Armando, an OTF courier on a fixed-gear, slid into a train support, cracking his frame and breaking his wrist. Bones went down on the Canal Street Bridge. While falling, he grabbed the grating and broke a few bones in his hand. Joe Hunt, an Apex courier of two years, rolled out into Western as a Ryder truck tried to catch a yellow. His bike flew two hundred feet and he went down with a set of crushed vertebrae.

On every level, winter was crippling. As its chill slowly broke, I was hoping the political turmoil of the community would just melt away with the dirty ice and the closed-off, defensive attitudes of the city. I was hoping that the sun would shine and everything would be different; that is, everything would just be perfect—magically. I wanted to attach a happy ending to this horrible season and forget that it ever happened.

THE FIRST RAIN of spring fell like the spill-off of unanswered prayers from heaven, filling the gutters, falling off the low rooftops in thick streams, pouring into drains so eagerly that the air from the sewers bubbled out of the iron grilles.

I was at a café sitting out the thunderstorm with a friend on a Tuesday morning when I heard the news that there had been a death. A messenger had been killed out on West Washington Street and Lockwood, a neighborhood street that I'd never once had to travel down. The sheet of rain just kept coming as we talked about the apprehensions we'd both had about being messengers. *One mistake could indeed be your last, you know? What's it all for?*

The news was a little distant at first. I assumed the victim was one of the bikers that we tend to forget about, the empty-bucket riders who run ten packages a day on beat-up Huffys. Some of them live in rough neighborhoods; many of them are hooked on rough habits. These are guys who might work for a week and then disappear. As hard as they struggle, they often don't have the time to develop the skills they need for the job. Because there was every chance that it was simply an accident, unavoidable, the news sort of rolled off my back. It was just a little sad and morbid and expected that a slipup would have fatal consequences.

"Did you know this guy?" I asked Marcus on the telephone the next day.

"Did I know him? Of course I knew him. It was Tommy. *Tommy McBride*," he said weightily. "He's been out here longer than I have, like *six years,* man."

"Tommy?" A few faces from the past crossed my memory and then it clicked. LaSalle and Washington, the asshole pit stop. Wells and Monroe, a friendly introduction. He'd asked my name and told me that it was "good to be back." He was strong, healthy, jovial, bright. He was one of the best. His eyes were ecstatic and full of brilliant reflections of the streets he knew well. Yes, I remembered him.

"Was it a bad move? A wrong turn? What?" I asked.

In a simple, straight-up way, Marcus then told me what he'd heard from the street and read in the morning papers about the incident. Tommy had been murdered. The papers called it an act of "road rage."

The rain broke sometime that morning and so, after talking to Marcus, I decided to take a ride to shake off the complicated thoughts that were messing with my head. The idea was difficult to process. I had found a combination of streets down in the Loop that made a rough figure eight. To clear my head, I decided to revisit this hidden track.

The course made a tight series of turns with good roads and legal lefts going up the South Water ramp and down the Fairbanks Bridge. Then there was a series of right turns around the North

Water area that connected beneath the Tribune Building. Crossing the river on the bottom of the duplex Michigan Avenue Bridge, the track came full circle, leading me to the South Water again. Falling into this pattern was like attaching the bike to an electrical rail in a macabre quarter-mile fun house. My mind wandered and my bike kept its line round and round through the industrial matrix.

Most of the course was underground. My eyes would have to adjust every few minutes between bright sunlight and underground shadows. Every two or three blocks I was being blinded by sunlight and then blinded by the shadow of the covered street again. The flashing of light made me forget about watching the road. I trusted the bike and its intelligence. I let my shoulders and wrists carry me through the course by memory. My mind slipped off into a trance of speed, balance, and rhythm.

Meditating on the collision of flesh and steel, flesh and asphalt, flesh and blood, blood and rain, I tried to imagine the murder from Marcus's description and the facts as he found them in that morning's *Sun-Times*. I tried to reconstruct it from my own experience of working on the common highway.

A MAN DROVE UP behind Thomas McBride, angered by a confrontation they'd had a few blocks back. Even in the rain, Tommy could hear the heavy engine revving up behind him. He was being taunted, and that is not unusual. Cyclists are always getting fucked with. In most cases, a few hard words go back and forth and the driver speeds ahead, using his accelerator, symbolically telling you to fuck off.

This happens all the time. In fact, for me, incidents like this would run together in the panorama of an average ride. Most drivers don't ever seem to understand or respect the minimum of space that a cyclist needs. The unusual thing about Tommy's encounter was that his confrontation happened in the pouring rain, only a little after eight in the morning. Most drivers won't bother in the rain. Indeed, drivers with especially aggressive appetites tend to drive like puppies in a serious downfall. The rain is meditative; it makes a driver feel and reflect. They have to be unusually upset or aggressive to challenge someone in that setting.

But then Tommy couldn't have been in good spirits either. Going out into bitterly cold rain after a night of comfortable, warm sleep is rarely a welcome transition. In heavy rain, it takes only a few minutes for the water from the street to come up from beneath the bicycle and drip down along the calves of the cyclist. From there it seeps along the ankles and then into tightly laced cycling shoes. Having a stream of cold water fill the shoe and puddle beneath the toes is just an uncomfortable, shitty feeling. It is the same with the layers of clothes. The process of soaking clothes in strong rain might take a few minutes longer, but Tommy was only a few minutes from his house when he and the 1997 Chevy Tahoe came to a stop to settle their differences.

I don't know why they stopped. Perhaps the Tahoe was pinching Tommy into the line of parked cars. This would mean that Tommy would knock on the hood of the vehicle to let the driver know that he needed room. Generally this is not done in spite but with seriousness. The thump is meant to wake a driver up when they are just being blind or inconsiderate.

After the argument, if it was seriously rude or aggressive, Tommy might have ridden into the center of the lane. He has a right to do this at any time, but drivers don't tend to agree. To them, a biker in the street is just *in the way*. The motorist approached threateningly. The grille of his Chevy Tahoe could be seen only a few feet back as Tommy glanced down between his arms. The sound of the engine gave a short delay between the driver's intention and the machine's response. He was threatening, but Tommy wasn't going to budge.

He'd seen too much of this. He couldn't back down to a pigheaded, SUV-driving son of a bitch like that. It was a matter of principle. They are just too blind, too selfish, too fat, and too numerous. *Fuck him.* That is what he said and that's what I would have said too. *I have a right to the road.*

I remember Donny telling me about a similar episode. An SUV was following him too closely over a small bridge on Chicago Avenue. Donny had taken a lane because there were traffic cones on the right shoulder. This meant that the traffic behind him would have to go the speed limit until he crossed the small bridge. Once he cleared it, the drivers behind him could speed all they wanted to, no problem. The SUV hit the accelerator as Donny came off the bridge and swung right, hitting Donny broadside, knocking him off his bike. The SUV then pulled over. The driver got out. He was a well-dressed professional carrying a twenty-ounce coffee cup. When Donny thought he was going to get a hand up, he got a double Starbucks coffee splashed in his face. Before he could react, the driver had climbed back into his truck and driven off, alone, the sole passenger in his heavily subsidized vehicle.

There again, I see this sense of imbalance. The Tahoe that ran down Tommy was carrying only one man. Yet something gave that man the idea that he alone, because he was driving, owned the road.

The Tahoe revved up behind Tommy a second time, driving his bumper as close as he could get to the biker's back tire, but the biker didn't back down. Tommy was fighting for his space. Facing, every day, so many drivers who think we are *in the way,* I have learned to fight this way too. I got swept into it. I guess it is natural to be assertive, even demanding, when you are publicly assaulted and abused on a daily basis. Of course I began to stand up. I learned to get serious about my place in public life. Just as Pat felt compelled to smash in the window of the taxicab, I learned to stand behind my liberties because no one has the right to take them away.

Tommy got hit for the first time, lightly. It was a test. A pulse shot through Tommy's hands as his heart jumped, pulling the blood the wrong way through his arms for an instant. Tommy stood up and pushed forward harder. Now the fear set in. Because the grille was so close, it was more difficult to veer out of the way. He had one escape: forward. And so, like a bull, he lunged, but the truck lunged with him and contact was made a second time.

This time the high bumper flattened Tommy's back tire, held on to it, and pushed it forward, skidding it into the street. As the driver drew back, Tommy was able to pedal again. Tommy looked back, worried. He kept his weight on the front tire so that the bike stayed in motion. He tried to speed up and get out of the way, but the Tahoe came again. He could hear the accelerator sounding like rocks being churned into dust. The bike was slowing down, and the truck was not. This sound kept coming at a steady speed.

Tommy looked back just for a second to see if this was really happening. The twist of his spine pulled his bike off balance just enough so that he felt the point of no return come up and grab him. At that instant the eyes of the young man met the eyes of his murderer. He was no more than a face with intense eyes, a man's face, and a layer of splashing water.

The feeling of falling came right through his cold hands, his lungs, and his face. Dropping the bike, he dove forward, arms spinning to catch the ground. When the ground was close enough, he could feel the speed of the pavement folding his right arm underneath his body and he fell onto his handlebars and right wheel as it slid forward in the rain like a raft overcome by heavy surf. For a moment, the bumper of the truck was pushing Tommy, and he was dragging the bike along beneath him.

His left hand swung back to catch hold of the truck, and he managed to hang on to something. It wasn't the bumper or the grille. It was the license plate that gave *this man* the privilege of operating a motor vehicle.

In jerky motions the bike was being pulled beneath the Tahoe as it rode over the small bumps of the street. The truck was still accelerating and the bike was disappearing and the license plate was just strong enough to hold on to. But swinging back and forth above the asphalt, the bike got caught beneath a wheel. The wheel pinned the bike to the ground and the truck pulled it under. The plastic frame of the license plate cracked and was torn from the front of the truck.

Witnesses said the driver of the 1997 Chevrolet got out of his vehicle a few blocks down, disconnected the bicycle from the back bumper, got back in the truck, and drove away. In the last minutes of Tommy's life, he stuffed the license plate beneath his body. And so, though he had no name to his murderer, the murderer would have a name for us: Carnell Fitzpatrick. He'd turned himself in that afternoon, having noticed that his plate was missing from his front bumper.

I CONTINUED—LEFT ON Michigan—taking care to avoid the steel pillars holding up the city. Accelerating on the underside of the duplex bridge before the light turned red, I burned my thighs and picked up enough momentum to carry me up the South Water ramp again. My mind was closed to the world, and my arms, legs, and memory led me through the maze, but my spirit was looping the events of Tommy's death. I felt like I was spinning sideways in the road, wearing injuries I too would never understand. There were thousands of times that I could have been Thomas McBride; thousands of my own confrontations could have gone that wrong.

It could have been any of the bikers in the community, messengers or otherwise. It is the nature of an anonymous murder; the injury spreads to everyone the victim could have been. Yes, for godsakes, it could have been me.

I took the Fairbanks hill down—right on Illinois—right at the first curb so that I could slip below the surface of the Peacock and connect the figure eight again. Instead of running the loop again, I stopped and looked around at the underground architecture of lower Michigan Avenue, the part that no one sees. The street, fully enclosed in cement and steel, was hollow and painted, like a still from an old movie, in gradations of soot.

WHEN I GOT HOME I found that Bobcat had sent me an e-mail entitled "What the Fuck Is Wrong with This World?" In it, he described roughly what I'd already learned about the murder, and in the last sentence of his message, he invited me out to the wake. I wrote back accepting the invitation.

Bobcat met me the next day at a designated time and place. Messengers do things like that. We don't say "I will pick you up at your place three-ish." We say things like "1100 North State at three-ten." I arrived at 3:02 after leaving my place at 3:00 because I knew he'd be early. Arriving at 1100 North State I found Bobcat waiting in his white Volvo hatchback, packing weed into a small pipe. It was about eighty degrees and the two of us were squinting at each other in the glaring sunlight.

Bobcat was a stiff-lipped guy. He spoke little, listened seriously, and stared for long periods of time. His eyes were always a little foggy. Every gesture was under his own careful scrutiny as if life, for him, was a process of refinement. It seemed hard to excite him and impossible to shock him, but Bobcat could catch me off guard with a comment or gesture that would erupt, stretching him from limb to limb, like an alligator yawning.

We drove due west all afternoon and pulled into the funeral home in St. Charles as the sun began to set over the small farming town. There were only a few other bikers present. I went inside. Recognizing a few of the faces in the room from my time on the street, I took a place in line, to pay my respects.

Bobcat took a seat and stared at Tommy from across the room. "Are you coming?" I asked.

"No, that's too close."

I understood Bobcat's need to keep a distance, though I wanted to know, learn, and see *everything*. This was a chance to look upon the murder of a man, a young man who'd been struggling, like me, to find his place in the world and to earn his respect.

In the room with us were about fifty people, the bits and pieces of Tommy's family, school friends, girlfriends, and a few bikers. Each of us knew an aspect of Tommy that was completely different. As they stepped up to visit with him, they exchanged that memory for a private question that no one else could hear.

His parents, who looked much like mine, stayed at the head of the line and greeted friends. The line was long at first, but it kept growing longer. Inside of half an hour the history of this young man's life continued through the other room—and then, to the door—and then, out of the door, and out of the funeral home entirely.

Framed photographs of Tommy's life stood on a small table near the line so that people could remember him. There were pictures of his childhood. I saw what he looked like when graduating from high school. I saw what he looked like wrestling with his brother. In the most recent picture, three messengers were standing at the railings above an industrial street. Tommy stood on the right side, half removed from the shot. In the center, standing proudly, was the messenger king, Cap'n Jack Blackfelt. His hair, almost a Mohawk, was dyed red and blond; he smiled brightly from beneath the mixing strands. On the strap of Jack's bag was a yellow pin that read I AM NOT A THIEF.

That is when I really understood that this murder took from us one of the best bikers out here, one of us who loved and believed in the work and the workers. A biker who was part of the solidarity I had come to depend on.

As I turned around I saw, standing in line, wearing a black beret, the Cap'n himself, the messenger guru who shook the Chicago streets into awareness, tightened the diffuse and anarchistic bunch into a proud people. He had flown in from Manhattan for the wake. Everybody knew Blackfelt and everybody knew how far he'd come. His presence woke up the whole room and made us all feel like family.

The parents, as I approached them, seemed surprised by how many messengers were there. It seemed clear to them now that Tommy was not just a rebellious kid. He was a part of something. He'd shown that he could work hard and that he could make challenging experiences work for him. He'd developed strong bonds with many different kinds of people here, regardless of color or background. Tommy was a fighter. Like the best of us in that room, he was a man who would not quit.

I gave my condolences to his parents and then I told them about a Critical Mass vigil ride that was being held in their son's honor. They had already received a call about it, they said, from a guy named T. C. O'Rourke. I smiled. It was good to hear that T.C., a strong advocate in the mass, had taken the initiative. Tommy's brother Robert assured me that he would be attending.

I moved on and knelt near Tommy's body. He was handsome, pale. I wondered, *Were his eyes to open, what would he see? A young man who he knew but vaguely—a friend, an implicit friend?* I hoped so. Were I in his place, wouldn't he too be sharing this moment with me? Of course he would. I knew he would. It was chance alone that drew these boundaries between the dead and the living. Only sad, meaningless chance was to blame.

Not long after I stepped away from the casket, a priest brought the room together in prayer. I could hardly see him through the crowd of bikers that I was standing among. I was looking between the wide shoulders of Vergil, who had brought his daughter along; Ryan, who held Zoe, his fourteen-month-old daughter, curled up quietly against his shoulder; and the Twelve-Guy, Rod Richardson, a father of two.

These couriers, many of them not really knowing what to do, bowed their heads gently at the appropriate times. But when the priest came upon the word "reincarnation," the word stood in the room like a dare, like a ghost pleading to the living, and I looked up. The priest said that Tommy would live on through eternity in the hearts and minds of the people he had touched. Honestly, it was a little strange to be in the room with a priest. He kept talking, and I could hardly hear him. While these strange feelings rose in my gut I began to ask cynical questions: *What does he think he's doing, this priest? Can he fix anything? For him, I know, it is just another day at work.* But then Ryan stepped away quietly and I could see the minister's face, his somber, pious posture, and his deep eyes.

Suddenly tears fell from my eyes and I noticed that they were falling from the eyes of the hard-living men and women around me. Whose tears were they? I couldn't imagine, but they were intense, and through them I began to say to myself, silently: *Yes, dammit, I am angry!* I suddenly found myself confessing.

I took a breath and tried to contain myself but the words kept coming. *Yes, I admit, Father, I am angry!* I looked up for a moment to see other guys with their heads bowed, eyes clenched, and tears falling from their cheeks to the floor. It was a fear we were facing. We'd lived with this fear for the hardest years of our lives. And as much as we worked to avoid such a fate, now we were angry that it had not taken us, each of us, instead.

Heaving and shouting to myself in blackness, I made out the words: *Please, God, do something with my anger because I want to be a good man. I feel that I need something to change here and I want to make it happen with my own hands—goddamn it, I am angry! Please, Father—tie my hands, give me peace, and help me to be a good man. Tell me: How can I forgive anyone when everyone seems responsible?*

I opened my eyes and took a few long breaths. In the silence, I could feel the messengers in the room declaring unto God, some of us for the first time in our lives, that we who battle cities, we who have worked and bled in vain, have a responsibility to redeem the harsh world we've chosen.

In our clenched hands and drawn faces, a second life was given—a life of knowledge, the realization that death can catch us too, that we are not immortal, but that we are of a class that will never die. We will live on together, Tommy and all who have fought for the protection of our common spaces, the safety of our streets, and the well-being of the very world that discounts us.

CHAPTER TWELVE

THE REMAINS OF PUBLIC SPACE

The right to have access to every building in
the city by private motorcar in an age when everyone possesses
such a vehicle is actually the right to destroy the city.

Lewis Mumford

*T*HE TURNOUT AT DALEY PLAZA WAS UNCOMMONLY STRONG for an off-schedule ride. There were more than a hundred bike commuters there and nearly one hundred messengers who had come to remember Tommy publicly and to show support to his family.

For the first time since winter, all the differences between these two groups could be set aside. In one group there were the messenger types like Jimbo, Matt Number 6145, Donny, Greenfield, Guenivere from Apex, John from Quicksilver, and others. They were spread out and sharing time with the Critical Mass riders like Jim Redd and his son Adrian, James Longfield, BigHorn, Digital Dan, Nick Jackson, Katherine, Gareth, and Ephraim—every month or so new faces would come into the core of the mass.

It was interesting to see us all come together. We were a cult that saw the bicycle as a lifestyle, a political choice, an economic necessity, and an ecological vision. We straddled our rigs. They varied. I saw road bikes, racing bikes, mountain bikes, old-style English cruisers with baskets. Each bike had unique traits. Some had stickers, some had been scraped down to steel, some had curious attachments like toys and fans and tassels. As I walked through the group, I could see the hands of the riders holding their bikes. They had tight hands, muscular hands, fingers lined with oil and dirt. The spirit was somber; all the heads seemed to look away from the center of the group, watching cars pass around us on Washington and Clark. Washington Street is a long one-way stretch that cuts right through the city. From the West Loop neighborhoods looking back, the skyscrapers align right along the roadway such that the entire vertical world seems cleanly parted by it. Farther out still on Washington was our destination, the calm, residential street where Tommy's body had been found. After a few short speeches were made at the foot of the Picasso, we mounted up and took Randolph westbound.

It was not a short ride. We kept a decent pace, riding faster than we would for an average mass because the messengers would speed through us, shooting ahead and weaving among themselves like flies. Massers tried to timidly keep a pace and let the conversation flow, but the messenger influence was there, getting the ride more aggressive. I would spend time with both groups. I would run up with the hotties to splash around the chopped-up West Side intersections, then I would hang back to talk with the massers. For a while I rode along with Amy from the Chicago Bicycle Federation and Adam, a red-bearded, bright-eyed bike advocate who was working with the Chicago-based Center for Neighborhood Technology.

Amy and Adam were friends who'd met on a Critical Mass ride. I thought it was interesting to see where their missions merged. The

CBF fights for bike-oriented legislation and raises awareness for cyclists' needs. The CNT is an organization founded to make our urban communities work on economic and environmental levels.

Together they were working to change the world and improve urban neighborhoods by cycling. *Is such a thing possible?* I wondered. The farther out we moved, the more I seemed to doubt it. Out here, the line of cyclists drew the attention of all the communities we passed through. They had never seen anything like us before. Bikes in this neighborhood seemed to be used only as toys. The ones that I saw adults riding had flat tires and rusted rims. Most people traveled by bus and train. Some pushed their old cars mile by mile, as if each mile was their last. Occasionally I would see a shining black SUV in a line of parked cars. It seemed that a car was a luxury, not a necessity. It was a thing of pride to be able to drive, a declaration of the respect they were after. But this community had little room for these luxuries. Their neighborhoods were neither ecological nor economical. They were suffering, holding on to every day carefully.

We were a diverse group, but we didn't feel so diverse entering these aggressively poor sectors of the city. We were a group of nameless faces in the villages of social neglect. Going past the families walking on the crumbling sidewalks, we were aliens to each other, having nothing to share and no excuse to cross the cultural boundaries between us.

Did Adam and Amy really think it was possible to transform these neighborhoods into cleanly operating districts that maximized energy use and community interaction? How would they do it—come out here with signs and pamphlets? I couldn't see the people in this neighborhood taking some greenie's pamphlets seriously.

"Poverty is the first problem. You can't be ecological if you are scrambling for your primary resources. Once you have maximized energy use," Adam continued, "then you will find that these communities are able to stretch their resources further."

I thought I saw his point, but then I rode past buildings with blown-out windows and boarded-up storefronts that had been kicked in. *How did our poverty get this severe?* I wanted to ask Adam and Amy what they thought, but I had lost track of them in the swarm of gently swaying bicycles.

I didn't need their input. I could see it from here on the sloping rooftops and the gutted buildings along West Washington: on one end towering skyscrapers, on the other end miles of uniform suburban rings and plush towns moving into the countryside. Between them sat this whole world of the poor and the underrepresented. They were still "innumerable, patient as the darkness of night." This is what Carl Sandburg wrote of the same communities nearly a hundred years earlier. Things hadn't changed much.

Back in the early 1900s, these ghettos were carefully situated between freight and elevated train lines on the South Side. They stayed alive because there was work to be had in the factories. While the early strikes of the American labor movement abounded in these industrial sectors of the city, the blacks in the community, many of whom had recently arrived from even more severe conditions in the South, were able to get work as scabs. This undermined the labor movement and gave big business the advantage of having their workers quarrel. Wages could be cut, because now there was sufficient competition for the few jobs that were available.

At the time, the ghettos accounted for 90 percent of the city's black population. But it has been a long hundred years, and a lot has happened. There has been a strong civil rights movement and unprecedented economic expansion; there have been technological advances like the telephone and the television, which should have given these communities a capacity to interact with and be a part of the progress of the times. But somehow, despite all these advancements and improvements, the ghetto has grown.

These buildings around us were not built for the families that were using them. They were built at a time when prosperity seemed assured. They were built for town folk who needed to be near work. They would never have been built to then be boarded up or inhabited by families on public aid. Many of these same houses once had leasing restrictions that, as late as the 1940s, made it illegal to sell or lease property to black families. Today's slums are the ruins of a domestic struggle that has created an exodus of personal resources and left an entire sector of the American workforce without choices, without opportunities, and without political representation.

The farther you go west or southward into the industrial sectors of the city, the more and more the effects of this exodus become apparent. It can be seen in pockets where poverty and race merge into truly despairing images of unclothed children on sidewalks, fields of trash and upturned shopping carts, razed foundations that still have parts of the house lying around, toys and clothes that were never cleaned up after the wreckage. Collecting these images as I rode past the broken windows and burned-out facades, I could unfold this saga of exclusion. The interplay of social instability and industrial omnipotence has turned the American urban experiment into something unhealthy, undemocratic, and ecologically unsound.

TO CREATE THE Interstate Highway System in the late 1950s, the federal government needed to acquire thousands of miles of privately owned urban space. So that these highways could be built cheaply and quickly, they were designed to run through the urban slums of America. It was a tried-and-true technique, mastered by Robert Moses and the early highway developers of the Depression era.

Who would notice? The land was cheap and the landowners were easy to subdue. Where the landowners were black they had little political savvy. We are talking about space that most whites had never been in because of their heavy concentrations of blacks and minorities. Once enclosed in miles of concrete, naturally, the area felt more "comfortable."

All across the country, while cement was poured and cars were sold, the plight of living on the *wrong side of the tracks* simply adjusted to accommodate car culture. The result was areas where black families found it more difficult to move, to work, or to get help fighting fire and crime. Often they were very near the commercial sectors of the city, yet they were cut off by miles of expressway, rivers of burning oil, through which the privileged could reach the young suburban developments of the time.

In 1950, 68 percent of Chicago's population was white. In 1970, that percentage had dropped to 39 percent. There was a 17.3 percent drop in Chicago's population between 1970 and 1990, while in the same period, the population of suburban Cook County increased by 10.9 percent and the population of Cook County's five collar counties jumped by 45.2 percent. Between 1950 and 1990 the population of Chicago dropped by 837,000 people.

While the white and wealthy took their degrees with them into the cornfields, the spiral of economic decline kept swirling down. In time, businesses picked up and made this migration too. Today, the tech industry has emerged on the outskirts and edge cities of Chicago, to employ this migrant and wealthy white population.

And what became of the city? Well, you can look at it. Chicago, today, has to court businesses to the downtown area with tax incentives and undue levels of citywide cooperation. The neighborhood parks and sidewalks are quiet. The city's swing sets are unused and its schools have fallen to embarrassing, often tragic lows. The term "inner city" has become a code word for "black and poor." Whole new wastelands of overgrown yards and razed foundations lie dormant in the southwest side of the city, only a mile or so from downtown in places, and yet it stretches as far as the eye can see.

Even in healthier areas, few people are willing to step out of their cars or their homes and experience the space around them. Because of the imbalance in resources, Americans have been made fearful and resentful of one another. There is no communication in the public arena to calm our fears and loosen our sense of inequity. The private car, being ideologically anti-urban, has reinforced the poverty of the past hundred years by separating our communities and steamrolling our commons. The car protects the public from public space—the last frontier where our ideas can be openly challenged and improved upon, where—forget happiness—*democracy* can be actively pursued.

---

312   WHEN WE PULLED INTO the intersection of West Washington and Lockwood Avenue, in a working-class neighborhood that sat smack between projects and slums, we laid our bikes on the asphalt, stopped traffic in both directions, and sat down to have a few minutes of silence for Thomas McBride. As I closed my eyes and felt the crowded street around me, giving prayers and taking a moment to meditate, I heard a voice, a loud one, a cry or a shout from the distance.

Then, one by one, people stood and addressed the group to talk about Tommy or the feelings and thoughts that his death had brought up. These speeches were interrupted by a few shouting voices. At first I thought it was motorists trying to get through, but it wasn't that. A spectator on one of the nearby street corners was shouting at the group. An officer who had been helping redirect traffic tried to quiet the woman, but his influence only made it worse. Now there were more voices shouting indecencies. A small crowd had grown, keeping a vile and angry pitch. The only words I could make out were: "He's dead. He's dead. What *can* you do about it now?"

Robert McBride, Tommy's brother, then stood up from the mass of sitting bikers and asked us all to "remember kindness." The whole group of us sat in silence, probably thinking—just like me— *What would it matter? How would they hear it? What can we actually do to show these people that we have kindness? WHAT DO WE DO?*

We sat and thought about it for a minute or two. As the group stood, stretching their legs and preparing their bikes for the ride back home, I went over to the corner where that upset family stood, and I addressed them: "I have some literature about the event. Would you take some of these flyers so that you can see what this whole thing is about?" A man's long black hand reached out to me, and I gave him a flyer. He glanced at it, crumpled it in his big hand, and dropped it on the sidewalk.

Seeing this, a small group of children gathered around me, eager to do the same. I gave them each a flyer and they promptly turned around and tore their flyers to pieces.

"Can I have another one?" an eight-year-old girl asked boldly.

"I just gave you one."

"But I want another one!" she demanded.

"Me too!" her younger brother shouted, with an outstretched arm.

I handed another flyer to each of the children. They turned, tore them up, and turned back for more. I gave them more, handing them small stacks of three or five and watching the flyers get torn up and dropped on the sidewalk by their feet.

A young woman shouted, "Don't take shit from that man," but the children kept reaching out and I kept filling their palms, letting them get more and more passionate about ripping them up at my feet. The woman walked off angrily while a small cloud of torn-up paper littered the ground where she stood. I continued to feed the children's anger, handing them larger stacks. I had thousands of flyers; they couldn't possibly have taken them all from me, so I kept giving, wanting them to feel the futility of their anger. The young woman who had walked off turned back and shouted from a distance, "He is already in jail. What can you do now? What is it you're trying to do?" She was furious, screaming and waving her hands in the air. "Your man should not have been on the road in the first place! What do you think you're going to accomplish here!" Two of the children ran to her to keep her calm.

Just then, John, a medical student who was riding in the mass,
314   tapped my shoulder and told me to get moving, since most of the mass had already started heading back downtown. As I followed, he

told me that I'd just been talking to the extended family of Carnell Fitzpatrick. I looked back and saw the woman and the children walking away from the pile of torn-up flyers, which had begun to spin in the road, turned up by a light wind.

"So much for strangers," John said in a heavy voice. The hit-and-run had become something of a marriage.

FUCK THIS PLACE, I thought, riding away from the scene. With my head bowed between my shoulders and my knees keeping a steady pace, I wondered if I, between its angry people and its scorched-earth politics, could really live in a city anymore. *Maybe I should just pick up and go live in a shack on a mountain, go back to Dixon, Illinois, where I can sit by the Rock River and hear the grass crackling beneath my feet. Why don't I just run away and take care of my own shit like an anarchist, a cynic, and save myself from the heartache of the city as it is today.*

But as I thought about it, I realized that if I picked up and went to the hills, I'd have to drive there. The automobile would win, and the city would weaken behind me. What if I needed to get back to the city for work? Then I'd be stuck in the middle, in the suburban wastelands that would never have existed without the automobile. Again, the car would win against the city. It would master me by becoming my only link between the conflicting impulses of running up and running out, of ascending and escaping. This is a well-paved path, one that would be a continuance of the slow death of the city.

Low-density suburban areas are where the majority of Americans live today, and with them the footprint of our developed space has expanded. The more widely we spread, the more we have to drive; and, architecturally, the more we drive, the wider we are forced to spread. The ecological implications of this expansion over the land make the present shape of our cities worthy of serious reconsideration.

Simply to accommodate the car and its migration outward, our forests have been razed, our wildlife has been consumed, much of our country's agricultural capacity has been built over, and many of our natural streams have been turned into storm sewers collecting oil, gasoline, antifreeze, and the runoff from fields of impervious asphalt and concrete. Our air has been sickened with pollutants that do as much harm to the atmosphere as they do to us.

But I won't get into the specifics because I can't, because they are obvious, because I am sick of the car being criticized merely for its effects on the earth. The environmental impact of the automobile is an important issue and it should be well discussed, but too few people in America seem to care.

And why should they care? The highways were built for these Americans. Gasoline is subsidized for these Americans. Suburbs were made cheap and accessible for these Americans. The message is clear: *Americans are to drive cars.* No strictly environmental rhetoric is going to beat that. As it stands today, most people think they need to drive, and they do need to drive, because there is nothing but a massive sprawling highway between them and the city; nothing but cement sidewalks and cracked asphalt roads and *dangerous* neighborhoods; nothing but exit-only lanes and Chevrolet billboards; nothing but old grocery stores and abandoned cars.

America today is locked down tight in the tinted glass and the environmental controls that filter, cool, and falsify the air of the common man. The driver is neither white nor black, male nor female. The driver is not even present because *it,* the driver, would only get in the way of the largest industry the world has ever seen. In order to protect its supremacy, the car—and the city with it—has had to divide our communities, spread them so far across the country that the city has become decentralized and incomplete. Once the city was sufficiently off balance, the car itself became necessary to hold it all together.

I have seen it from the bridges that arch over the Eisenhower Expressway: thousands of cars, each holding a person in the front seat, a person who is having to navigate their own path. Meanwhile, the whole, the body of one hundred million machines lined bumper to bumper, keeps its shape and continues its cycle of invading the city and then retreating to the country again. Each time through, the sanctity of public space is undermined. Each trip takes some part of the city with it, tearing out the spirit of the place.

It is said that the only time a person feels more important than the whole of his community is when he is insane—or when he is driving. This is the basis of car culture, the idea that the world and all of the world's people are merely *in its way.* This is the arrogance that makes our big businesses stronger and our failing democracy weaker. This is the arrogance that has made the spirit of our country so proud and yet so blind to the acute poverty, the blanket levels of illiteracy, and the social disinvestment that we have, ourselves, set in motion.

By allowing the impulse toward greater privatization to usurp our public spaces, democracy itself becomes endangered. It is happening in Congress, in city hall, on the Internet, in the real estate of suburban residential repositories that skirt exit ramps on major highways, and in the advertisements that glorify the car's rule over the earth and man: the idealism of private ownership becomes a public disavowal. Underneath these corporate pressures, public life, like public schools, public housing, and public transportation, has become sick with cruelty and flagrant disregard. The effect of this isolationist campaign leads to a denial of our civic sense, which, like a personal secession from the Union, becomes a blockade against the very idea of responsible action.

If we continue on our path by committing ourselves to the protected environments of the automobile, the idea of community becomes impossible. America, the most socially diverse country in the world, becomes a lonely place, even among the masses.

As I see it, there is no solution to the social or environmental problems of our age if we cannot give a new shape to our urban spaces that will make living without a car feasible for the average American family. And while reducing the country's dependency on the car will certainly help the environment, we should not be motivated by ecological concerns alone. We should be working toward the development of our communities and let these immediate improvements have their long-term, earth-friendly consequences.

By restoring our existing urban areas, we can draw the steam out of the ever-growing residential regions that are sprawling around our cities and give them the opportunity to be developed into more autonomous neighborhoods. This drawing back, or drawing in, of our metropolitan districts will mean integrating a new level of diversity into our communities and our schools. If we can achieve this level of social integration, the government programs that are needed to educate our children can be paid for by a range of taxpayers (rich and poor), which can then benefit an equally diverse student body. This economic integration will help curb the problems of acute poverty, while the spatial integration of residential and commercial zones will make it possible for average, working people to enjoy a higher quality of life without being dependent on the automobile.

The struggle would not so much be *against* the private car as it would be *for* the more appropriate use of urban space. Working toward appropriate use, we will find appropriate technology. The truth is that the closer we live to one another, the easier it is to walk, to bike, and to pay for trains that will reduce the need for an automobile. It is only with residential and commercial density that the bicycle becomes appropriate and thereby necessary. The diseases of our current living environment, our public life, will begin to lessen only when the bicycle becomes the measure of the city, and clean-burning human energy becomes the primary source of fuel.

I don't pretend to think that these changes can happen overnight, but for the sake of our families, our communities, and our environment, they need to happen soon. Our cities today are crying for improvements, and our communities are not being adequately served, managed, or represented by the social services of our current political environment. To transform these communities into working neighborhoods, we have got to step outside and learn about the social dynamics that make up our country on a firsthand level. We have got to set aside our fears of the people we don't know, and we need to stand up and be proud of our place in public life.

From all that I have seen as a cyclist and a messenger, I have learned that there are good people out here, hidden beneath the highways and behind the dashboards of America. These people have heart; even the suffering are living as honestly as they are able. They might be starving, they might be singing, but if we let them do it alone, if we do it ourselves alone, then we are not doing our job as people, empowered people in a truly free country. If we let the machine age put sanctions on the city, then we keep the public from expressing their concerns openly. In avoidance, we are sacrificing our own freedoms and letting the opportunity to reclaim them pass unnoticed between us. Democracy disintegrates once you leave the community scale.

ON THE WEST SIDE, even under the train tracks and over the potholes on Racine, the city is undergoing a transition. The staid urban ideal of a ring of commercial buildings cut off from residential and industrial areas has faded. The buildings nearby are of every order: warehouses, small offices, produce distributors, and restaurants. But also, nearby, are a host of newly converted condominiums and apartments. The functions of this space have merged.

Much of these residential spaces are themselves integrated, as businesspeople are finding it easier to work from home. Architecturally, by integrating and revitalizing this industrial area, we are looking at a principle of spatial recycling. Why build when we can rebuild? In a similar light, why cordon off this old industrial area when it can still be shared, used, and profited from in many different ways?

On these streets, loading trucks line up behind traffic signals, taxis rage, and couriers rattle—all of us moving for purposes of commerce. Yet here, people jog and walk dogs; tourists line up around Harpo Studios and patronize nearby vendors. Some of the foot traffic here is made up of actors and models going to casting calls for commercials that are being shot in studios right down the street. Trains pass above me, bringing workers to the city. This is a multiuse space and it is financially better off for it.

Many of these people have returned to the city after living or being raised in the suburbs and the exurbs of the countryside. They have come back now with money and resources. They have populated old warehouses and encouraged local businesses to thrive. They have stacked up, one upon the other, in midrise developments minimizing the actual, if not ecological, footprint of their urban experience. Detractors call this process gentrification, but these new residents contribute important tax money to the city, which uses it to improve parks and transit lines. Their added density allows the city to make and upgrade tired parks and unkempt alleys. Chicago today is making improvements to neighborhood areas and working toward the ideal of a bike-friendly city. As more density is created in and around the Loop, these neighborhood measures, bike lanes, and bike racks become essential.

It may still be a long time before the average family will be a bicycling family, but Chicago is, the closer we come to its center, quickly becoming a place where an average American family can raise children and get to work without the use of a motor vehicle. The exodus is being reversed and so the question then becomes: how well can it be managed?

As I crossed above the highway with a line of cyclists, I could see bikes building up in greater numbers in the neighborhood. I saw a couple of guys riding into work, wearing shirts with matching emblems. They crossed right in front of me and about twenty other cyclists still coming in from the west. I could see these young men's faces, I could see their eyes gleam as they carried on a conversation in Spanish. I nodded, they waved. The mass moved on.

All the people I was riding alongside had faces that I knew and trusted. It was not a happy day, but we were glad to be together where we could stand up for the safety of our streets and the possibility of a cleaner future—a future of many colors, many *real* working places, and many kinds of transportation alternatives. There are people like this in every city in the world. They are concerned about their planet, their neighborhood, and their families. To their credit, I saw that this group had found a way to benefit the environment, protect public funds, encourage interaction with different backgrounds and social strata. They had found a way to change the world with a simple pulley system, a frame, a set of wheels, and a smile. I was proud to follow in their wake.

WE ARE STANDING around quietly on the courtyard of Daley Plaza between skyscrapers and government buildings. A few messengers talk about the idea of having an hour of radio silence Monday in Tommy's name. "Let the work mount up, who cares?" Jimbo advocates. "It's just an hour."

"Just an hour! Are you crazy? Companies are going to freak. Besides, catching up is going to be insane!" another messenger contends.

I have walked off and begun looking at the skyline soaring up above me. To me, the city is a majestic work of art. Every detail is honest and unconcealed. The moment I step out of its maniacal pace, I can see it. It moves like a massive kinetic sculpture. Some parts move quickly; some don't move at all. Landmarks like the Art

Institute and the Board of Trade have tremendous weight. They seem to pull the rest of the city streets into their gravitational force. Block-length crowds of people seem to swim past their moving parts fluidly. Tiny airplanes fly between the buildings. Some travel right up Washington Street; some choose Oak. Above the taxicabs they launch and descend over old buildings, and they merge into their own reflections on the surface of the skyscrapers. Each detail of the city seems carefully chosen to represent the various attitudes and characters of city life. Pigeons in flanking maneuvers expand into the volume of a public sky. Above the intersection, as their wings pound in the worship of open space, they seem the lords of men.

The city is a fluid text, meant to be read, seen up close and far away, scrutinized at leisure by the very people who fuel its overwhelming scale. These peculiar spectacles make the city a place of provocative insights and accidental passages that, in foot and meter, show us the naked honesty of our own condition.

The city is a story. In it are times of tremendous tension and inequity, conflicts that may never find complete redemption without the work of every hand involved. But as we live in this moment and we find ourselves a part of the often sullen masterpiece that is our world, we can still be active. Even in all the madness of urban life there is still room and reason to consider our public space on a personal level. We can use the city's history to our favor and make the changes that will reflect the spirit of our times. We simple people with our big dreams and our many struggles—we are the city as we are part of its story.

Uninterrupted by the light surrounding conversation, I have shut my eyes and begun to listen. I am trying to imagine what it could be like, to live both dense and peaceful. I am trying to see it as I scroll through her tired streets in my mind, a *sustainable Chicago* covered with bike-only streets, quiet trains, and a patient, car-free, delivery-based roadway. I envision inner-city schools that thrive and parks that are in use. I see a rich, diverse, and colorful city, where the blackness that we now fear can just be sprayed off our buildings with a high-pressure water gun.

Chicago, the world that I have mapped into the back of my mind, the towers and the gutters that have become so much a part of me—I know that she is tired and I know that she is strong. I have adopted her every talent, her every wound, her every complaint by a kind of spiritual contagion. And though as a messenger and as a cyclist, I feel as plagued by neglect as some of her broken asphalt surfaces, I will not give up on these streets.

Her strength, her conviction, and her hunger to persist are indefatigable. Her grit and forbearance fuel the very model of my own courage. Her posture and ambition mark my determined stance. I—and many of these other riders, messengers and commuters alike—have inherited her conviction to survive, to stand out, and to succeed. For the bicycle and for the culture that supports it, we are helping to give the city a resurrection, a second coming of the City Beautiful, a second chance at really *working.*

ABOUT THE AUTHOR

After taking a year off in Philadelphia to write *The Immortal Class,* TRAVIS HUGH CULLEY has returned to Chicago and has picked up an old job working in the industry of small-package delivery. His new biker number at Service First Courier is Five-oh.

PHOTO CREDITS

daniel@metrodigital.com © 1998: pages ii–v, 142, 278, 304

Butch Connelly: page 2

Lenyr Muñoz: pages 26, 80, 172, 202, 228

Jimbo Daniels: pages 50, 110

ed@metrodigital.com © 1998: page 250